NACH BILDENDE KUNST

AFTER FINE ART

WORKS PRESENTED IN THE GERMAN LANGUAGE
ARBEITEN VORGESTELLT IM DEUTSCHSPRACHIGEN RAUM

LAWRENCE WEINER

GABRIELE WIX (ED./HG.)

HATJE
CANTZ

CONTENTS

INHALT

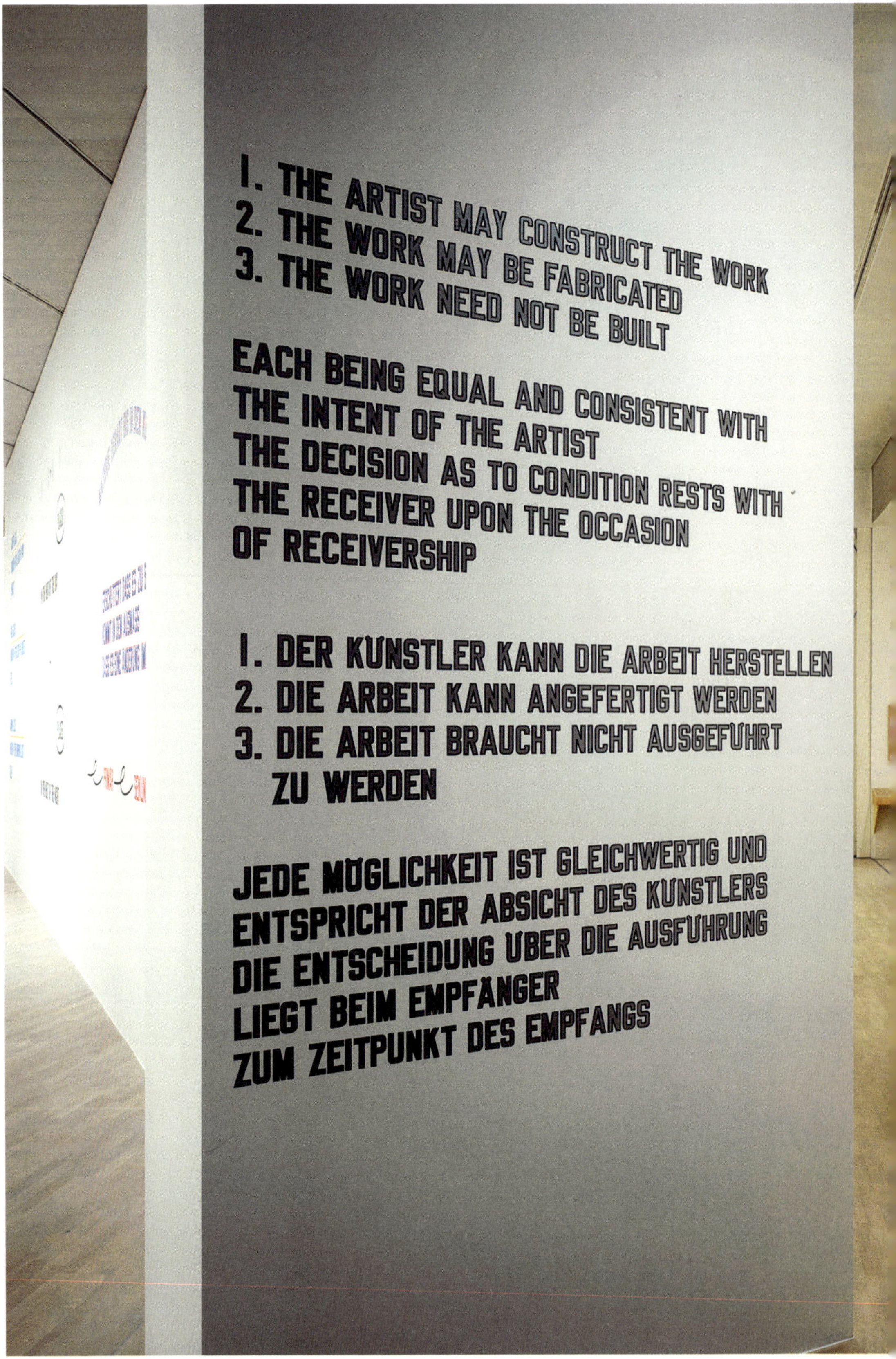
1. THE ARTIST MAY CONSTRUCT THE WORK
2. THE WORK MAY BE FABRICATED
3. THE WORK NEED NOT BE BUILT
EACH BEING EQUAL AND CONSISTENT WITH
THE INTENT OF THE ARTIST
THE DECISION AS TO CONDITION RESTS WITH
THE RECEIVER UPON THE OCCASION
OF RECEIVERSHIP
1. DER KÜNSTLER KANN DIE ARBEIT HERSTELLEN
2. DIE ARBEIT KANN ANGEFERTIGT WERDEN
3. DIE ARBEIT BRAUCHT NICHT AUSGEFÜHRT
ZU WERDEN
JEDE MÖGLICHKEIT IST GLEICHWERTIG UND
ENTSPRICHT DER ABSICHT DES KÜNSTLERS
DIE ENTSCHEIDUNG ÜBER DIE AUSFÜHRUNG
LIEGT BEIM EMPFÄNGER
ZUM ZEITPUNKT DES EMPFANGS

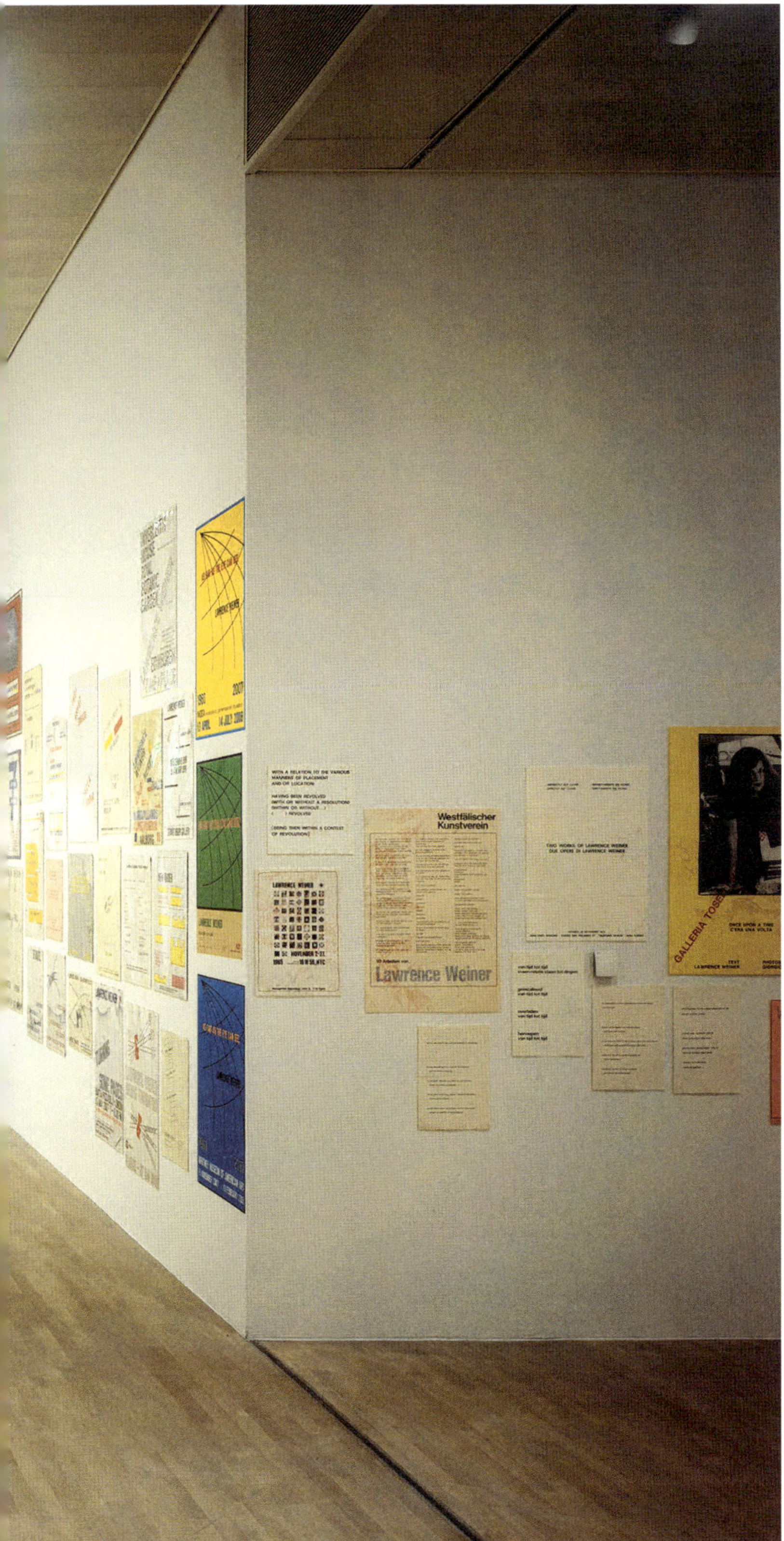
Westfälischer Kunstverein
Lawrence Weiner

Previous page:
As Far as the Eye Can See,
K21 Kunstsammlung Nordrhein-Westfalen, Düsseldorf, 2008; front wall: Lawrence Weiner's Statement of Intent (1968); back wall: Lawrence Weiner Poster Archive
Vorherige Seite:
As Far as the Eye Can See,
K21 Kunstsammlung Nordrhein-Westfalen, Düsseldorf, 2008
Vordere Wand: Lawrence Weiners Absichtserklärung (1968);
hintere Wand: Lawrence Weiner Poster-Archiv

UNCLAIMED THINGS

Gabriele Wix

In spite of all the incantations about a "material turn," a new materialism, to the contrary nothing proves as obstinate as the paradigm of the immateriality of text. And no one is as obstinate as artist Lawrence Weiner in using language as a material to make art, and making manifest the very materiality of text. He describes his art as sculpture. Though art history has classified Weiner within the realm of Conceptual Art, literary studies barely takes notice of him; this in spite of the universal popularity of interdisciplinary cultural studies and its now fundamentally revised concept of the parameters of text. Walter Benjamin's observations on writing heralded the reception of such an art based on language. While interpreting the "blizzard" and "dictatorial perpendicular" of the new media of the city as a threat to the "archaic stillness of the book" and an expression of a deficient cultural process, Benjamin viewed text in terms of its materiality.

> Printing *[Schrift]*, having found in the book a refuge in which to lead an autonomous existence, is pitilessly dragged out onto the street by advertisements and subjected to the brutal

VON HERRENLOSEN DINGEN

Gabriele Wix

Allen Beschwörungen eines »material turn« zum Trotz: Nichts hält sich so hartnäckig wie das Paradigma der Immaterialität des Textes. Und niemand besteht so hartnäckig wie der Künstler Lawrence Weiner darauf, Sprache als Material zu verwenden, um Kunst zu machen und damit auch die Materialität des Textes greifbar zu machen. Seine Kunst beschreibt er als Skulptur. Während die Kunstgeschichte Weiner der Concept Art zuordnet, nimmt die Literaturwissenschaft ihn kaum wahr, und dies ungeachtet ihrer heute weltweit eher kulturwissenschaftlichen und interdisziplinären Ausrichtung und eines grundlegend gewandelten Textbegriffs. Wegweisend für die Rezeption einer auf Sprache basierenden Kunst sind die Beobachtungen Walter Benjamins zur Schrift. Zwar wertet er deren »dichtes Gestöber« und »diktatorische Vertikale« durch die neuen Medien der Großstadt als Bedrohung für die »archaische Stille des Buches« und als Ausdruck eines defizitären kulturellen Prozesses, aber er beachtet sie als solche in ihrer Materialität.

> Die Schrift, die im gedruckten Buche ein Asyl gefunden hatte, wo sie ihr autonomes Dasein

heteronomies of economic chaos. This is the hard schooling of its new form. If centuries ago it began gradually to lie down, passing from the upright inscription to the manuscript resting on sloping desks before finally taking to bed in the printed book, it now begins just as slowly to rise again from the ground. The newspaper is read more in the vertical than in the horizontal plane, while film and advertisement force the printed word entirely into the dictatorial perpendicular. And before a child of our time finds his way clear to opening a book, his eyes have been exposed to such a blizzard of changing, colorful, conflicting letters that the chances of penetrating the archaic stillness of the book are slight. Locust swarms of print, which already eclipse the sun of what is taken for intellect for city dwellers, will grow thicker with each succeeding year.[1]

Weiner's art fearlessly enters the "locust swarms of print." It seeks out public spaces beyond established art galleries and museums to appear, for example, in relief on the exterior of buildings, painted on walls as tattoos, and in everyday street scenes, as posters. In a general sense, the fact that a text is rarely presented "in an unadorned state"[2] has been known since Gérard Genette's exploration of paratexts, the "thresholds" that facilitate the reception of a text: "And although we do not always know whether these productions are to be regarded as belonging to the text, in any case they surround and extend it, precisely in order to present it, in the usual sense of this verb but also in the strongest sense, to make present, to ensure the text's presence in the world."[3] Weiner demonstrates this on a

führte, wird unerbittlich von Reklamen auf die Straße hinausgezerrt und den brutalen Heteronomien des wirtschaftlichen Chaos unterstellt. Das ist der strenge Schulgang ihrer neuen Form. Wenn vor Jahrhunderten sie allmählich sich niederzulegen begann, von der aufrechten Inschrift zur schräg auf Pulten ruhenden Handschrift ward, um endlich sich im Buchdruck zu betten, beginnt sie nun ebenso langsam sich wieder vom Boden zu heben. Bereits die Zeitung wird mehr in der Senkrechten als in der Horizontale gelesen, Film und Reklame drängen die Schrift vollends in die diktatorische Vertikale. Und ehe der Zeitgenosse dazu kommt, ein Buch aufzuschlagen, ist über seine Augen ein so dichtes Gestöber von wandelbaren, farbigen, streitenden Lettern niedergegangen, daß die Chancen seines Eindringens in die archaische Stille des Buches gering geworden sind. Heuschreckenschwärme von Schrift, die heute schon die Sonne des vermeinten Geistes den Großstädtern verfinstern, werden dichter mit jedem folgenden Jahre werden.[1]

Weiners Kunst begibt sich furchtlos in die »Heuschreckenschwärme von Schrift«. Sie sucht den öffentlichen Raum jenseits etablierter Kunstgalerien und Museen und tritt als Inschrift auf Gebäuden, auf Wände gemalt als Tattoos oder im alltäglichen Straßenbild als Plakate in Erscheinung. Ein Text präsentiert sich »selten nackt«, das wissen wir spätestens, seit sich Gérard Genette den Paratexten gewidmet hat, den »Schwellen«,[2] die eine Rezeption von Texten überhaupt erst ermöglichen. »Von ihnen weiß man nicht immer, ob man sie dem Text zurechnen soll; sie umgeben und verlängern ihn jedenfalls, um ihn im üblichen, aber auch im vollsten Sinn des Wortes zu *präsentieren,* very elementary basis: in his use of typography. How a text, a work in language is presented does indeed play a role. Helvetica? “It's one of the typefaces that I absolutely detest . . . It's telling you that this is cultural, this is intellectual, and this is intelligent. I'm rather afraid that words don't start off being cultural, intellectual, or intelligent. So I found a typeface that I like, which was Franklin Gothic Extra Condensed. It reminded me of the working class Dutch letters that I am intrigued by.”[4] Benjamin distanced himself at the start of the twentieth century in a similar fashion from the classic German typeface Fraktur, which he had used for the title of his 1928 book *Origin of German Tragedy.* For *One-Way Street,* a volume that appeared the same year, he selected Grotesque for the titles of his aphorisms, which, like the title of this collection, he had collected on the street—signs like “Tankstelle” (filling station), “Betteln und Hausieren verboten” (no vagrants), or “Galanteriewaren” (fancy goods).[5]

Weiner chooses the typography of the street, time-tested and plain typefaces that were designed at the start of the twentieth century and became fixed components of everyday culture in America and Europe due to their practicality: capital letters of the typeface Franklin Gothic Extra Condensed, designed in 1904 by Morris Fuller Benton from the American Type Founders Company—the unadorned sans serif font, strong, masculine—and occasionally Stencil, a typeface developed in 1937 by Gerry Powell with serifs. Since the late nineties, Weiner has also been using another sans serif stencil typeface, FF Offline, designed by the Dutch graphic designer and artist Roelof Mulder in 1998.

ihn *präsent* zu machen.«[3] Weiner zeigt es uns auf einer ganz elementaren Basis, der Typografie. Es spielt durchaus eine Rolle, wie ein Text, eine Arbeit aus Sprache, präsentiert wird. Helvetica? »Das ist eine der Schriften, die ich zutiefst verabscheue. Sie sagt, das ist gebildet, das ist intellektuell, und das ist intelligent. Ich fürchte aber, dass Worte zunächst einmal nicht gebildet, intellektuell oder intelligent sind. So habe ich eine Schrifttype gefunden, die mir gefällt: Franklin Gothic Extra Condensed. Sie erinnerte mich an die holländische Schrift der Arbeiterschicht, die ich sehr mag.«[4] Ebenso setzte sich Benjamin zu Beginn des 20. Jahrhunderts von der klassischen deutschen Frakturschrift ab, in der er den Titel seines 1928 erschienenen Buchs *Ursprung des deutschen Trauerspiels* noch hatte setzen lassen. Für das im selben Jahr erschienene Bändchen *Einbahnstraße* wählte er eine Groteskschrift für die Überschriften seiner Aphorismen, die er – wie den Titel der Sammlung – sozusagen auf der Straße aufgelesen hatte, Schilder wie »Tankstelle«, »Betteln und Hausieren verboten« oder »Galanteriewaren«.[5]

Weiner nimmt die Typografie der Straße, bewährte, einfache Schriften, zu Beginn des 20. Jahrhunderts entworfen und ihres hohen Gebrauchswerts wegen fester Bestandteil der Alltagskultur in Amerika und Europa: Versalien der Schrifttype Franklin Gothic Extra Condensed, 1904 von Morris Fuller Benton von der American Type Founders Company entworfen – serifenlos, streng, männlich – und gelegentlich Stencil, eine 1937 von Gerry Powell entworfene Schablonenschrift mit Serifen. Seit Ende der 1990er-Jahre benutzt Weiner auch eine andere serifenlose Schablonenschrift, FF Offline, 1998 von dem holländischen Grafiker und Künstler Roelof Mulder entworfen.

> Each letter is broken up in an unusual way. Imagine a horizontal and a vertical space slicing through the center of the letters. In the case of a letter Y or Z or M or any other that includes a 45-degree angle, a space also angled at 45-degrees interrupts the connection between the lines. . . . The font has the look of the stenciling you might find on an industrial shipping crate, except less gritty, which puts you in mind of the international movement of goods.[6]

Despite all its elegance, as a stencil font it retains the immediacy of the street, evoking associations of sprayed or tagged graffiti on walls. And Weiner has designed his own sans-serif font: Margaret Seaworthy Gothic, which conveys the raw character of the die-cut letters that Weiner utilizes to design his distinctive posters, first and foremost

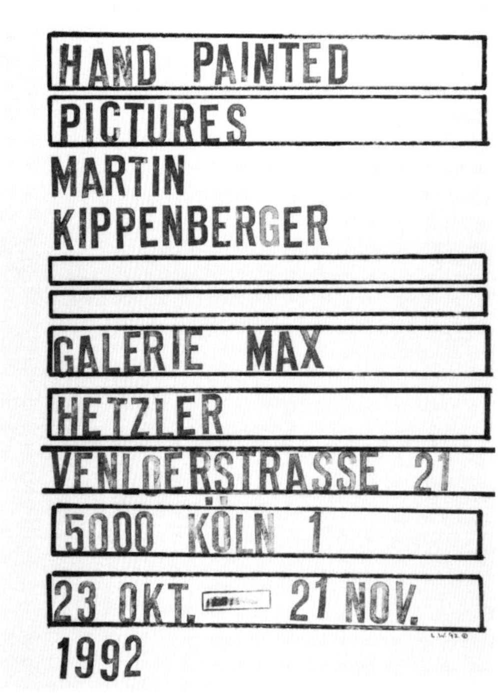

Exhibition poster designed by Lawrence Weiner, *Martin Kippenberger: Hand Painted Pictures*, Galerie Max Hetzler, Cologne, 1992
Ausstellungplakat, entworfen von Lawrence Weiner, *Martin Kippenberger, Hand Painted Pictures*, Galerie Max Hetzler, Köln, 1992

> Jeder Buchstabe ist auf eine ungewöhnliche Art aufgebrochen. Sie müssen sich einen horizontalen und einen vertikalen Leerraum vorstellen, der die Buchstaben in der Mitte durchschneidet. Bei einem Y oder einem Z oder M oder einem anderen Buchstaben, in dem es einen 45-Grad-Winkel gibt, wird die Verbindung zwischen den Linien durch einen Leerraum unterbrochen, der ebenfalls im 45-Grad-Winkel angeordnet ist. [...] Die Schrift erinnert an die Schablonenschrift, wie man sie, nur in gröberer Form, auf Frachtkisten finden kann. Man denkt dabei unwillkürlich an den internationalen Warenverkehr.[6]

Trotz aller Eleganz bewahrt sie als Schablonenschrift durch die Assoziation mit Sprühen und Wandgraffitis die Unmittelbarkeit der Straße. Weiner selbst hat schließlich eine serifenlose Schrift gezeichnet: Margaret Seaworthy Gothic, die den rohen Charakter des Stempeldrucks transportiert, mit dem Weiner unvergleichliche Plakate gestaltet hat, allen voran das berühmte Plakat für eine Ausstellung von Martin Kippenbergers Bildern 1992 in der Galerie Max Hetzler, Köln. Charakteristisch für Weiners Schrift sind die unregelmäßigen Abstände zwischen den Buchstaben, die so den Eindruck erwecken, einzeln von Hand gestempelt zu sein (was vielleicht sogar der Fall war). Die nahezu geradlinige Binnenzeichnung der runden Buchstaben verleiht ihnen eine gewisse Irritation, aber auch Präzision. Auffallend ist darüber hinaus die Gestaltung der diakritischen Zeichen, vor allem der Umlautzeichen als besonderem Merkmal der deutschen Sprache. Sie schweben nicht über, sondern sitzen kreisrund an den oberen Ecken der Buchstaben fest, fast wie Mickeymaus-Ohren. Das ist auf dem Siebdruck **NACH BILDENDE** the famous poster for a 1992 exhibition of Martin Kippenberger's paintings at Galerie Max Hetzler in Cologne. A prominent feature of this typeface are the irregular gaps between the letters, giving rise to the impression of their being individually stamped by hand (and maybe they were); the practically straight inner profiles of the rounded letters endow them with an unsettling quality, but also a certain air of decision. What is also striking in his typeface is the design of the diacritics, especially the umlauts common in the German language. Weiner's umlauts do not float above the letters, as is customary, but are rendered instead as small circles affixed on the outside upper "corners" of the letters; they look like Mickey Mouse ears. The umlauts appear in **NACH BILDENDE KUNST | AFTER FINE ART**, Weiner's special edition silkscreen produced for a boxed set of this volume. One of these "ears" can just be made out, on the left side of the *ü* in *Künste;* a red slash covers the other ear. In addition to their "seaworthiness," they issue a signal of irony in relation to the printing process, questioning cultural values behind the practice of typesetting according to rules of design while, at the same time, establishing an aesthetic all their own.[7] Typography has always been important to Weiner's work, and he continues to expand his vocabulary of form and structure, which will be apparent to the reader by merely leafing through this volume.

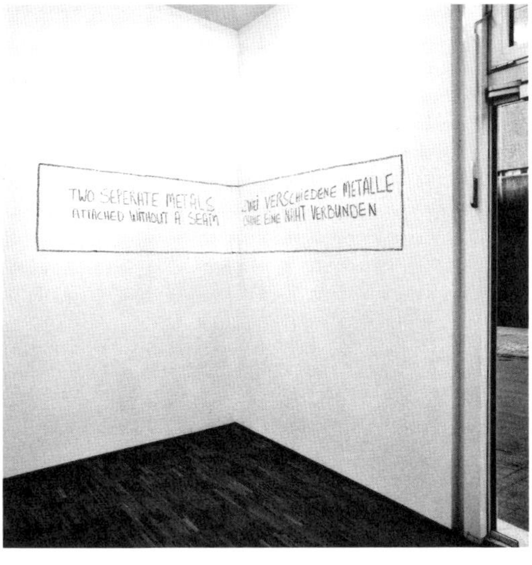

5 *Sculptures*, Konrad Fischer Galerie, Düsseldorf, 1985
5 *Sculptures*, Konrad Fischer Galerie, Düsseldorf, 1985

KUNST | AFTER FINE ART, den Weiner als Sonderedition zu dem vorliegenden Buch entworfen hat, trotz des roten Schrägstrichs auf der linken Seite des Ü in *Künste* ein Stück weit zu erkennen. Neben ihrer »Seetüchtigkeit« setzen sie in Verbindung mit der Aura des Stempeldrucks ein Ironiesignal. Damit sind die Wertmaßstäbe infrage gestellt, die hinter der kulturellen Praxis des Setzens nach Gestaltungsrichtlinien stehen, gleichzeitig wird aber selbst wieder eine eigene Ästhetik begründet.[7] Der Blick auf die Typografie ist in Weiners Werk von Anfang an wichtig und setzt sich in der kontinuierlichen Erweiterung seines Formenvokabulars fort, was allein schon beim Durchblättern dieses Bandes sinnfällig wird.

Das Paradigma des immateriellen Textes steht auch hinter der weithin nicht hinterfragten Praxis des Zitierens, der Übertragung eines Textes von einem Kontext in einen vollkommen anderen. Das Gewaltsame dieses Vorgangs wird deutlich, wenn man ihn auf der materiellen Ebene nachvollzieht: Ein Text wird aus seiner Schrifttype und -größe herausgelöst, von der Papierqualität und seinem Satzspiegel getrennt und wie selbstverständlich in die Schrifttype und -größe, auf die Papierqualität und den Satzspiegel des Zieltextes transformiert. Wenn Weiner in diesen Übertragungsprozess verwickelt ist, wenn seine Arbeiten aus einem Kontext in einen anderen gesetzt werden wie zum Beispiel in diesem Buch, beanspruchen seine Sprachskulpturen nicht den Schutzraum der Lyrik, deren letzte textsortenspezifische Bastion die Versgrenze oder typografisch gesprochen der Zeilenumbruch ist. Ein fester Zeilenumbruch ist bei Weiner in der Regel nicht zu beobachten. Aber die konsequente Entscheidung für Versalien, die Weiners Arbeiten nach der Erprobung verschiedener typografischer

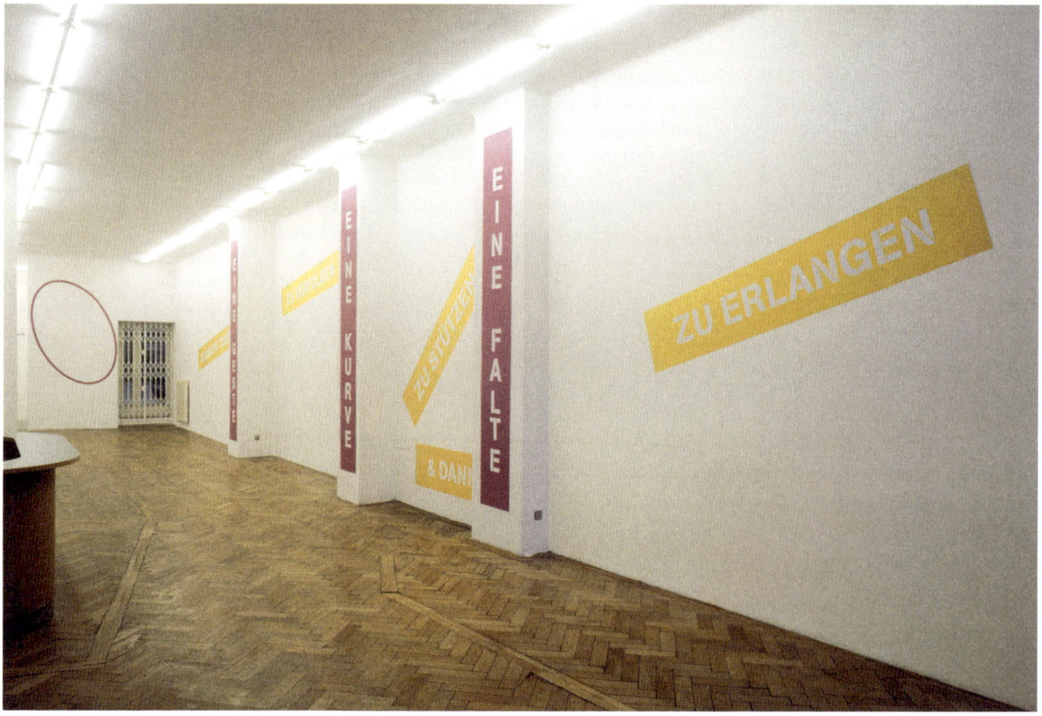

Full Circle, Galerie Hubert Winter, Vienna, 2000
Full Circle, Galerie Hubert Winter, Wien, 2000

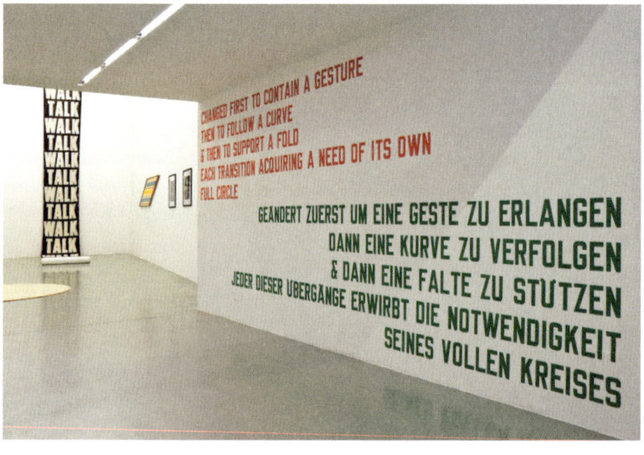

Filmschönheit, Galerie Mezzanin, Vienna, 2010
Filmschönheit, Galerie Mezzanin, Wien, 2010

The paradigm of the immateriality of text, the idea that it may be easily divorced from the form in which it appears, is what enables the largely unquestioned practice of quotation, the transfer of text from one context into an entirely different context. The act of appropriation, of violence inherent in this act is made clear by following the actual material process of the act: a text is removed from its typeface and size, paper quality and print area and rendered matter-of-factly in the destination text's typeface and size, paper quality and print area. When Weiner is caught up in this "transfer" process, when his work is removed from its context to be placed in another such as this book, his sculptures do not claim the protected space of poetry, where the last text-specific bastion is at the end of the verse, or, typographically speaking, at the line break. We do not see a consistent method or rule to the line breaks in Weiner's work. The use of capital letters, which has marked Weiner's work since his earlier exploration of the possibilities of typography,[8] represents an initial stumbling block for the reader/viewer. His works are never completely typographically assimilated into the body of a text; as a rule they are quoted in capital letters, a very unusual sign of respect for the materiality of the text used. Weiner does not make Conceptual Art, an "art of ideas," but works within it, as a sculptor.[9]

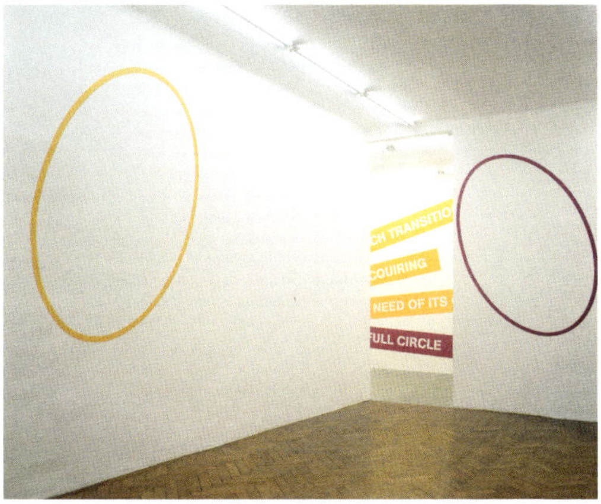

***Full Circle*, Galerie Hubert Winter, Vienna, 2000**
Full Circle, Galerie Hubert Winter, Wien, 2000

Gestaltungsmöglichkeiten kennzeichnet,[8] bildet eine erste Stolperschwelle für den Leser / Betrachter. Durch sie leisten Weiners Sätze dieser Einverleibung im Zitat Widerstand: Seine Arbeiten werden dem Fließtext nicht gänzlich angepasst, sondern in der Regel in Versalien zitiert, was ein ganz ungewöhnlicher Respekt vor der Materialität des übernommenen Textes ist. Weiner macht keine Konzept-, keine Ideenkunst, sondern arbeitet in ihr als Bildhauer.[9]

Die Materialität der als Skulptur verstandenen Schrift betont Weiner mit der haptischen Qualität von Gusslettern in Stahl- oder Bronzeplatten, von Schablonenschriften, die in Stahl geschnitten oder in Papier gestanzt sind, oder von Materialien wie Plastik. Dies ist leicht in seiner Arbeit **BUILT UP WITH STONES FALLEN DOWN FROM THE SKY DOWN ON | AUFGEBAUT MIT VOM HIMMEL GEFALLENEN STEINEN HERUNTER HINAUF** nachzuvollziehen, die auf dem grauen monolithischen Stein eines repräsentativen Hauses in Düsseldorf angebracht ist und sich über die gesamte Breite der Fassade erstreckt. Die Arbeit fügt sich problemlos in ihre bürgerliche Umgebung ein. In seinem unerschütterlichen Glauben an die Gleichwertigkeit aller Materialien wählte Weiner Plastik in himmelblauer Farbe für die Buchstaben. Der Kunststoff wird zweifellos ebenso lange überdauern wie der Stein. Auf die Buchbanderole um den Katalog der 2010 im Haus der Kunst in München gezeigten Sammlung Daled ist **A BIT OF MATTER AND A LITTLE BIT MORE** nicht nur gedruckt (in Franklin Gothic Extra Condensed), sondern auch aus dem Papier herausgestanzt (in FF Offline). Die beiden Statements laufen parallel und lassen sich als visuelles Wortspiel über Fragen der Simultaneität lesen.[10] An den Tastsinn appelliert auch die Präsentation einer Arbeit in der Galerie Hubert Winter in Wien,

The materiality of text understood as sculpture is accentuated in Weiner's work by the seemingly haptic quality of, for example, cast in steel or bronze; stencil cut-outs in steel, aluminum, or paper; or materials like plastic. This concept is easy to discern in the work **BUILT UP WITH STONES FALLEN DOWN FROM THE SKY DOWN ON | AUFGEBAUT MIT VOM HIMMEL GEFALLENEN STEINEN HERUNTER HINAUF**, with its placement on the gray monolithic stone of a stately home in Düsseldorf as it stretches across the broad façade. The work has integrated into this bourgeois neighborhood with ease. Weiner, ever true to his belief in the equality of all materials, chose plastic for those letters, in a sky blue color. The plastic will undoubtedly last as long as the stone.

Weiner's belly band for the Daled Collection catalogue at Munich's Haus der Kunst (2010) functions much the same way. **A BIT OF MATTER AND A LITTLE BIT MORE** is not only printed (in Franklin Gothic Extra Condensed) but also die-cut (in FF Offline); the two statements run parallel, or perhaps are a visual pun on simultaneity.[10] These characteristics relate to the presentation of work in 1996 at Galerie Hubert Winter in Vienna. Removing wall material, letters are chiseled into the gallery wall to create the work: **ROWS OF BROKEN BOTTLES SET INTO BADLY MIXED CONRETE | REIHEN VON ZERBROCHENEN FLASCHEN IN SCHLECHT GEMISCHTEN BETON GESETZT**. This installation recalls an earlier language work of Weiner's: **A 36" X 36" REMOVAL TO THE LATHING OR SUPPORT WALL OF PLASTER OR WALLBOARD FROM A WALL | EIN 36 X 36 INCHES GROSSER AUSSCHNITT BIS AUF DEN GRUND DES LATTEN- ODER MAUERWERKS AUS EINER GIPSWAND ODER WANDPLATTE**. It was first

die 1996 durch Abtragung von Material entstand, indem Buchstaben aus der Wand herausgemeißelt wurden: **ROWS OF BROKEN BOTTLES SET INTO BADLY MIXED CONCRETE | REIHEN VON ZERBROCHENEN FLASCHEN IN SCHLECHT GEMISCHTEN BETON GESETZT.** Diese Installation erinnert an eine frühere Spracharbeit, **A 36" X 36" REMOVAL TO THE LATHING OR SUPPORT WALL OF PLASTER OR WALLBOARD FROM A WALL | EIN 36 X 36 INCHES GROSSER AUSSCHNITT BIS AUF DEN GRUND DES LATTEN- ODER MAUERWERKS AUS EINER GIPSWAND ODER WANDPLATTE** und ihre erste Umsetzung in Europa, 1969 bei Harald Szeemanns Ausstellung

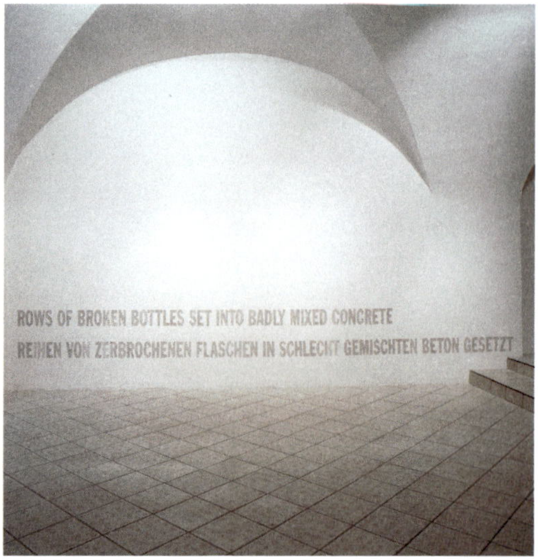

Badly Mixed Concrete, Galerie Hubert Winter, Vienna, 1996
Badly Mixed Concrete, Galerie Hubert Winter, Wien, 1996

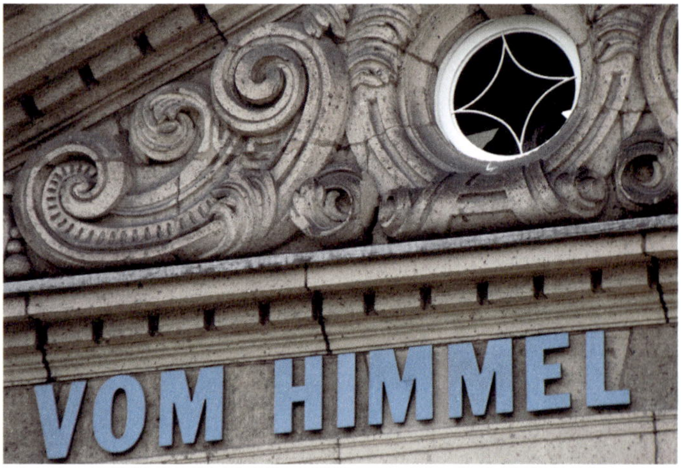

Work detail, Düsseldorf, 1997, Ursula Schulz-Dornburg Collection
Werkausschnitt, Düsseldorf, 1997, Sammlung Ursula Schulz-Dornburg

shown in Europe in 1969 at Kunsthalle Bern, in Harald Szeemann's *When Attitudes Become Form.* Or another example is the installation arrangement of the work **STONES & STONES & STONES & STONES | STEINE & STEINE & STEINE & STEINE** in 1995 at Leo Castelli Gallery in New York.

The presentation of a sculpture composed of text—or language—requires a showplace, a stage. This is yet another crucial moment in the insistence on the materiality of text. "Mise en scène / Setting the Stage" is a leitmotif in Weiner's work. The lexical field "to place" is one found frequently in his language sculptures; for example, take the following three works strung together: **THAT WHICH SETS THE STAGE FOR WHAT . . . PUT ASIDE OR PUT AWAY . . . PUT INTO A CONTEXT NOT PREVIOUSLY KNOWN WHERESOEVER,** or **IN SEARCH OF WHERE TO PLACE WHAT AND WHY EN ROUTE TO DOCUMENTA XIII.**[11] Without a "stage" there is no entry to a cultural context. What Weiner reduces to a very elementary level with the terms "stage" or "place" masks out the question of the sculpture and plinth in a narrow sense—so central to art history—as secondary, and is actually such a broad and complex component of his oeuvre that it is difficult to develop discursively in an essay.

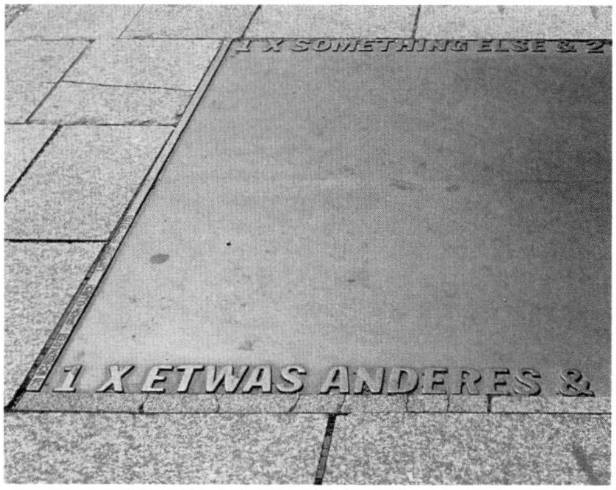

Work detail, *To Build a Square in the Rhineland*, Cologne Cathedral Square, 1995, Gift to the City of Cologne in the framework of the Wolfgang Hahn Prize, Ludwig Museum
Werkausschnitt, *Ein Quadrat im Rheinland bauen*, Domplatte, Köln, 1995, Geschenk im Rahmen des Wolfgang-Hahn-Preises, Museum Ludwig, an die Stadt Köln

When Attitudes Become Form in Bern. Ein weiteres Beispiel ist die Installation der Arbeit **STONES & STONES & STONES | STEINE & STEINE & STEINE & STEINE** 1995 in der Galerie Leo Castelli, New York.

Die Präsentation einer Skulptur aus Text oder Sprache braucht einen Schauplatz, eine Bühne. Dies ist ein weiteres entscheidendes Moment im Beharren auf der Materialität des Textes. »Mise en scène« oder »Setting the stage« ist ein Leitmotiv von Weiners Arbeit. Das lexikalische Feld »to place« ist in seinen Sprachskulpturen häufig vertreten wie bei den folgenden drei aneinander gereihten Arbeiten **THAT WHICH SETS THE STAGE FOR WHAT ... PUT ASIDE OR PUT AWAY ... PUT INTO A CONTEXT NOT PREVIOUSLY KNOWN WHERESOEVER** oder bei **IN SEARCH OF WHERE TO PLACE WHAT AND WHY EN ROUTE TO DOCUMENTA XIII.**[11] Ohne Bühne gibt es keinen Eintritt in den kulturellen Kontext. Aber was Weiner mit den Begriffen »Stage« oder »Place« auf eine ganz elementare Ebene herunterbricht und damit auch die im kunstgeschichtlichen Diskurs zentrale Frage von Skulptur und Sockel im engeren Sinne als sekundär ausblendet, ist in seinem Œuvre tatsächlich ein so weit gefasster und komplexer Begriff, dass es schwierig ist, ihn diskursiv zu entfalten.

Als eines der grundlegenden Elemente in Weiners Œuvre muss die Entscheidung betrachtet werden, die Arbeit selbst ohne ein anderes Trägermaterial direkt auf der Wand aufzubringen. Sie ergab sich in den 1970er-Jahren aus der Präsentation einer Arbeit Weiners, die Giuseppe Panza, ein passionierter Sammler von Weiner, in seinem Haus in Mailand hatte umsetzen lassen:

> Ich kam in sein Haus, um die Sammlung anzusehen, und da stand eine von meinen Arbeiten

The decision to place work directly on the wall without any support should be considered a fundamental element of Weiner's oeuvre. It began in the early seventies with the presentation of a Weiner work that Giuseppe Panza, an avid collector of his, had carried out in his home:

> And there was a work of mine either painted or presstype, I never figured it out, on the wall. I think I was a little distressed, walked around Milano for a while, and realized that it was just as good as anything else. It wasn't anything I figured out, it was something that just came about by someone using the work. I think I was also tired of carrying these wrinkled typewritten papers.[12]

By adopting this manner of exhibition for much of his oeuvre, Weiner's work has gained its lasting imprint, even if the artist himself constantly subverts this device, as seen in large-format floor installations that he began exploring in 1981 at Leo Castelli Gallery and that reached their pinnacle in terms of size in the 2011 collaboration with Liam Gillick on a literally conceived 1,600-square-meter exhibition floor at MUHKA in Antwerp.

The formative experience of his attempt to work in a traditional sense as a sculptor, which ended (or possibly began!) with placing a found piece of stone on a rough sawn table built of plain pine two-by-fours, is a story that is repeated in almost all writing on Weiner. While it would seem to exhibit all the traits of the myth of a conflicted artist, it in fact reflects the significance of the plinth or the stage for the approach to language as sculpture from the very beginning.

> an der Wand, entweder mit Farbe oder mit Klebebuchstaben, das habe ich nie erfahren. Ich glaube, ich war zuerst etwas irritiert, lief eine Zeitlang durch Mailand, und erkannte dann, daß es wohl genausogut war wie irgend etwas anderes. Ich hatte es nicht selbst erfunden, es kam von jemandem, der die Arbeiten gebrauchte. Ich war es inzwischen wohl auch leid, diese zerknitterten Schreibmaschinenblätter mit mir herumzutragen.[12]

Durch Übernahme dieses Ausstellungsmodus für viele seiner Arbeiten hat das Werk Weiners eine nachhaltige Prägung erfahren, wenngleich er dieses Dispositiv selbst immer wieder unterwandert wie beispielsweise mit großformatigen Bodeninstallationen, die er 1981 bei Leo Castelli erprobte und die – zumindest hinsichtlich der Größe – 2011 einen Höhepunkt in Zusammenarbeit mit Liam Gillick auf 1.600 Quadratmetern wörtlich genommener Ausstellungsfläche im MUHKA in Antwerpen erfuhren.

Mit der Entscheidung, einen gefundenen Stein auf einen rau gesägten Tisch zu stellen – Kanthölzer aus einfacher Kiefer, 5 x 10 Zentimeter –, endete (oder begann) Weiners Versuch, im traditionellen Sinn als Bildhauer zu arbeiten. Dieses Schlüsselerlebnis ist eine in nahezu allen Texten über Weiner wiedergegebene Geschichte, die fast die Züge eines

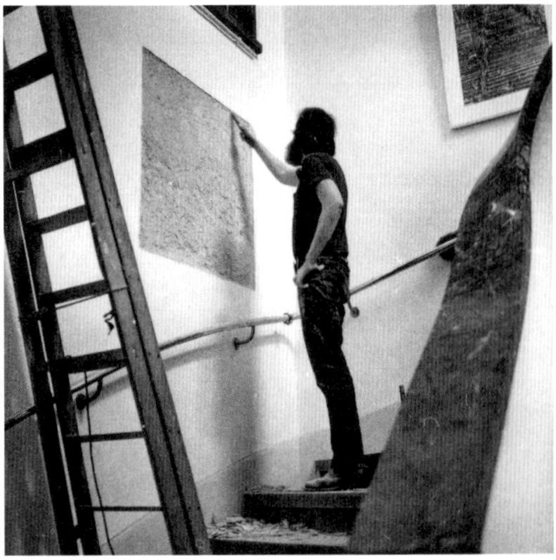

Lawrence Weiner constructing his work at *When Attitudes Become Form*, Kunsthalle Bern, 1969
Lawrence Weiner bei der Installation seiner Arbeit *When Attitudes Become Form*, Kunsthalle Bern, 1969

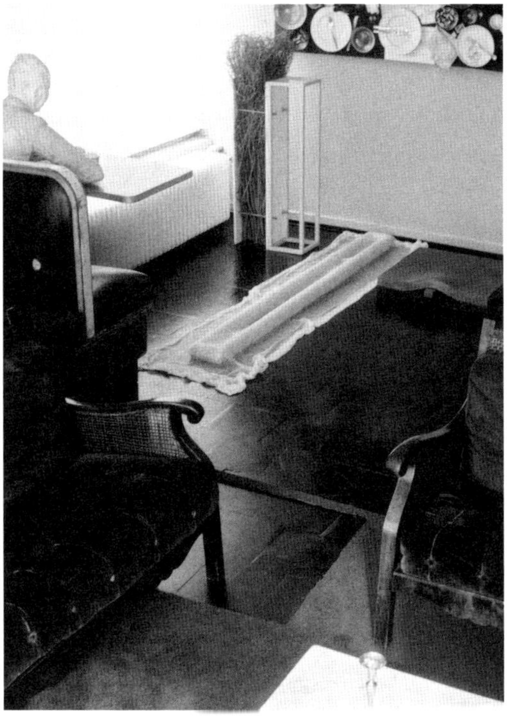

Work detail, Cologne, 1969, Wolfgang Hahn Collection, Ludwig Museum, Vienna
Werkausschnitt, Köln, 1969, Sammlung Wolfgang Hahn, Museum Ludwig, Wien

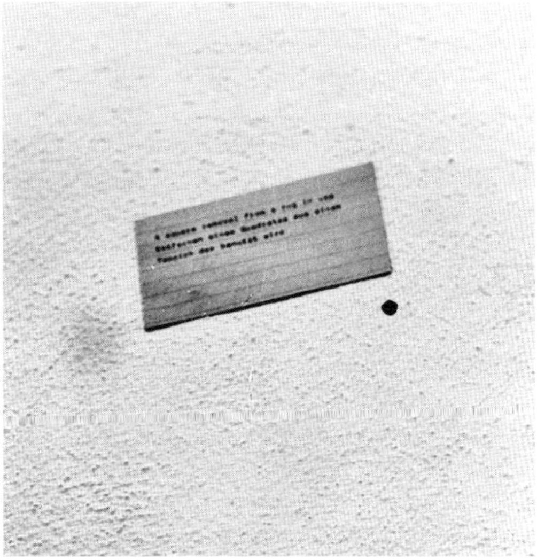

***Lawrence Weiner*, Konrad Fischer Galerie, Düsseldorf, 1969**
Lawrence Weiner, Konrad Fischer Galerie, Düsseldorf, 1969

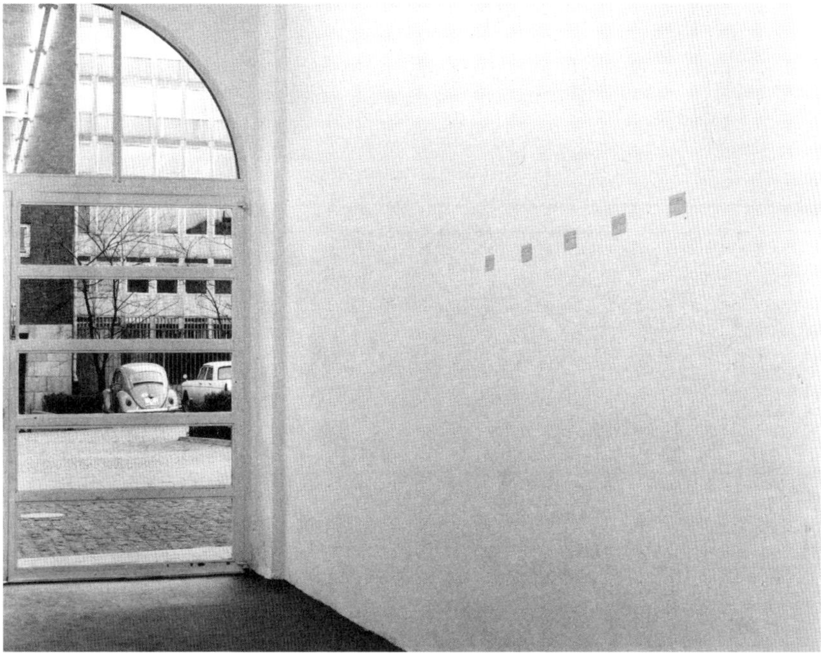

***Lawrence Weiner*, Konrad Fischer Galerie, Düsseldorf, 1969**
Lawrence Weiner, Konrad Fischer Galerie, Düsseldorf, 1969

> I realized sculpture was about "Put in Place," volume or mass put in place. It's a matter of transportation; you move it from one place to the other, which was a rejection of the Duchampian ethic. I still find myself engaged in rejecting the idea that changing the context of a material constitutes an aesthetic gesture. I think that all materials normally change their context and it's not necessarily an aesthetic gesture.[13]

Weiner responds to epistemological or ontological doubts about reality and its accessibility to human perception and cognition in the title of his contribution to the recent Documenta 13 *100 Notes—100 Thoughts* notebooks, *If in Fact There Is a Context*, and thus knocks the theory off the table to be able to place "something" on it.

The Rhineland can claim to have provided one of the culturally most significant and at the same time controversial stages for a work by Weiner: a 7,000-square-meter open square of light-gray granite in front of a UNESCO World Heritage Site, the so-called Domplatte (Cathedral Square or "Pavement"), a term that in German clarifies the brutality behind the leveling of the originally labyrinthine urban architecture that once surrounded it. Later on, Gerhard Richter was commissioned to design the south-facing window at the Cathedral itself.

To Build a Square in the Rhineland / Ein Quadrat im Rheinland bauen was a gift of the Friends of the Ludwig Museum to the City of Cologne in 1994. Weiner, a recipient of the museum's Wolfgang Hahn Prize, could be seen as making a tribute to Hahn, the collector. The work consists of four

ihm eher widersprechenden Künstlermythos trägt. Tatsächlich spiegelt sie die Bedeutung des Sockels oder der Bühne für den Umgang mit Sprache als Skulptur von Anfang an.

> Mir wurde klar, daß es in der Skulptur um das »Put in Place« geht, darum, Volumen oder Masse an einem Ort zu plazieren. Es geht um Transport, etwas von einer Stelle an eine andere zu versetzen, und das bedeutete eine Ablehnung der Duchampschen Ethik. Ich lehne auch heute noch die Idee ab, daß es eine ästhetische Geste ist, den Kontext eines Materials zu verändern. Ich meine, alle Materialien wechseln normalerweise ihren Kontext, und das ist nicht unbedingt eine ästhetische Geste.[13]

Auf alle erkenntnistheoretisch oder ontologisch begründeten Zweifel an der Realität und ihrer Zugänglichkeit für die menschliche Wahrnehmung und Erkenntnis antwortet Weiner im Titel seines *dOCUMENTA (13) Notebook* mit: *If in Fact There Is a Context* und fegt damit die Theorie vom Tisch, um etwas – »something« – darauf platzieren zu können.

Das Rheinland darf für sich beanspruchen, eine der kulturell bedeutendsten und zugleich umstrittensten Bühnen für eine Arbeit von Weiner zur

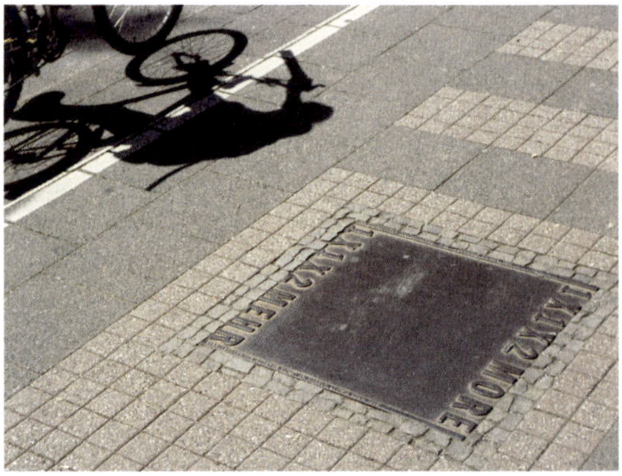

***To Build a Square in the Rhineland*, Venloer Strasse, Cologne, 1995, Gift to the City of Cologne in the framework of the Wolfgang Hahn Prize, Ludwig Museum**
Ein Quadrat im Rheinland bauen, Venloer Straße, Köln, 1995, Geschenk im Rahmen des Wolfgang-Hahn-Preises, Museum Ludwig, an die Stadt Köln

quadratic steel plates in different sizes, a return to a central motif of Weiner's earlier work where the square is a component in numerous works from the sixties, as in Szeemann's *When Attitudes Become Form* exhibition in 1969 where he hammered out a square from a wall in the museum. Shortly after, Weiner began working with his first German gallery, Konrad Fischer Galerie,

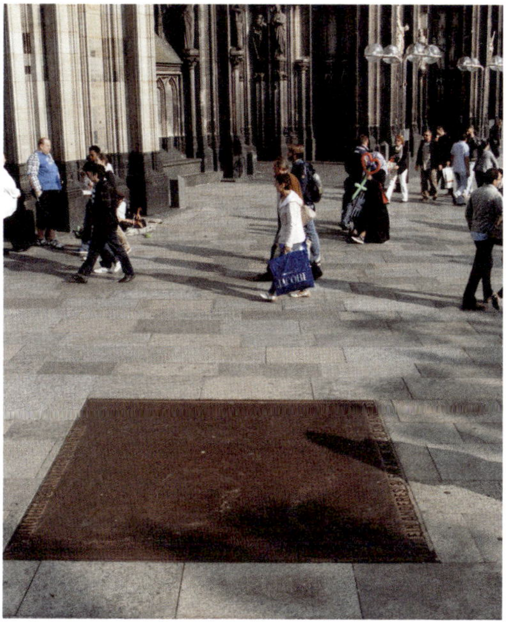

***To Build a Square in the Rhineland,* Cathedral Square, Cologne, 1995, Gift to the City of Cologne in the framework of the Wolfgang Hahn Prize, Ludwig Museum**
Ein Quadrat im Rheinland bauen, Domplatte, Köln, 1995, Geschenk im Rahmen des Wolfgang-Hahn-Preises, Museum Ludwig, an die Stadt Köln

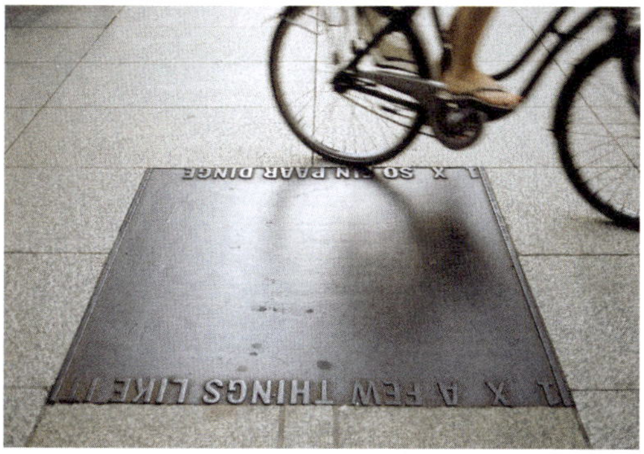

***To Build a Square in the Rhineland,* Cathedral Square, Cologne, 1995, Gift to the City of Cologne in the framework of the Wolfgang Hahn Prize, Ludwig Museum**
Ein Quadrat im Rheinland bauen, Domplatte, Köln, 1995, Geschenk im Rahmen des Wolfgang-Hahn-Preises, Museum Ludwig, an die Stadt Köln

Verfügung gestellt zu haben, und das lange bevor Gerhard Richter mit der Gestaltung des Südfensters im Kölner Dom beauftragt wurde: Eine rund 7.000 Quadratmeter große Freifläche in hellgrauem Granit vor einem UNESCO-Weltkulturerbe, der sogenannten »Domplatte«, ein Begriff, der die Brutalität der Planierung des ursprünglich verwinkelten Areals um den Kölner Dom verdeutlicht.

To Build a Square in the Rhineland / Ein Quadrat im Rheinland bauen wurde 1994 der Stadt Köln als Geschenk der Gesellschaft für Moderne Kunst am Museum Ludwig übergeben, von der Weiner auch den Wolfgang-Hahn-Preis erhielt, sodass die Arbeit als Hommage an den Sammler Hahn betrachtet werden kann. Mit der Gestaltung von vier quadratischen Stahlplatten in unterschiedlichen Größen greift Weiner auf ein zentrales Motiv seines Œuvre zurück. Es ist Gegenstand zahlreicher Arbeiten aus den 1960er-Jahren, wie etwa das Quadrat, das er 1969 in Bern bei Harald Szeemanns Ausstellung *When Attitudes Become Form* aus der Wand des Museums hämmerte. Kurz darauf begann die Zusammenarbeit mit seiner ersten deutschen Galerie, der Konrad Fischer Galerie in Düsseldorf.[14] Wolfgang Hahn, der erste rheinische Sammler Weiners, erwarb **A SQUARE REMOVAL OF A RUG IN USE | ENTFERNEN EINES QUADRATES AUS EINEM TEPPICH DER BENUTZT WIRD** in der Ausstellung.[15] »Und wann immer Weiner ein Wort entbindet,« so Reiner Speck, ebenfalls ein Kölner Sammler von Weiner, »schwebt ihm das Werden einer Skulptur vor; und die hat Köln nun – so radikal und adäquat wie diese Stadt es verdient: Wo immer man sie betrachtet, verbeugt man sich vor dem Dom und blickt auf die Klarheit eines Quadrats.«[16] Weiner betrachtet diese Arbeit nicht als »site-specific«, sondern im Kontext einer, so Speck, »durch Mittelalter, Bomben und Klüngel

Düsseldorf.[14] Wolfgang Hahn, the first collector of Weiner in the Rhineland, had purchased **A SQUARE REMOVAL OF A RUG IN USE | ENTFERNEN EINES QUADRATES AUS EINEM TEPPICH DER BENUTZT WIRD**[15] from the exhibition. According to Reiner Speck, another Weiner collector from Cologne, "And whenever Weiner gives birth to a word, he has in mind the creation of a sculpture, which Cologne now has—as radically and as adequately as this city deserves: Wherever one chooses to observe it, one must bow before the Cathedral and look at the clarity of the square."[16] Weiner does not consider this work site specific, but rather sees it in the context of what Speck calls a "crooked city deformed by the Middle Ages, bombs, and corruption": "A work is capable of being Stadt specific not site specific. It doesn't in fact matter where the squares fall as long as they fall within the Rhineland."[17]

Over twenty thousand people walk by the Domplatte each day; this means over seven million viewers per year. What Weiner has to say to them on the squares laid in the ground is the following:

1 X ANOTHER & ANOTHER & ANOTHER
1 X EIN ANDERES & EIN ANDERES & EIN ANDERES

1 X SOMETHING ELSE & 2 OTHER THINGS
1 X ETWAS ANDERES & 2 ANDERE DINGE

1 X A FEW THINGS LIKE IT
1 X SO EIN PAAR DINGE

and somewhat further away from the Cathedral, on Venloer Strasse in front of the Stadtpark:

1 X 1 X 2 MORE
1 X 1 X 2 MEHR

ungeformten, krummen Stadt«: »Work is capable of being Stadt specific NOT site specific. It doesn't in fact matter where the squares fall as long as they fall within the Rhineland.«[17] Egal wo die Platten fallen, Hauptsache, sie fallen im Rheinland.

Über 20.000 Menschen passieren täglich die Domplatte, das sind über 7 Millionen Betrachter im Jahr. Was Weiner ihnen auf den im Boden eingelassenen Platten zu sagen hat:

1 X ANOTHER & ANOTHER & ANOTHER
1 X EIN ANDERES & EIN ANDERES & EIN ANDERES

1 X SOMETHING ELSE & 2 OTHER THINGS
1 X ETWAS ANDERES & 2 ANDERE DINGE

1 X A FEW THINGS LIKE IT
1 X SO EIN PAAR DINGE

Und etwas entfernt vom Dom in der Venloer Straße vor dem Stadtpark:

1 X 1 X 2 MORE
1 X 1 X 2 MEHR

Bemerkt man die Aussage? Nimmt man die Stahlplatten überhaupt wahr? Sind sie nicht Teil all der Kanaldeckel, Abdeckungen, Lüftungsschächte, die den städtischen Grund in die Unterwelt perforieren, Teil des Abwehrmechanismus, auf den Landschaftsarchitekten wie Adriaan Geuze nachdrücklich verweisen, indem sie genau mit den Materialien arbeiten, die Bestandteil der Stadtkultur sind: Stahl, Beton, Gusseisen?[18]

Weiners Beitrag für die *Skulptur. Projekte in Münster 1997* bestand aus zwei dicken Stahlplatten, wie

Does one notice the statement? Are the steel plates perceived at all? Have they not become a part of all the manhole covers, grates, and vents that perforate Cologne's streets and that lead underground, the very protective measures to which landscape architects like Adriaan Geuze explicitly refer by working with materials that are an integral part of urban culture: steel, concrete, cast iron.[18]

Weiner's contribution to Skulptur Projekte in Münster 1997 consisted of two thick steel plates identical to those used in construction to cover excavations, for safety. One of the plates has the work stenciled in German, the other, English. Weiner's instructions for placing the plates refers explicitly to their bi-functionality; they were to be "installed" wherever necessary, to cover excavations, to protect pedestrians.

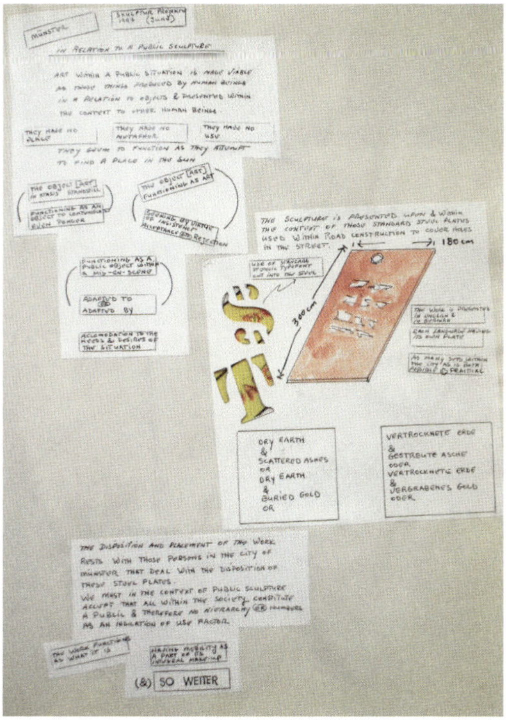

Sketchbook, 1997–98
Skizzenbuch, 1997/98

sie im Tiefbau zur Abdeckung von Baugruben eingesetzt werden. Die Spracharbeit ist mit Schablonenschrift in der einen Platte auf Englisch, in der anderen auf Deutsch geschnitten. Auf ihre doppelte Funktion weist Weiners Konzept für die Ausführung der Platten explizit hin. Sie sollten dort installiert werden, wo immer sie zur Abdeckung von Baugruben, zum Schutz der Fußgänger notwendig waren. Während der Ausstellung wurden 1997 die Bodenplatten mit Weiners Schriften in ihrer tatsächlichen Funktion in aktuelle Baustellen integriert. Später, 2010, installierte man ein Plattenpaar neben dem Eingang des Westfälischen Landesmuseums auf dem Bürgersteig, sodass sie in einem bürgerlich-kulturellen Kontext platziert sind, der ihre ursprüngliche Funktion im Straßenbau unterwandert.

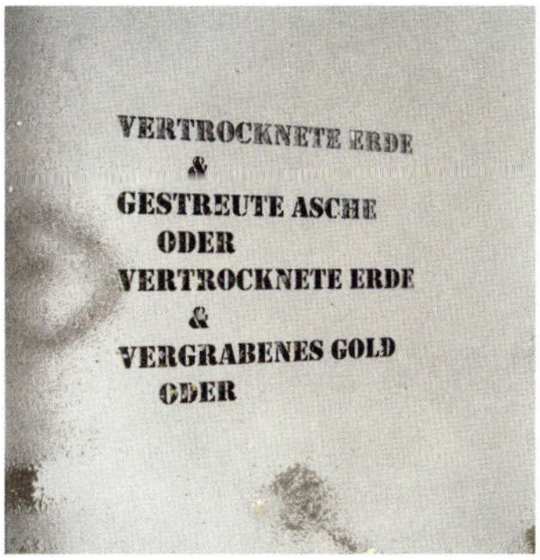

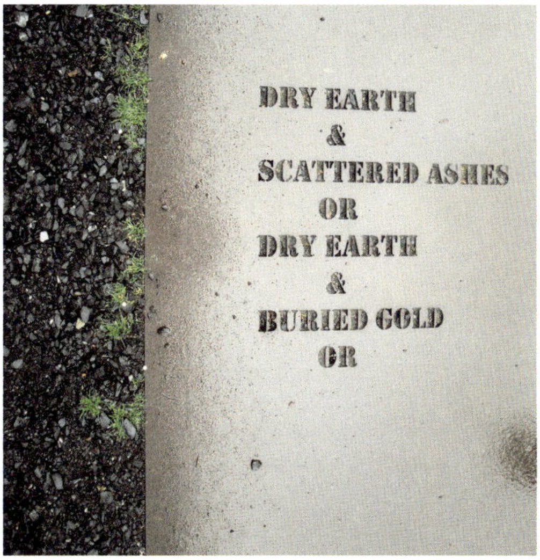

***Skulptur. Projekte 97*, Münster, 1997; new installation at Westfälisches Landesmuseum, Münster, 2010**
Skulptur. Projekte 97, Münster, 1997, neu installiert am Westfälischen Landesmuseum, Münster, 2010

Weiner's inscriptions were integrated into Münster construction sites during the exhibition, where needed. Later, in 2010, one set of plates was reinstalled on the sidewalk adjacent to the entrance to the Westfälisches Landesmuseum; this location, in a more bourgeois-cultural context, subverted their original function, i.e. to be placed at construction sites. The display resisted the transience of painted walls, making a different claim to duration and validity due to the materiality of both support and text. (In a 1988 catalogue essay, Marja Bloem referred to the historical tradition of gestures of domination linked to inscriptions on stone and metal within the context of a proposed work Weiner later inserted into an unused sandstone frame in the front of the Stedelijk Museum façade in 1988.[19]) In 1997, however, the reaction to Weiner's contribution to the Münster Skulptur Projekte was divided. Thomas Wagner, a critic at the *Frankfurter Allgemeine Zeitung,* deplored Lawrence Weiner's "poeticization of the steel slabs from the public works administration," the work showing how "tired the concept of sculpture that works with site-specificity has become." Amber Sayah, of the *Stuttgarter Zeitung,* in contrast, wrote, "And thus, in the midst of the art hullabaloo, the old classical sculptures and installations are given new importance beyond all 'site-specificity': quiet

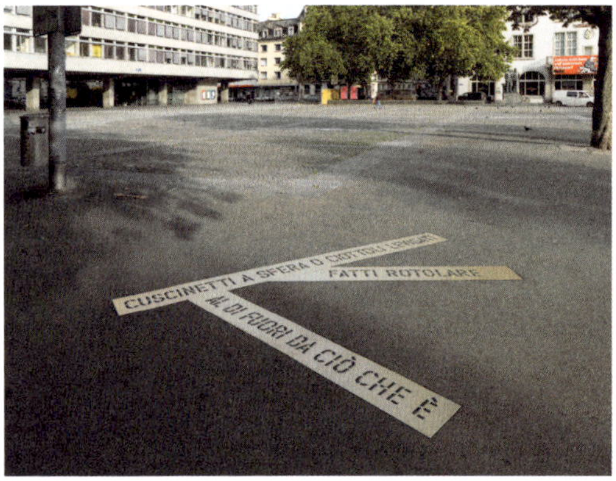

Helvetiaplatz, Zurich, 2007, public commission by the City of Zurich, Hans Hüssy Collection, Zumikon
Helvetiaplatz, Zürich, 2007, im Auftrag der Stadt Zürich, Sammlung Hans Hüssy, Zumikon

Das Display ist insofern ungewöhnlich, als es sich der Flüchtigkeit bemalter Wände widersetzt und aufgrund der Materialität von Träger und Schrift einen anderen Anspruch auf Dauer und Gültigkeit erhebt. (Im Zusammenhang mit einer 1988 von Weiner für einen leeren Sandsteinrahmen auf der Fassade des Stedelijk Museum vorgeschlagenen Arbeit verweist Marja Bloem in einem Katalogbeitrag auf die historische Tradition der mit Inschriften auf Stein oder Metall verbundenen Herrschaftsgesten.)[19] 1997 war die Reaktion auf Weiners Beitrag zu den *Skulptur. Projekten* gespalten. Thomas Wagner von der *Frankfurter Allgemeine Zeitung* kritisierte Lawrence Weiners »Poetisierung von Stahlplatten des Tiefbauamtes«, die Arbeit zeige, wie »sehr das Konzept einer site-specific arbeitenden Skulptur in die Jahre gekommen« sei. Amber Sayah, *Stuttgarter Zeitung,* dagegen schrieb: »Und so kommt es, dass inmitten dieses Kunstrummels die alten klassischen Skulpturen und Installationen jenseits aller ›site-specificity‹ zu neuen Ehren gelangen: stille Arbeiten wie Ulrich Rückriems in den Boden eingelassene Granitplatten vor dem Schloss, die ihr Pendant in Lawrence Weiners an Baustellen verwendeten Stahlplatten haben […].« In Zürich wurden drei Bodenarbeiten Weiners an innerstädtischen Verkehrsknotenpunkten und Plätzen sehr unterschiedlichen Charakters installiert. Sie nehmen den Rhythmus und das Sich-ineinander-Verkeilen der Wege von unzähligen Menschenströmen auf und sind in Englisch, Deutsch und Italienisch realisiert.[20]

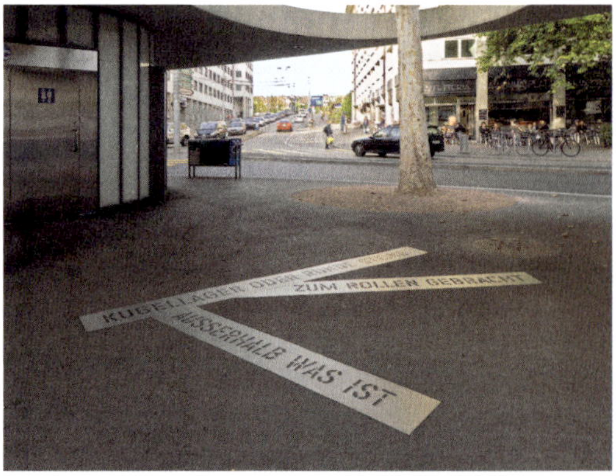

Bellevue, Zurich, 2007, public commission by the City of Zurich, Hans Hüssy Collection, Zumikon
Bellevue, Zürich, 2007, im Auftrag der Stadt Zürich, Sammlung Hans Hüssy, Zumikon

works like Ulrich Rückriem's granite plates in the ground before the castle have their counterpart in Lawrence Weiner's steel plates, used at construction sites." In the city of Zurich, in 2007, Weiner installed three surface works at different intersections and squares in the city. Realized in English, German, and Italian, they take up the rhythm and the converging, intertwining paths of the endless flow of pedestrians.[20]

In exhibitions and catalogues, Weiner's work is usually accompanied by the statement "language + the materials referred to." The beholder is thus reminded that the work is not just a linguistic presentation but about objects themselves, about the "things" in this world. Contrary to postmodern theories and the skepticism of linguistic philosophy, the referentiality of language is an absolute requirement from Weiner's realistic and materialistic standpoint; today this view finds consensus from linguistics and carries over to the philosophy of language.[21] His work on a tram, realized in 2008 as part of the Düsseldorf retrospective, could be read as paying homage to the philosopher, logician, and mathematician Gottlob Frege: **A LINE DRAWN FROM THE FIRST STAR AT DUSK TO THE LAST STAR AT DAWN | EINE LINIE GEZOGEN VOM ERSTEN STERN DER ABENDDÄMMERUNG BIS ZUM LETZTEN STERN DER MORGENDÄMMERUNG**. For Frege, sense is reference.[22] The difference between the key terms "reference" and "sense" in his approach to the philosophy of language is clarified in the famous example of the two names of the planet Venus: "The reference of 'evening star' would be the same as that of 'morning star,' but not the sense."[23] Weiner's work names a line that is drawn from the Morning Star to the Evening Star, and thus perhaps nothing other

Den Arbeiten Weiners ist in Ausstellungen und Katalogen immer der Zusatz beigestellt: »language + the materials referred to« (Sprache + die benannten Materalien). Der Betrachter wird dadurch darauf hingewiesen, dass die Arbeit nicht einfach eine Sprachpräsentation ist, sondern von den Objekten selbst, von den »Dingen« der Welt, handelt. Entgegen aller postmodernen Theoreme und sprachphilosophischen Skepsis ist die Referenzialität der Sprache von Weiners realistischem und materialistischem Standpunkt aus unabdingbare Voraussetzung, und er trifft damit heute wieder auf einen Konsens, der von der Linguistik aus in die Sprachphilosophie hineingetragen wird.[21] Seine 2008 anlässlich der Düsseldorfer Retrospektive auf einer Straßenbahn ausgeführte Arbeit lässt sich als Hommage auf den Philosophen, Logiker und Mathematiker Gottlob Frege lesen: **A LINE DRAWN FROM THE FIRST STAR AT DUSK TO THE LAST STAR AT DAWN | EINE LINIE GEZOGEN VOM ERSTEN STERN DER ABENDDÄMMERUNG BIS ZUM LETZTEN STERN DER MORGENDÄMMERUNG**. Für Frege ist Bedeutung Referenz.[22] Den Unterschied der in seinem sprachphilosophischen Ansatz zentralen Begriffe »Sinn« und »Bedeutung« verdeutlicht er an dem berühmt gewordenen Beispiel der beiden Namen des Planeten Venus: »Es würde die

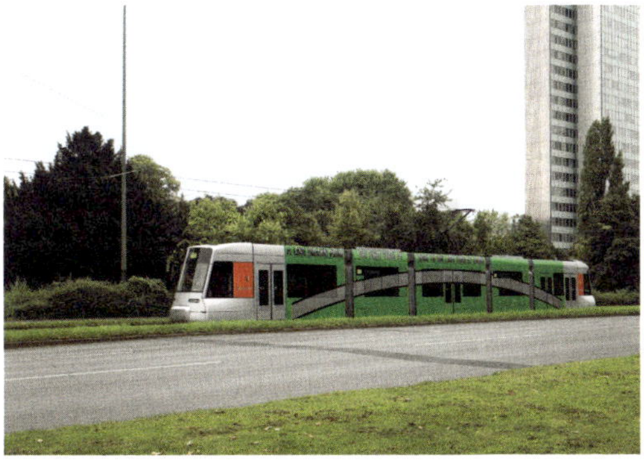

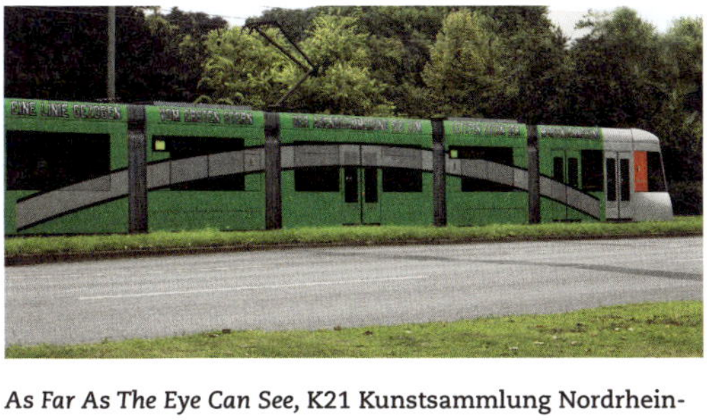

***As Far As The Eye Can See*, K21 Kunstsammlung Nordrhein-Westfalen, City tram, Düsseldorf, 2008**

As Far As The Eye Can See, K21 Kunstsammlung Nordrhein-Westfalen, Straßenbahn, Düsseldorf, 2008

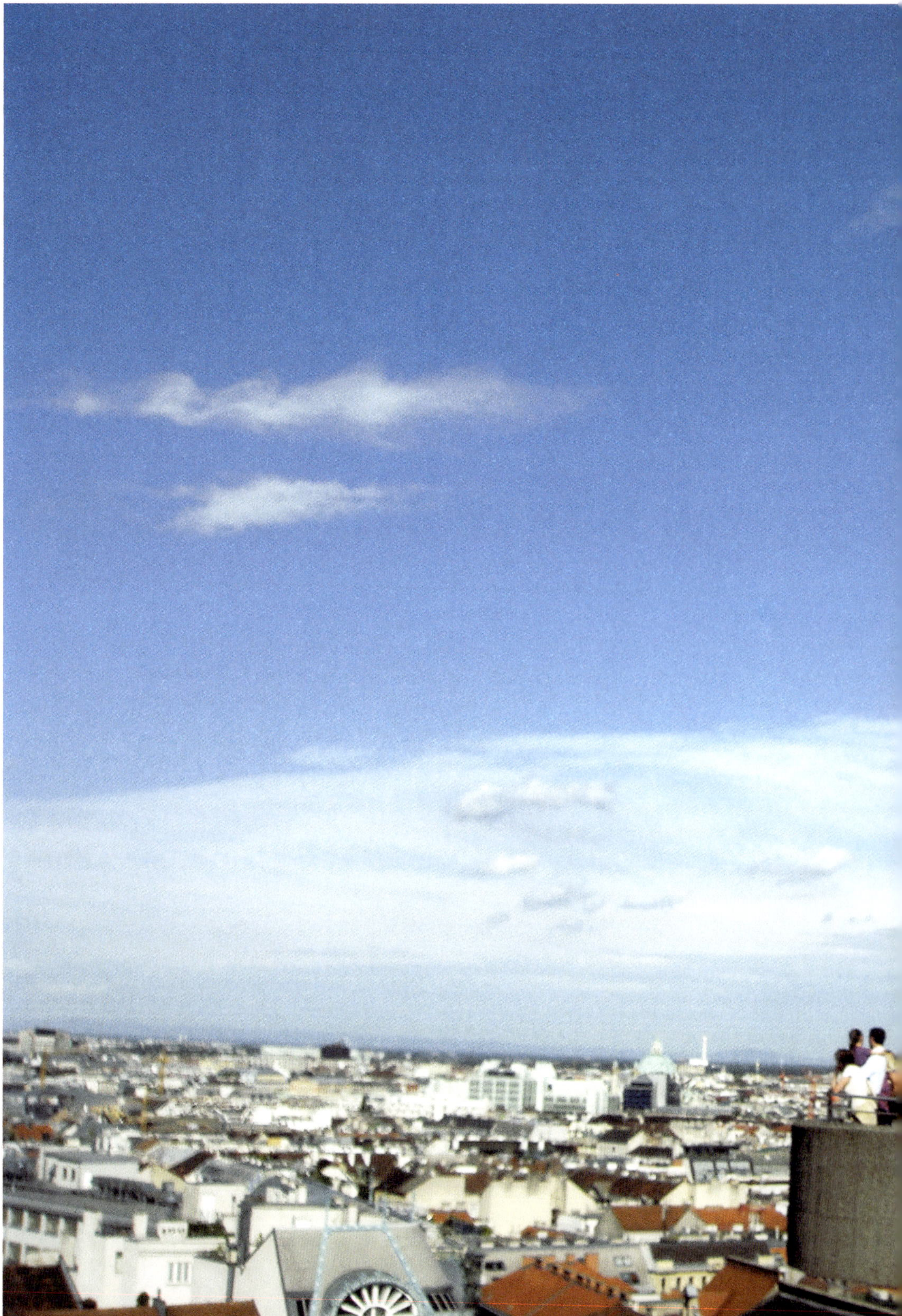

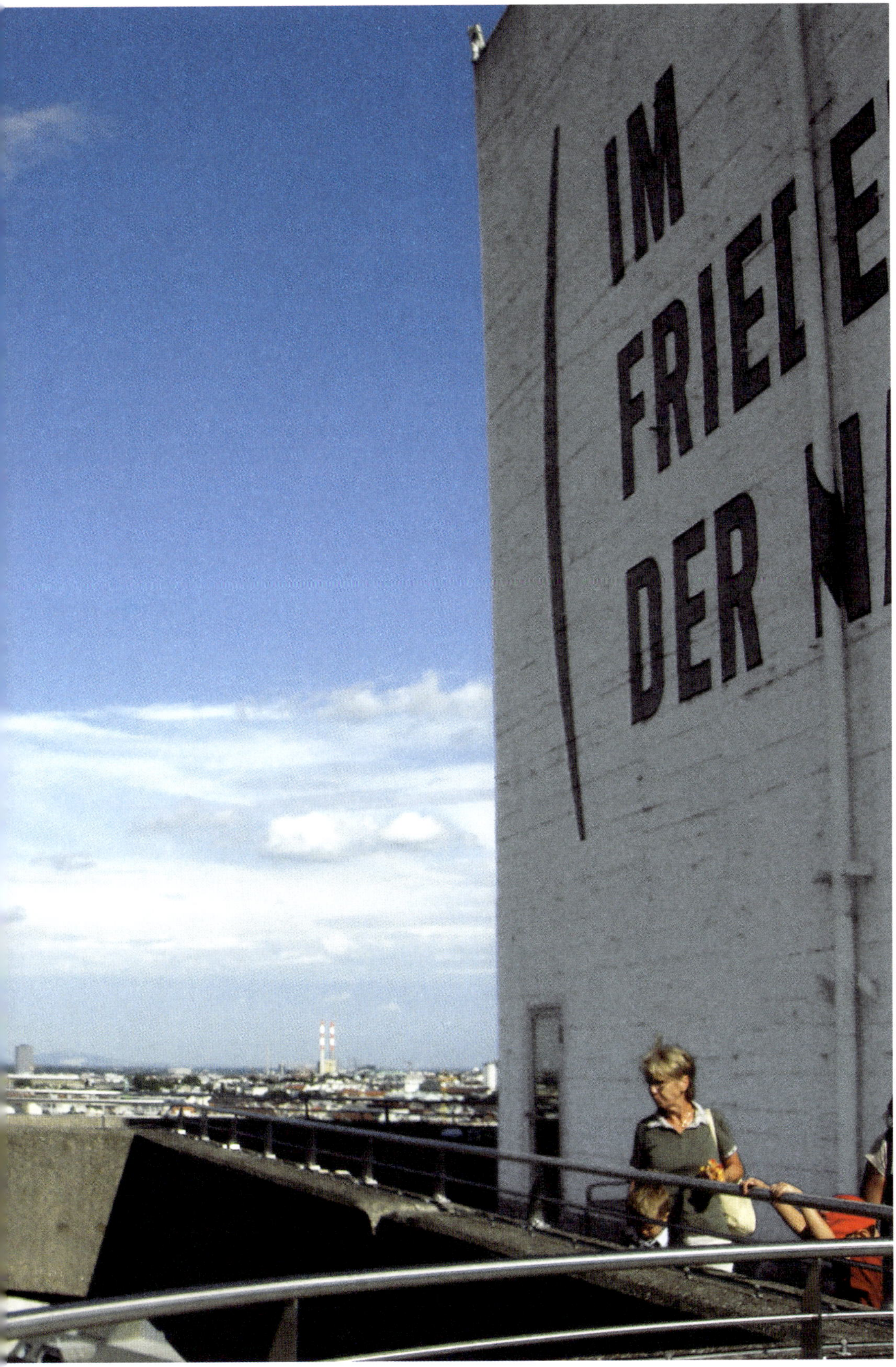
IM
DER

than the conceptual figurative of the *Full Circle* as seen in 2000 in Hubert Winter Gallery.

The reference to the object seems to emerge on its own in the installations in public spaces by way of choosing a concrete stage, while at the same time remaining in highly complex linguistic territory. For example, the case with Weiner's spectacular work **SMASHED TO PIECES (IN THE STILL OF THE NIGHT)**, sited on a former flak tower in Vienna's Esterházy Park. Nearly fifty meters high, the English section of the work shows a common phrase that the passerby views by chance on the street, is superimposed upon, and can find themselves thrust into new, uncharted perspectives. The work was translated into German by the Austrian poet Ferdinand Schmatz as **ZERSCHMETTERT IN STÜCKE (IM FRIEDEN DER NACHT)**. As Schmatz himself comments on this disturbing translation, "**IN THE STILL OF THE NIGHT**: that is an idiom from poetry, pop music, etc. That everyone thinks he or she knows. But is it 'understood'? Does he or she know what 'in the still of the night' means, given the connotation of the German translation (piece = peace, still (English) = Stille (German))."[24] What he does not reveal to the reader in his contribution to the catalogue is his virtuosic play with sound, which he took from the English phrase and translated in a literal sense. Just as Weiner avoids the parallels of "piece" and "peace" and instead uses "still of the night," Schmatz avoids the alliteration of *Stücke* and *Stille* and uses the word *Frieden*. The expressions in the source language and target language are thus so complementary that the connotations from the English text are present in the German translation and both texts are linked to one another by the avoidance of clumsy alliterations.

Bedeutung von ›Abendstern‹ und ›Morgenstern‹ dieselbe sein, aber nicht der Sinn.«[23] Weiners Arbeit benennt eine Linie, die vom Morgen- zum Abendstern gezogen ist, und damit vielleicht nichts anderes als die Denkfigur des *Full Circle*.

Der Gegenstandsbezug scheint sich bei Installationen im öffentlichen Raum durch die Wahl einer konkreten Bühne von selbst herzustellen, während sie gleichzeitig auf einer höchst komplexen linguistischen Ebene verbleiben, beispielsweise Weiners spektakuläre Arbeit **SMASHED TO PIECES (IN THE STILL OF THE NIGHT)** auf dem ehemaligen Flakturm im Esterházypark in Wien. In fast fünfzig Metern Höhe zeigt der englischsprachige Teil des Textes eine gängige Wendung, die ein Passant zufällig sieht und so in einem anderen Kontext wiederfindet, der sich dann mit dem abgespeicherten Wissen überlagert. Ins Deutsche übersetzt wurde die Arbeit von dem österreichischen Dichter Ferdinand Schmatz: **ZERSCHMETTERT IN STÜCKE (IM FRIEDEN DER NACHT)**. Er selbst kommentiert seine irritierende Übersetzung: »**IN THE STILL OF THE NIGHT** – das ist ein Idiom aus der Poesie, der Pop-Music etc., das jeder zu kennen meint, aber ›versteht‹ er es? Weiß er, was ›in der Stille der Nacht‹ bedeutet, noch dazu, wo es auf Deutsch dann ›im Frieden der Nacht‹ heißt (das sich aufgrund der englischen Konnotation von ›pieces‹, dt. Stücke mit ›peace‹, dt. Frieden auf ›still‹, dt. Stille übertragen ließ).«[24] Was er in seinem Katalogbeitrag dem Leser nicht enthüllt, ist sein virtuoses Spiel mit dem Klang, den er aus dem englischen Statement aufgenommen und fast im wortwörtlichen Sinne *über*setzt hat. So wie Weiner die lautlich naheliegende Parallele von »piece« und »peace« vermeidet und »still of the night« verwendet, vermeidet Schmatz die Alliteration von »Stücke« und »Stille« und setzt das Wort »Frieden«.

Previous page:
***Topografie I*, Flak tower, Vienna, 1991**
Vorherige Seite:
Topografie I, Flakturm, Wien, 1991

A poet's interest in Weiner's language sculptures and the analysis of his work from a poetic-literary perspective seem at first glance to violate the artist's approach, which is focused on the empirical, on what can be observed, and requires some explanation.[25] With American English as his native language and Dutch as a second language, Weiner can also communicate in many other languages. He learned them primarily in conversation, and his decided feel for the sound and rhythm of a language cannot be denied. And with his firm rejection of the expressive-literary in art, Weiner appears to increasingly grant space to the poetic as a moment inherent in language. At a 1969 conference held by Seth Siegelaub, he said the following:

> As for poetry, poetry is inherently involved in the medium of language as well as the content. I may utilize the medium in an attempt to get across *only* the content, in the most concise package I'm capable of that in that moment. Inherent beauty or exciting ramifications of

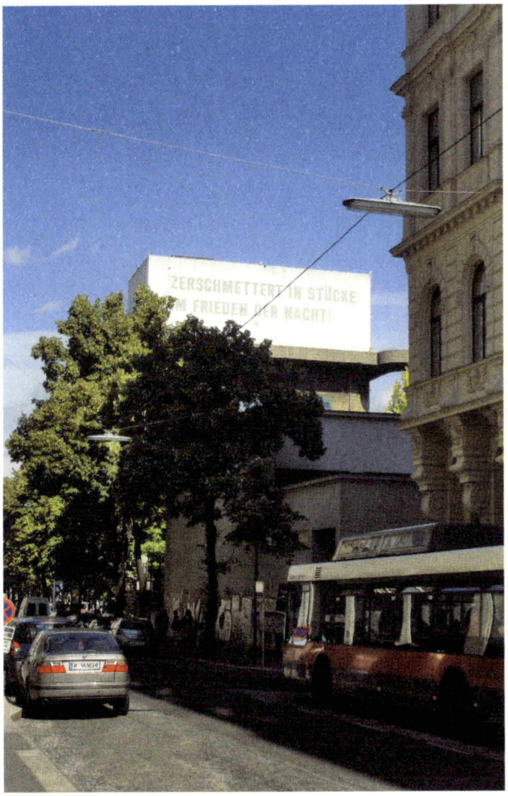

***Topografie I*, Flak tower, Vienna, 1991**
Topografie I, Flakturm, Wien, 1991

Ausgangssprachlicher und zielsprachlicher Ausdruck ergänzen sich so wechselseitig, indem die aus dem Englischen geweckten Konnotationen in der deutschen Übersetzung umgesetzt und beide Texte durch die Strategie der Vermeidung plumper Alliterationen miteinander verbunden sind.

Das Interesse eines Dichters an den Sprachskulpturen Weiners und die Analyse seiner Arbeit aus einer poetisch-literarischen Perspektive stehen auf den ersten Blick in Widerspruch zu dem auf die Empirie, auf das Beobachtbare konzentrierten Ansatz des Künstlers und erfordern an dieser Stelle einen Exkurs.[25] Neben dem amerikanischen Englisch als seiner Muttersprache und dem Niederländischen als Zweitsprache kann sich Weiner auch in vielen anderen Sprachen verständigen. Er hat sie überwiegend im Gespräch erlernt, und sein ausgeprägtes Gefühl für den Klang und den Rhythmus einer Sprache ist nicht zu leugnen. Und bei aller entschiedenen Ablehnung des Expressiv-Literarischen in der Kunst scheint Weiner dem Poetischen als einem der Sprache immanenten Moment zunehmend Raum zu geben. 1969 äußerte er auf einem von Seth Siegelaub geleiteten Symposium:

> Was Poesie betrifft, Poesie beschäftigt sich grundsätzlich mit dem Medium der Sprache *und* mit dem Inhalt. Ich kann das Medium benutzen, um nur den Inhalt mitzuteilen, in der prägnantesten Form, zu der ich im Moment in der Lage

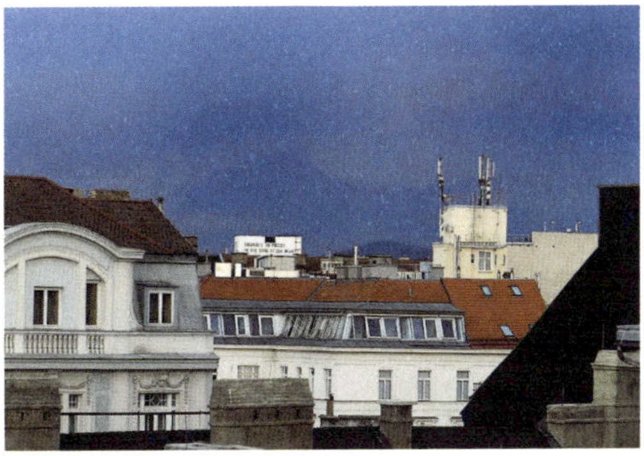

***Topografie I*, Flak tower, Vienna, 1991**
Topografie I, Flakturm, Wien, 1991

the language don't terribly interest me, but I don't see how you can differentiate poetry from art without the proper information. First you might see it as a poem, but with the correct information, you would accept it as it is intended.[26]

In 1985, when Michael Gibbs asked the artist, "Why do you call your work 'sculpture' and not simply paintings, poetry, or art philosophy?," Weiner replied:

That's easy to answer: the fact is, they are sculptures, since they show the relationship of object to object and that is the idea and purpose of a sculpture. I've got nothing against 'poetry,' but it's only resonance and tempo. Each of my works is perhaps also indeed a poetic sculpture. It's not that I think it's a bad word, poetry, but I'm not a poet, since a poet is concerned with the relationship of human beings to human beings.[27]

In one of his most recent conversations, "Talking Art at the Tate Modern," with John Slyce, Weiner once again went into the question of what distinguishes his works from poetry:

I love poetry, that's not the point. I like to read it. I really sometimes prefer poetry to prose. But I don't do poetry, and if I were a poet I'd be a really lousy one. . . . Let's put it this way: there is a certain aspect of me that tries to make things *clink*, sound well when they are read to people so that they can take it. There is no reason to be abrupt. But that's my own weaknesses, my own romantic nature, poetic nature, whatever it is. But it is not an essential

bin. Inhärente Schönheit oder überraschende Nebeneffekte der Sprache interessieren mich nicht besonders, aber ich weiß nicht, wie man ohne die notwendige Information Poesie von Kunst unterscheiden könnte. Vielleicht sieht man etwas erst einmal als Gedicht an, aber mit der richtigen Information begreift man es dann so, wie es intendiert ist.[26]

Auf die Frage von Michael Gibbs: »Warum nennen Sie Ihre Arbeiten ›Skulpturen‹ und nicht Gemälde, Poesie oder Kunstphilosophie?«, antwortete Weiner 1985:

Das ist nicht schwer zu beantworten: Sie sind nämlich tatsächlich Skulpturen, denn sie zeigen die Beziehung von Gegenständen zu Gegenständen, und das ist die Idee und die Absicht einer Skulptur. Ich habe nichts gegen »Poesie«, aber Poesie ist nur Klang und Rhythmus. Vielleicht sind meine Arbeiten auch poetische Skulpturen. Ich finde das kein schlechtes Wort, Poesie, aber ich bin kein Dichter, denn die befassen sich mit der Beziehung von Menschen zu Menschen.[27]

In einem seiner jüngsten Gespräche, *Talking Art* mit John Slyce in der Tate Modern, geht Weiner noch einmal auf die Frage nach der Abgrenzung seiner Arbeiten von der Poesie ein:

Ich mag Lyrik, darum geht es nicht. Ich lese sie gerne. Manchmal ist mir Lyrik lieber als Prosa. Aber ich mache keine Poesie. Und wenn ich ein Poet wäre, wäre ich ein lausiger. [...] Lassen Sie es mich so ausdrücken: Da ist etwas in mir, das möchte, dass die Dinge gut klingen, wenn sie jemandem vorgelesen werden, damit man sie part of the work. But it's there. I don't think it's a fault in the work.[28]

The aurality and cadence of language, also aspects of its materiality, resound in Weiner's work. Consequentially, he is able to characterize his language works in this context as "poetic sculptures" without in any way affecting their immediate link to the relation between things to things and things to people.

In regards to the concrete link to objects, Weiner's work on the flak tower depicts at first nothing more than the sound of destruction at night. This is at least true of the English version. In the German translation, the replacement of "still" with *Frieden* (peace) no longer provides this compelling reference. **(IN THE STILL OF THE NIGHT)** The parentheses here move the designated temporal framework from the realm of the factual to the realm of the possible, which makes the repetition of the expression in the parentheses in the installation seem plausible. The beholder of the installation in situ immediately relates Weiner's statement to the nightly bombing attacks during World War II, against which the three flak towers in Vienna were erected to defend. Weiner commented in conversation with Christoph Schenker on the work in 2007: "But you've never walked at night in the street and listened to something? Listened to a bottle being thrown and breaking in the street at night. It has a sound. Go to the same street, same bottle during the day—and it's a different sound."[29] In fact, this particular work—as is usually the case in Weiner's oeuvre—was not conceived as site specific, but was already shown in 1990 and 1991 at an exhibition marking the twenty-year anniversary of Galerie Hubert Winter.

versteht. Es gibt keinen Grund, abrupt zu sein. Doch das ist eine persönliche Schwäche von mir, meine eigene romantische Natur, poetische Natur, was auch immer. Aber es ist kein wesentlicher Teil der Arbeit. Trotzdem ist es da. Ich glaube nicht, dass es dem Werk Abbruch tut.[28]

Klang und Rhythmus der Sprache, ebenfalls Aspekte ihrer Materialität, finden ihren Widerhall in Weiners Werk. Folgerichtig kann er seine Spracharbeiten in diesem Zusammenhang auch als »poetische Skulpturen« bezeichnen, ohne dass damit in irgendeiner Weise ihr unmittelbarer Bezug auf das Verhältnis von Dingen zu Dingen und Dingen zu Menschen tangiert wäre.

Hinsichtlich des konkreten Gegenstandbezugs beschreibt Weiners Arbeit am Flakturm zunächst einmal nicht mehr als ein Geräusch der Zerstörung in der Nacht. Das gilt zumindest für die englische Version. In der deutschen Übersetzung ist durch das Ersetzen von »still« durch »Frieden« dieser stringente Bezug nicht mehr gegeben. Die Klammern um **(IN THE STILL OF THE NIGHT)** stellen den in ihnen benannten zeitlichen Rahmen von der Faktizität in den Bereich des Möglichen, was auch die Wiederholung des Klammerausdrucks in der Installation plausibel erscheinen lässt. Der Betrachter der Installation in situ bezieht Weiners Aussage sofort auf die nächtlichen Fliegerangriffe im Zweiten Weltkrieg, zu deren Abwehr die insgesamt drei Flaktürme in Wien ursprünglich errichtet worden waren. 2007 kommentierte Weiner im Gespräch mit Christoph Schenker die Arbeit mit der Erklärung, dass sich das Geräusch einer Flasche, die nachts auf der Straße zerschlagen werde, unterscheide von einer am Tag auf der Straße zerschlagenen Flasche.[29] Tatsächlich wurde die

> *Smashed to Pieces* was actually on view at that exhibition. Lawrence sent the work by fax with a note saying, "Birgit has to decide the size of the work." [Birgit is the artist Birgit Jürgenssen.] And Birgit placed the work on a small wall so that the work was no larger than perhaps 70 cm. A few months later, Wiener Festwochen invited Lawrence to contribute a work, and Lawrence chose this work as the one he wanted for the flak tower.[30]

By choosing a flak tower located in a park as a support for a sculpture, the work is given an enormous metaphorical charge in spite of the artist's hesitations about conceiving works in public space for a special location. By specifying placement on a structure that served primarily as a protective bunker for the population of Vienna (flak was not effective against air attacks by the time the tower was completed), the question of changing the world by people intervening, or, in Weiner's concrete language, the question of the relationship of people to things is moved into a context that could not be more existential. At the time of the installation of Weiner's work in 1991, the former flak tower had been an aquarium for more than thirty years. This initially detracted from some of the potential pathos of the language sculpture, even in situ, though it is perceived as a "memorial against war and fascism."[31] Due to its height and size, the tower is a sign that marks its location, visible from a distance. After the work was installed, the context has shifted once again: Weiner's work is now caught up in competition with its surroundings, getting crowded out by the erection of large advertising billboards and plans that will partially hide the work behind an external elevator. This shameless—and here

Arbeit – wie bei Lawrence Weiner die Regel – nicht »site-specific« konzipiert, sondern bereits 1990/91 in einer Ausstellung zum 20-jährigen Bestehen der Galerie Hubert Winter gezeigt.

> »Smashed To Pieces« war tatsächlich in dieser Ausstellung zu sehen. Lawrence hat die Arbeit per Fax gesandt mit der Anmerkung »Birgit has to decide the size of the work«. Mit Birgit war die Künstlerin Birgit Jürgenssen gemeint. Und Birgit Jürgenssen platzierte die Arbeit auf eine kleine Wand, sodass das Werk nicht größer als vielleicht 70 cm war. Ein paar Monate später fragten die Wiener Festwochen bei Lawrence an, und Lawrence nannte diese Arbeit als die von ihm gewünschte für den Flakturm.[30]

Mit der Wahl eines in einem Park gelegenen Flakturms als Träger für eine Skulptur findet eine gewaltige metaphorische Aufladung statt, trotz Weiners Zurückhaltung vor der Konzeption einer im öffentlichen Raum präsentierten Arbeit für einen besonderen Ort. Die Frage nach der Veränderung der Welt durch den Eingriff des Menschen, in Weiners konkreter Sprache: nach der Beziehung der Menschen zu den Dingen, gerät durch die Platzierung auf ein Gebäude, das der Wiener Bevölkerung im Zweiten Weltkrieg primär als Schutzbunker diente (Flaks waren schon bei Fertigstellung des Turms der fortgeschrittenen Flugzeugtechnik nicht mehr gewachsen), in einen Kontext, der

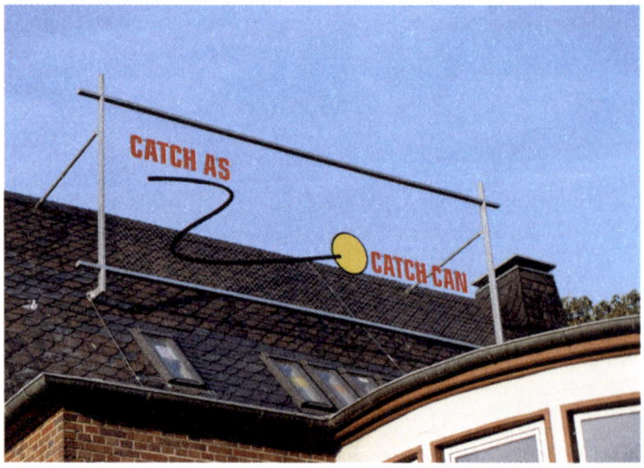

Ruhr.2010, BernePark, Bottrop, 2010, a collaboration with artist Mischa Kuball; Lawrence Weiner's component is shown here
Ruhr.2010, BernePark, Bottrop, 2010, eine Zusammenarbeit mit dem Künstler Mischa Kuball, hier ist Lawrence Weiners Beitrag zu sehen

a term from the realm of ethics is only appropriate, for the realm of aesthetics has long been left behind—exercise of commercial interests becomes a mirror of contemporary society's condition as a global **CATCH AS CATCH CAN**, a literal quote from Weiner's collaboration with Mischa Kuball for their contribution to *Ruhr.2010* located in BernePark.

The stage that a work enters is linked neither to institutional nor to national conditions, and works do not only cross from the English language to the most varied cultural contexts.[32] **DICHT BIJ**, for example, was developed based on a lexical peculiarity of the Dutch language. Written together as a single word, *dichtbij* possesses a broad spectrum of meaning, where the core, *dicht*, or "close," is understood in the sense of emotional closeness: *zeer dichtbij* is "very close." *Dicht bij*, written separately, means something spatial: "close by." Weiner uses the separate words. At issue here are relations of things to things and people to things. Nonetheless, emotional proximity also echoes here. The work went from the

existenzieller nicht zu denken ist. Zur Zeit der Installation von Weiners Arbeit im Jahre 1991 war aber aus dem ehemaligen Flakturm bereits seit über dreißig Jahren ein Meeresaquarium geworden. Das nahm der Sprachskulptur auch in situ von vornherein die Eindeutigkeit einer pathetischen Geste, wenngleich sie als »Mahnmal gegen Krieg und Faschismus«[31] wahrgenommen wird. Aufgrund seiner Höhe und Größe ist der Turm ein weithin sichtbares Kennzeichen des Ortes. Nachdem die Arbeit angebracht worden war, verschob sich der Kontext nochmals: Weiners Arbeit steht heute in einem Verdrängungswettbewerb, in den sie durch die Montage großer Werbeaufschriften und die Pläne, durch einen Außenaufzug das Kunstwerk teilweise zu verdecken, geraten ist. Dieser schamlos – und hier trifft nur eine Vokabel aus dem ethischen Bereich, da der ästhetische längst verlassen ist – zur Schau gestellte Vorrang kommerzieller Interessen wird zum Spiegel der heutigen gesellschaftlichen Situation eines globalen **CATCH AS CATCH CAN**, wörtliches Zitat von Weiners Zusammenarbeit mit Mischa Kuball in ihrem Beitrag zur Ausstellung *Ruhr.2010* im BernePark.

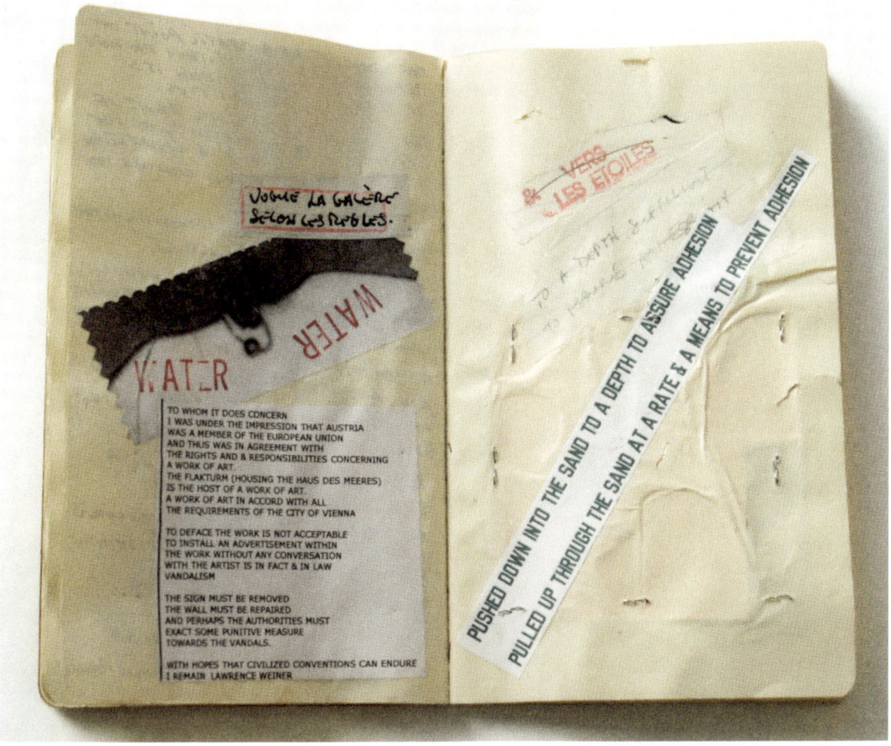

Sketchbook, 2008
Skizzenbuch, 2008

Netherlands to the Johanneskirche in Düsseldorf. A work by Weiner had been installed in the year 2002 but was destroyed when the church was renovated. The artist agreed to present a new work for the church congregation. The text reads: **BROUGHT FORTH BY THE RESONANCE OF A DISSONANCE | HERVORGEBRACHT DURCH DIE RESONANZ EINER DISSONANZ,** with a curvilinear line that links it to **DICHT BEI.**[33]

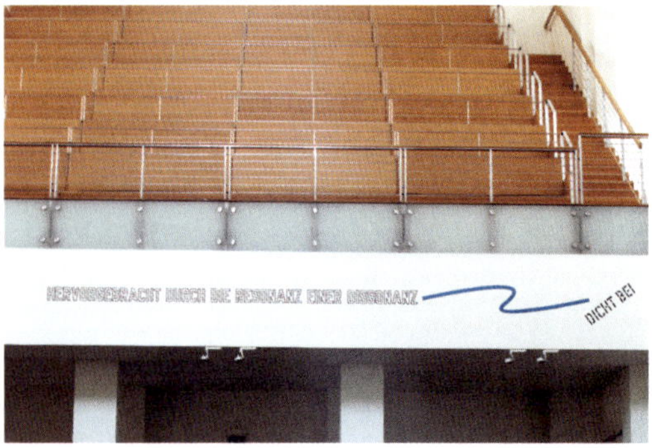

Johanneskirche, Düsseldorf, 2010
Johanneskirche, Düsseldorf, 2010

For Weiner, the act of placing his "language + the materials referred to" in various contexts is done explicitly to not function as an aesthetic gesture—just as every material provides a new context to emerge for his work. An example is a 2011 group exhibition *Through The Warp,* in Brooklyn, in which Weiner participated with a work from the early seventies. Here is a presentation of "seven different approaches to the same overarching structure—material building upon material via

Die Bühne, die ein Werk betritt, ist weder an institutionelle noch an nationale Gegebenheiten gebunden. Arbeiten wandern nicht nur von der

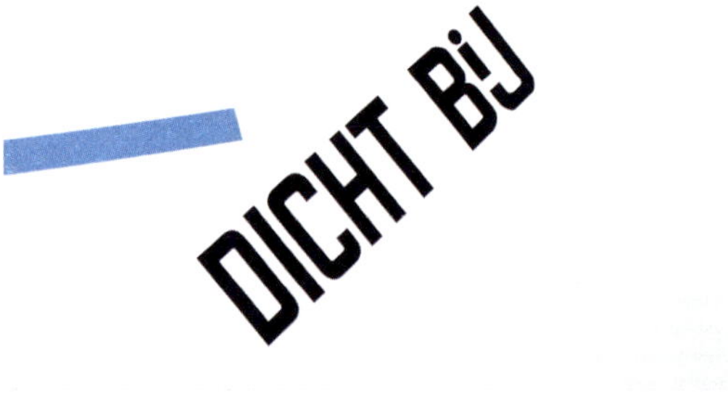

***Dicht Bij*, BAK, Utrecht, 2010**
Dicht Bij, BAK, Utrecht, 2010

englischen Sprache aus in die unterschiedlichsten kulturellen Kontexte.[32] **DICHT BIJ** wurde beispielsweise von einer lexikalischen Besonderheit des Holländischen aus entwickelt. Zusammen geschrieben besitzt »dichtbij« ein breites Bedeutungsspektrum, dessen Kern »nah« im Sinne der emotional empfundenen Nähe ist: »zeer dichtbij« ist »hautnah«. »Dicht bij« in Getrenntschreibung gibt eine räumliche Gegebenheit wieder: »in der Nähe von«. Weiner verwendet die Getrenntschreibung. Es geht um die Beziehung von Dingen zu Dingen und Menschen zu Dingen. Nichtsdestoweniger schwingt auch die gefühlte Nähe mit. Die Arbeit kam von den Niederlanden in die Düsseldorfer Johanneskirche, in der bereits 2002 eine

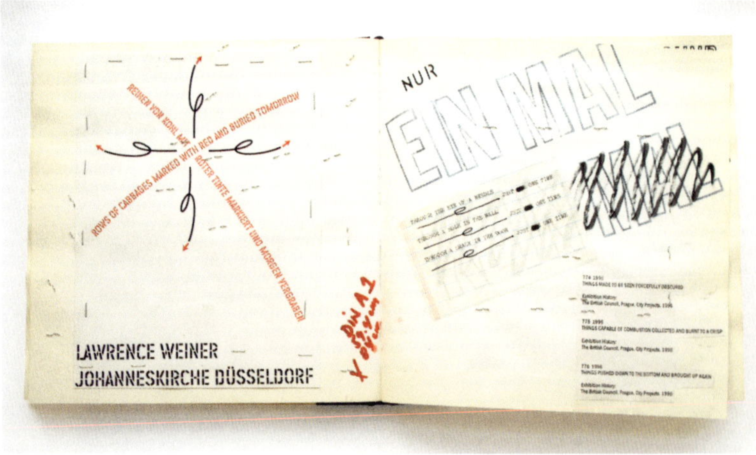

Sketchbook, 2002–3
Skizzenbuch, 2002/03

linear repetition and overlap."[34] Weiner's work can hardly be described in terms that are more concise than this. **OVER AND UNDER. UNDER AND OVER. AND OVER AND UNDER. AND UNDER AND OVER | UNTER UND ÜBER. ÜBER UND UNTER. UND UNTER UND ÜBER. UND ÜBER UND UNTER.** The work is an alternating series of two prepositions linked by a conjunction. In terms of etymology, the word "preposition" contains the Latin verb *ponere:* to place, to set, to put in place. In German, a preposition is also called a *Verhältniswort*, a "relation word." Used without nouns, this kind of word describes the relationship between things and people in the greatest possible openness: in, on, by, between, next to . . . **UNDER AND OVER.**

Sprachskulptur von Weiner installiert worden war. Diese wurde bei dem Umbau der Kirche jedoch zerstört. Der Künstler erklärte sich bereit, für die Gemeinde eine neue Arbeit anzufertigen. Ihr Text: **BROUGHT FORTH BY THE RESONANCE OF A DISSONANCE | HERVORGEBRACHT DURCH DIE RESONANZ EINER DISSONANZ**, und eine geschwungene Linie verbindet ihn mit **DICHT BEI**.[33]

Den Akt, seine Sprachskulpturen und damit die darin angesprochenen Materialien in unterschiedliche Kontexte zu setzen, begreift Weiner ausdrücklich nicht als eine genuin ästhetische Geste. Wie für jedes Material ergibt sich auch für seine Kunst immer wieder ein neuer Kontext, so zum Beispiel eine Gruppenausstellung in Brooklyn, an der sich Weiner 2011 mit einer Arbeit aus den frühen 1970er-Jahren beteiligt. »*Through The Warp* [Durch die Kettenfäden] präsentiert sieben unterschiedliche Annäherungen an dieselbe übergreifende Struktur – Material, das auf Material über lineare Repetition und Überschneidung aufbaut.«[34] Präziser als mit diesem Ausstellungskonzept ließe sich auch die konkrete Arbeit von Weiner kaum beschreiben **UNDER AND OVER. OVER AND UNDER. AND UNDER AND OVER. AND OVER AND UNDER. | UNTER UND ÜBER. ÜBER UND UNTER. UND UNTER UND ÜBER. UND ÜBER UND UNTER.** Sie besteht aus einer alternierenden Reihung zweier mit einer Konjunktion verbundener Präpositionen. Von der Etymologie her steckt in dem Wort »Präposition« das lateinische Verb

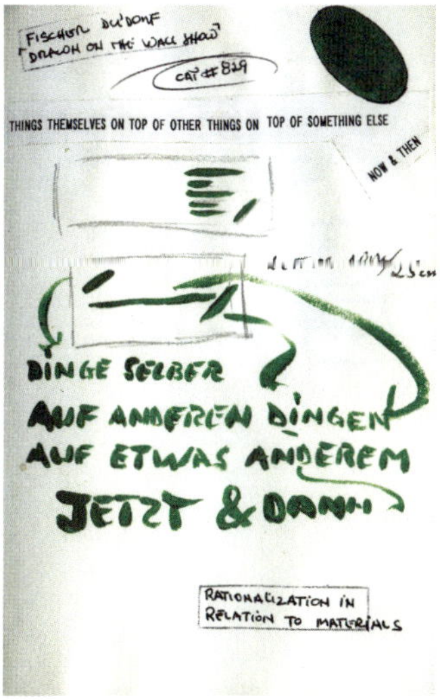

Sketchbook, 1999
Skizzenbuch, 1999

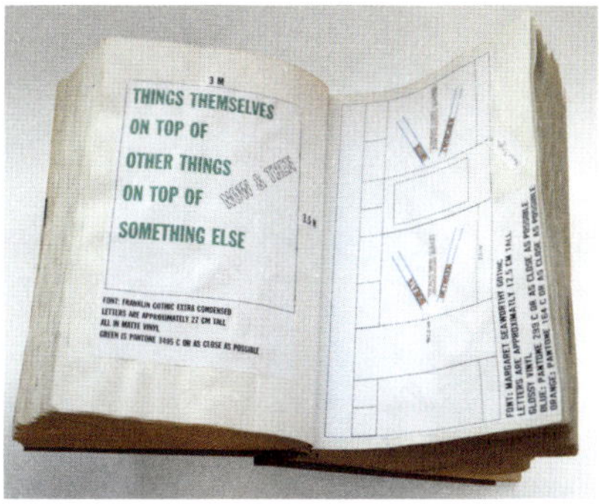

Sketchbook, 2005–9
Skizzenbuch, 2005–2009

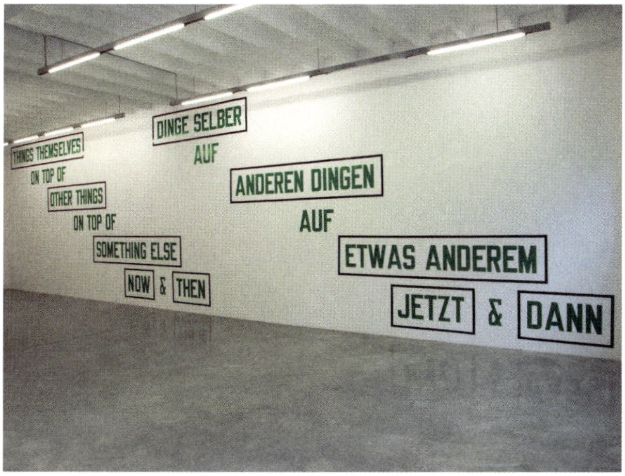

***Lawrence Weiner*, Konrad Fischer Galerie, Berlin, 2008**
Lawrence Weiner, Konrad Fischer Galerie, Berlin, 2008

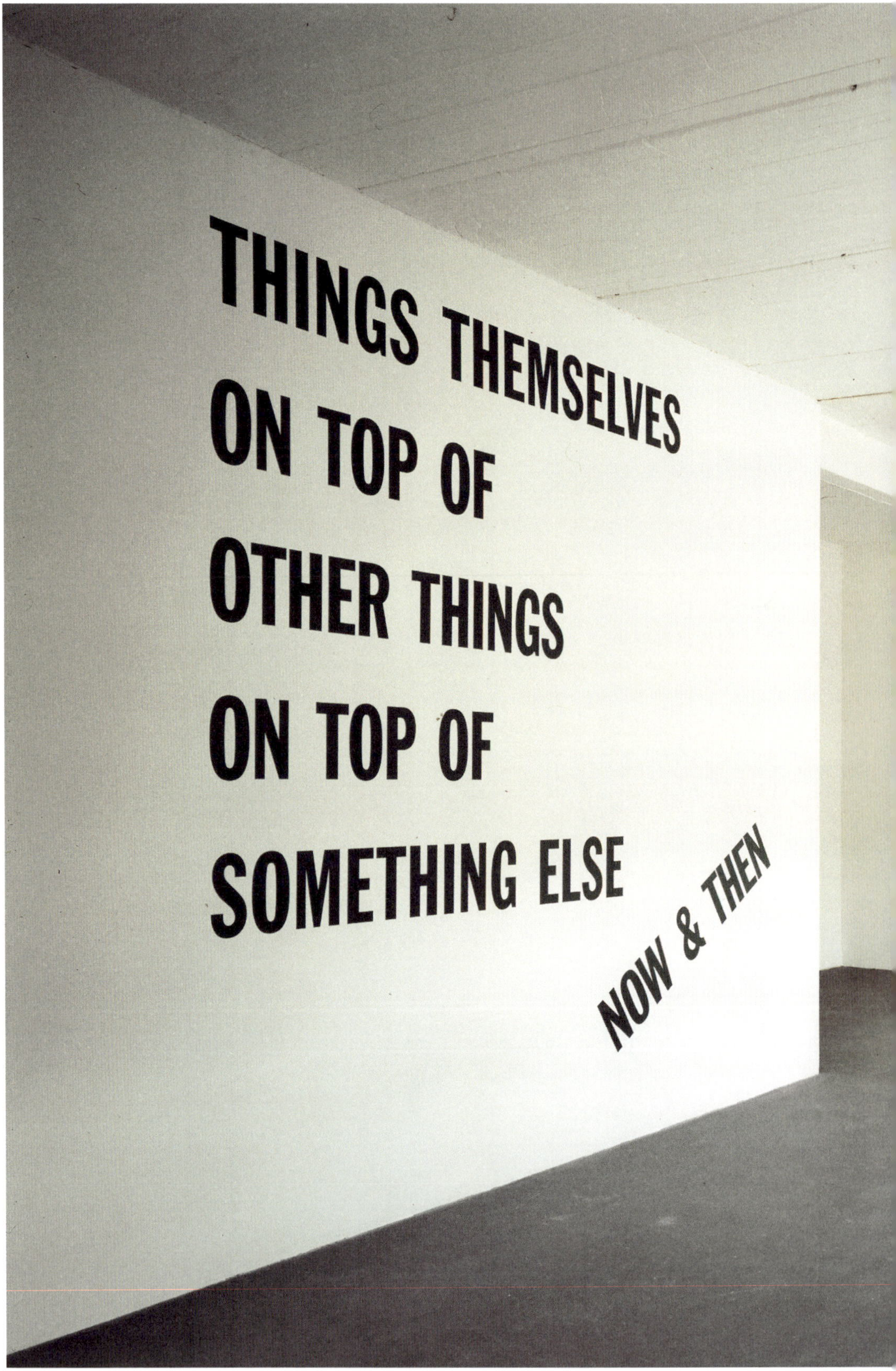
THINGS THEMSELVES
ON TOP OF
OTHER THINGS
ON TOP OF
SOMETHING ELSE
NOW & THEN

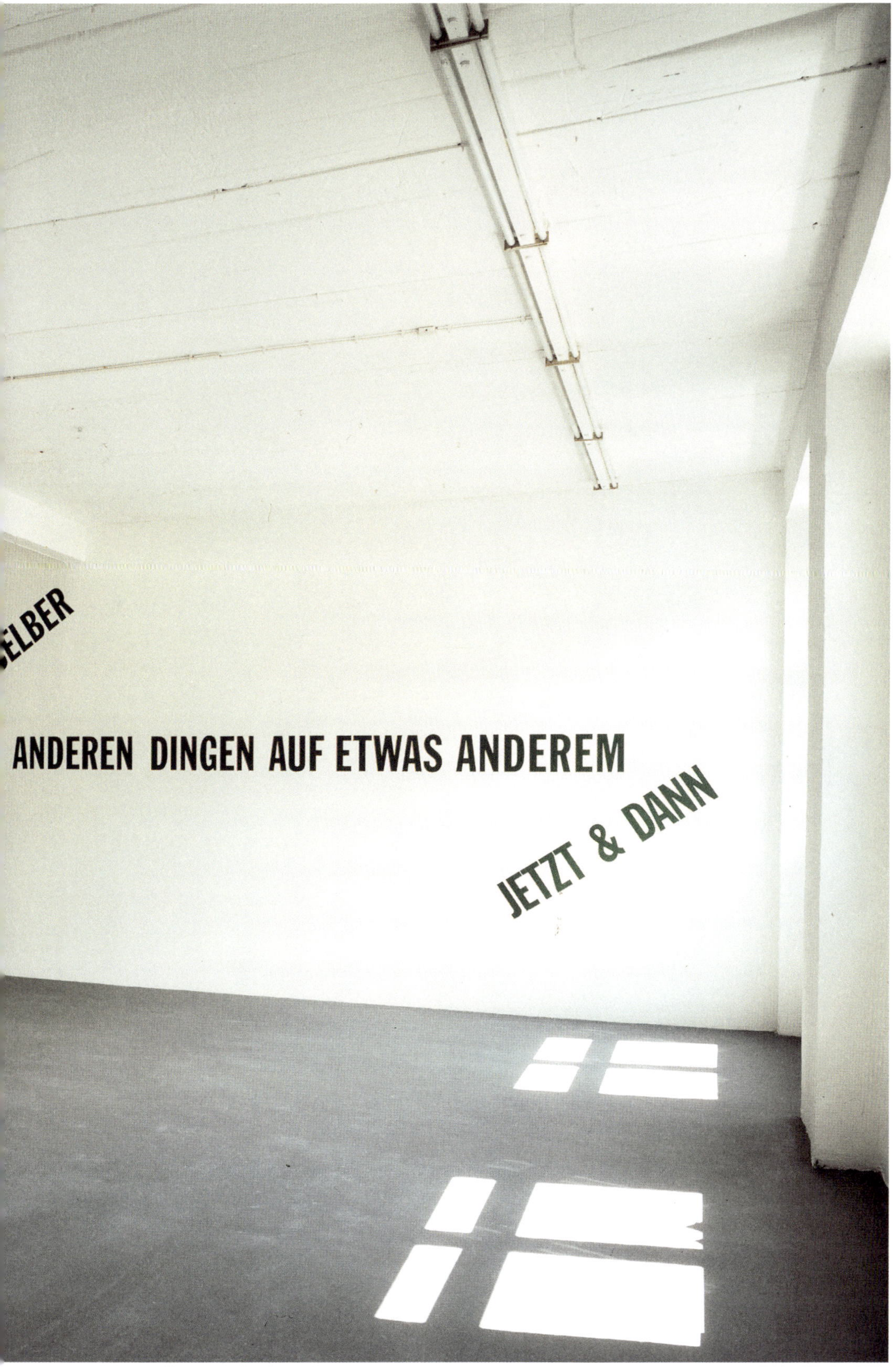
ELBER
ANDEREN DINGEN AUF ETWAS ANDEREM
JETZT & DANN

Previous page:
***Walls*, Konrad Fischer Galerie, Düsseldorf, 1999**
Vorherige Seite:
Wände, Konrad Fischer Galerie, Düsseldorf, 1999

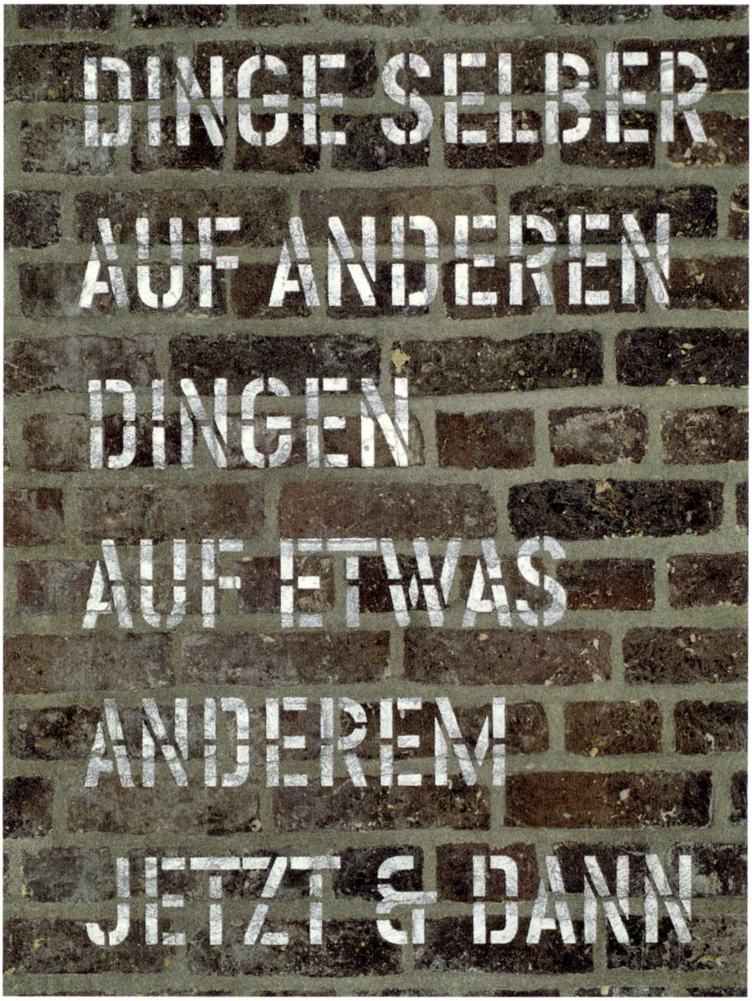

***Any Given Time*, Stommeln Synagogue, 2003**
Irgendwann, Synagoge Stommeln, 2003

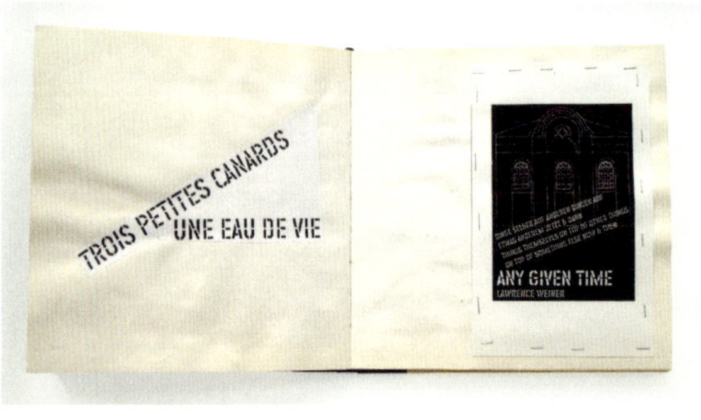

Sketchbook, 2002–3
Skizzenbuch, 2002/03

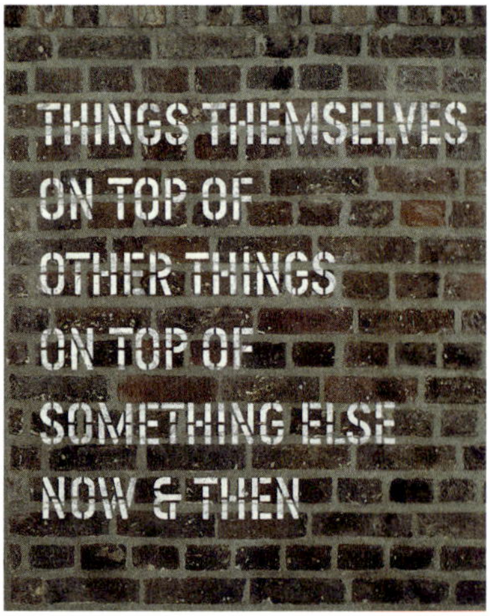

***Any Given Time*, Stommeln Synagogue, 2003**
Irgendwann, Synagoge Stommeln, 2003

The movement described in Weiner's work cannot only be read as a horizontal structure, as in this exhibition, but also as one constructed vertically. In this ambiguity—this would be the poetological, self-referential reading—the work represents a clear-cut characteristic of Weiner's multilayered and interwoven oeuvre: material building upon material via linear repetition and overlap.

THINGS THEMSELVES ON TOP OF OTHER THINGS ON TOP OF SOMETHING ELSE NOW & THEN | DINGE SELBER AUF ANDEREN DINGEN AUF ETWAS ANDEREM JETZT & DANN takes up this idea in a different formulation. Instead of being limited to prepositions lined up one after another, in this work the word *Ding*, or "thing," is placed at the center as an undefined, general description of an object. In English, the word "thing" is explicitly contained in the indefinite pronoun "something," which is never reflected in daily use. Weiner explores this kind of construct in his work at the Cologne Cathedral by the wordplay of **SOMETHING** and **A FEW THINGS**. The shift in the use of the word "thing" cannot be transferred to German. A further aspect is added by **THINGS THEMSELVES ON TOP OF OTHER THINGS**. Adding to it **ON TOP OF SOMETHING ELSE** sets itself apart from the things mentioned beforehand and again brings the question of the stage into play. Numerous variations in the presentation of the work repeatedly endow it with a different rhythm. The isolation of the preposition in particular slows the process described in the work and refers emphatically to the factor of time, which is explicitly mentioned in the final line. Something similar was achieved in the 2011 group exhibition *Through The Warp*, by placing periods after each pair of prepositions linked with "and" in **UNDER AND OVER**.

»ponere« (legen, setzen, stellen), das »Put in place«. Im Deutschen wird eine Präposition Verhältniswort genannt. Ohne Nomen beschreibt diese Wortart in größtdenkbarer Offenheit das Verhältnis von Dingen zu Dingen und Menschen zu Dingen: in, auf, bei, zwischen, neben … **UNTER UND ÜBER**. Die in Weiners Arbeit beschriebene Bewegung lässt sich jedoch nicht nur als horizontal ausgerichtete Struktur wie in diesem Ausstellungskontext lesen, sondern unabhängig davon auch als eine vertikal errichtete. In dieser Vieldeutigkeit, und das wäre die poetologische, selbstreferenzielle Lesart, stellt sie eine äußerst genaue Charakteristik von Weiners vielschichtigem und ineinander verwobenem Gesamtwerk dar: Material auf Material über lineare Repetition und Überschneidung aufgebaut.

Die Arbeit **THINGS THEMSELVES ON TOP OF OTHER THINGS ON TOP OF SOMETHING ELSE NOW & THEN | DINGE SELBER AUF ANDEREN DINGEN AUF ETWAS ANDEREM JETZT & DANN** greift diesen Gedanken in anderer Formulierung auf. Statt der Beschränkung auf reihend verbundene Präpositionen steht in dieser Arbeit das Wort »Ding« als unbestimmte, allgemeine Beschreibung eines Gegenstands im Zentrum. Im Englischen steckt das Wort »thing« explizit in dem Indefinitpronomen »something«, eine Wortbildung, die im täglichen Gebrauch nicht reflektiert wird, Weiner aber in seiner Arbeit am Kölner Dom im Spiel mit **SOMETHING** und **A FEW THINGS** thematisiert. Diese Verschiebung im Gebrauch des Wortes »thing« ist nicht ins Deutsche zu übertragen. Ein weiterer Aspekt kommt in **DINGE SELBER AUF ANDEREN DINGEN** hinzu. Die Beifügung **AUF ETWAS ANDEREM** setzt sich ab von den zuvor genannten Dingen und bringt wieder die Frage der Bühne ins Spiel. Zahlreiche Variationen in der Präsentation der Arbeit geben ihr immer wieder einen anderen Rhythmus. Insbesondere die Isolierung

By breaking down the complex relation of things to things into elementary structures, one can trigger linguistic notations with prepositions or words like "thing," and presume an exacting and enduring observation that embraces all of the senses:

THE WEIGHT OF IT ALL
THE LENGTH OF IT ALL
THE BREADTH OF IT ALL
THE SOUND OF IT ALL
THE SMELL OF IT ALL

DAS GEWICHT VON ALLEM
DIE LÄNGE VON ALLEM
DIE BREITE VON ALLEM
DER KLANG VON ALLEM
DER GERUCH VON ALLEM

Both the outwardly visible and the very process of seeing are in the foreground of the work. **AS FAR AS THE EYE CAN SEE**, the title of Weiner's first American retrospective (and a work of Weiner's) that traveled from New York and Los Angeles in 2008 to Düsseldorf, the only European city in which it was shown, is thus programmatic: it was translated by K21's staff as **SO WEIT DAS AUGE REICHT**. Weiner's translation, **SO WEIT WIE DAS AUGE KANN**, brings the idiomatic expression back to the literal ("as far as the eye can") and places the impetus on

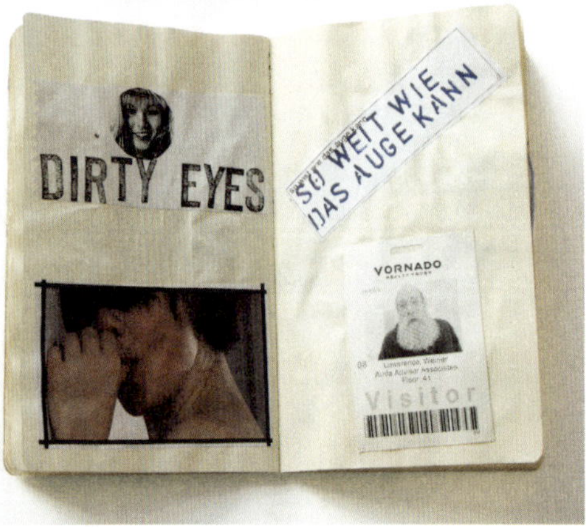

Sketchbook, 2008
Skizzenbuch, 2008

der Präposition entschleunigt den in der Arbeit beschriebenen Prozess und verweist nachdrücklich auf den Faktor Zeit, der in der Schlusszeile explizit genannt ist. Ähnliches erreichte er 2011 in der Gruppenausstellung *Through the Warp*, indem er in **UNTER UND ÜBER** jeweils nach einem mit »und« verbundenem Präpositionenpaar Punkte setzte.

Das Herunterbrechen komplexer Gegenstandsbeziehungen auf elementare Strukturen, deren sprachliches Notat sich mit Präpositionen oder einem Wort wie »Ding« begnügen kann, setzt ein genaues und geduldiges Beobachten voraus, das alle Sinne umfasst.

THE WEIGHT OF IT ALL
THE LENGTH OF IT ALL
THE BREADTH OF IT ALL
THE SOUND OF IT ALL
THE SMELL OF IT ALL

DAS GEWICHT VON ALLEM
DIE LÄNGE VON ALLEM
DIE BREITE VON ALLEM
DER KLANG VON ALLEM
DER GERUCH VON ALLEM

Sowohl das äußerlich Sichtbare als auch der Prozess des Sehens stehen jedoch im Vordergrund. Der Titel (gleichzeitig auch eine Spracharbeit) **AS FAR AS THE EYE CAN SEE** der ersten amerikanischen Retrospektive Weiners, die 2008 aus New York und Los Angeles nach Düsseldorf kam und dort als einziger Station in Europa zu sehen war, ist insofern programmatisch: Er wurde von den Mitarbeitern des K21 mit **SO WEIT DAS AUGE REICHT** übersetzt. Mit seiner Übersetzung **SO WEIT WIE DAS AUGE KANN** holt Lawrence Weiner den idiomatischen Ausdruck in

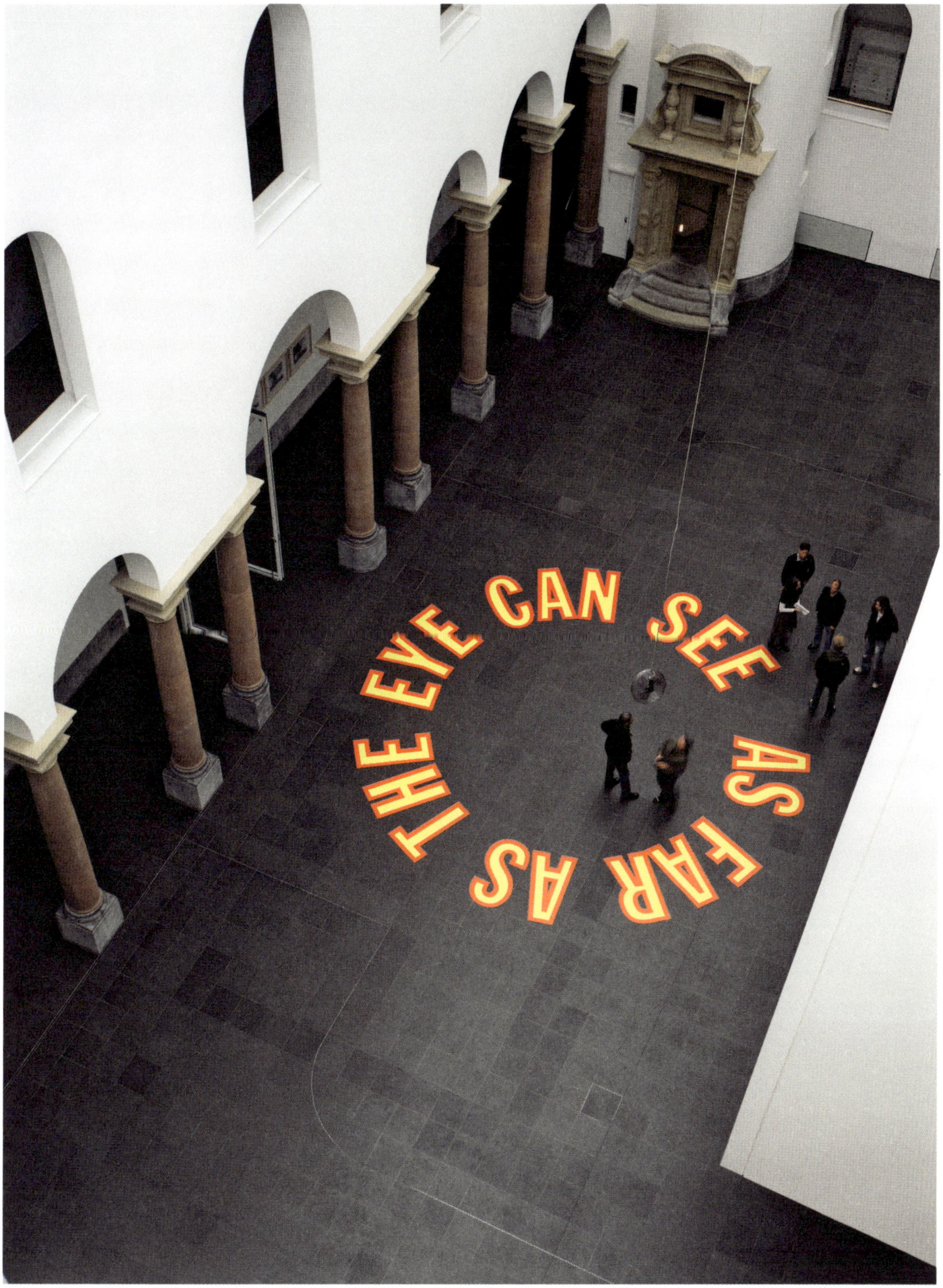

As *Far as the Eye Can See*, K21 Kunstsammlung Nordrhein-Westfalen, Düsseldorf, 2008
As *Far as the Eye Can See*, K21 Kunstsammlung Nordrhein-Westfalen, Düsseldorf, 2008

the visible, on the empirical. Or, to use an early Weiner term from the sixties, his translation is specific rather than general.

In the art magazine *Monopol*, Weiner writes "there is no metaphor" about Alberto Giacometti's *The Palace at 4 a.m.* (1932) at New York's Museum of Modern Art.[35] This maxim, clarifying Weiner's statement, was translated as "Keine Metapher in Sicht," i.e. "No metaphor in sight"; a claim that indeed can be questioned becomes immediately evident: metaphors are not visible, and art is only about the visible. The matter becomes more difficult in **AS TO BE IN PLAIN SIGHT**, a work that was presented to the public in 2009 on an exterior wall facing a heavily trafficked avenue in front of the Denver Art Museum. "In plain sight" is a police term "as to be" meaning that evidence was obtained legally, without an invasion of privacy, from what was readily apparent; "in plain sight" is to be visible, but also to be exposed to view; there is an inherent tension here that is conveyed by an American television crime series called *In Plain Sight*, which receives a further interpretation in the German title of the series, *In der Schusslinie*, "in the line of fire." The work takes on another spin in the questioning of the observed on a metalevel as captured by **AS TO BE**, which stands in tension with the claimed **PLAIN SIGHT**. Another Weiner work from the seventies reads: **WITH A PROBABILITY OF BEING SEEN | MIT DER MÖGLICHKEIT GESEHEN ZU WERDEN**.

Yet Weiner's "things" are "in plain sight." Early sketchbooks show a view of language that escapes a reading based on the immateriality of text. Weiner takes care in how words are placed, in what constellations they appear. He does not

die Wörtlichkeit zurück und setzt den Impetus nachdrücklich auf das Sichtbare, auf die Empirie, oder macht die Übersetzung eher spezifisch als allgemein, um auf einen frühen Begriff Weiners aus den 1960er-Jahren zurückzugreifen.

»There is no metaphor«, schreibt Weiner in der Kunstzeitschrift *Monopol* über Alberto Giacomettis *Palast um vier Uhr früh* (1932) im Museum of Modern Art in New York.[35] Die Aussage wurde, Weiners Statement verdeutlichend, übersetzt mit: »Keine Metapher in Sicht«, und eine durchaus infrage zu stellende Behauptung »There is no metaphor« wird mit einem Schlag evident: Metaphern sind nicht sichtbar, und nur um das Sichtbare geht es in der Kunst. Schwieriger wird der Sachverhalt in **AS TO BE IN PLAIN SIGHT**, ein 2009 der Öffentlichkeit übergebener Schriftzug auf einer Außenwand des Museumskomplexes des Denver Art Museum an einer dicht befahrenen Straße. »In plain sight« ist ein Begriff, der von der Polizei gebraucht wird. Er besagt, dass Beweise ohne Verletzung der Privatsphäre auf legale Weise aufgefunden wurden, allein aus dem, was unmittelbar offen lag. »In plain sight« bedeutet, sichtbar zu sein, aber auch, dem Blick des Beobachters ausgeliefert zu sein, eine Spannung, die *In Plain Sight* als Titel einer US-amerikanischen Krimiserie transportiert und die in der Übersetzung für das deutsche Fernsehen mit *In der Schusslinie* eine weitergehende Interpretation erfährt. Eine nochmalige Drehung erfährt die Arbeit durch die in **AS TO BE** formulierte Infragestellung des Beobachteten aus einer Metaebene, die wiederum in Spannung zur behaupteten **PLAIN SIGHT** steht. **WITH A PROBABILITY OF BEING SEEN | MIT DER MÖGLICHKEIT GESEHEN ZU WERDEN** heißt es in einer anderen Arbeit von Weiner aus den 1970er-Jahren.

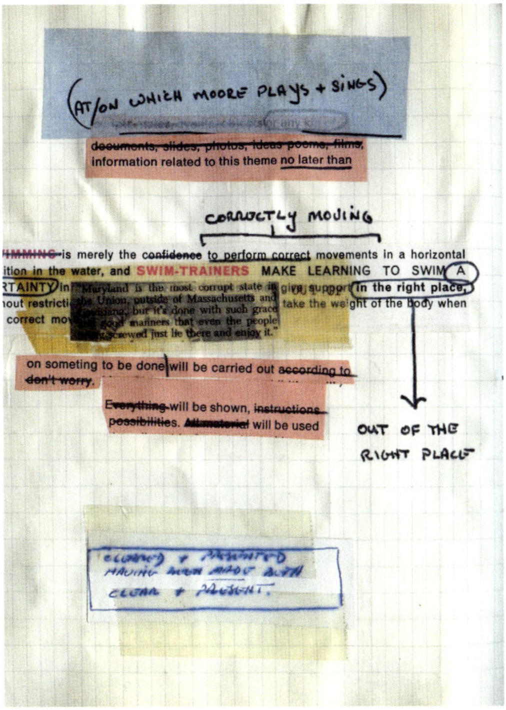

Sketchbook, 1973
Skizzenbuch, 1973

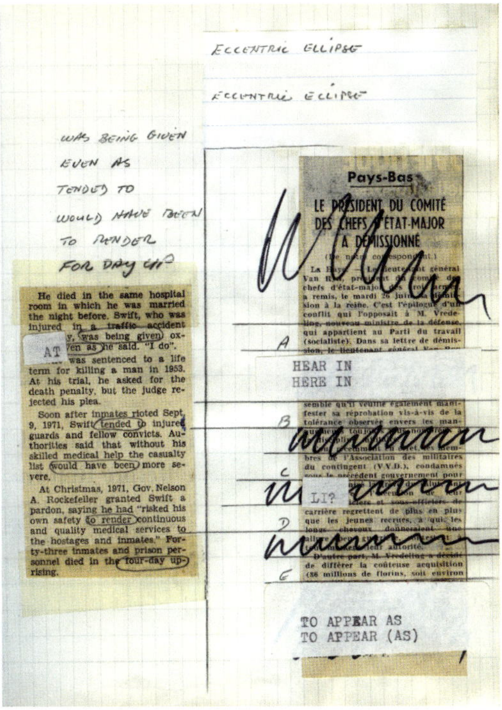

Sketchbook, 1973
Skizzenbuch, 1973

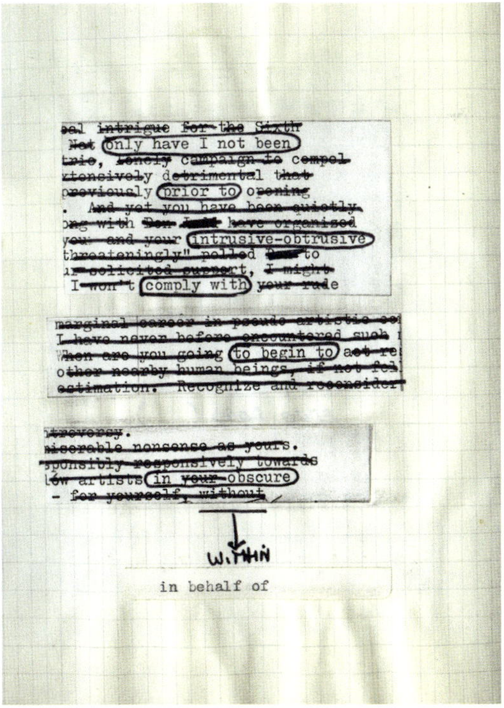

Sketchbook, 1973
Skizzenbuch, 1973

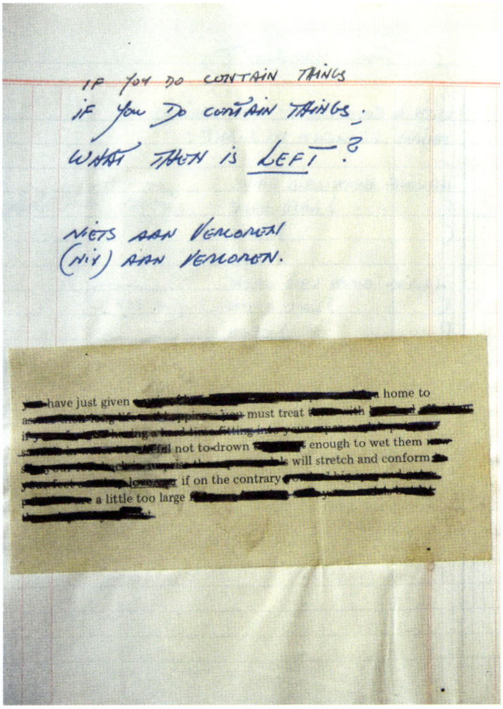

Sketchbook, 1975
Skizzenbuch, 1975

study concrete content, but the relationship of things to the world from a fundamental point of view, and how these words are placed in relation to one another on paper, or in Weiner's entire oeuvre. At issue here is not to represent historical, social situations, but the representation of what lies at their foundation. In so doing, it is not the search for ideas, but to show the use and function of materials, of things. This point cannot be seen more concretely than in the following two works: **THE SOUNDS MADE OF TREES MADE TO FALL | DAS KRACHEN VON ZU FALL GEBRACHTEN BÄUMEN** and **MATTER SO SHAKEN TO ITS CORE TO LEAD TO A CHANGE IN INHERENT FORM TO THE EXTENT OF BRINGING ABOUT A CHANGE IN THE DESTINY OF THE MATERIAL | MATERIE DERART BIS IN DEN KERN ERSCHÜTTERT DASS ES ZU EINER VERÄNDERUNG DER INHÄRENTEN FORM FÜHRT IN DEM AUSMASS DASS ES EINE ÄNDERUNG IM SCHICKSAL DES MATERIALS BEWIRKT**; the latter had its premiere at Essen's Kunstverein Ruhr in 2003, and was prominently featured in the 2005 Venice Biennale on the façade of the Italian Pavilion.

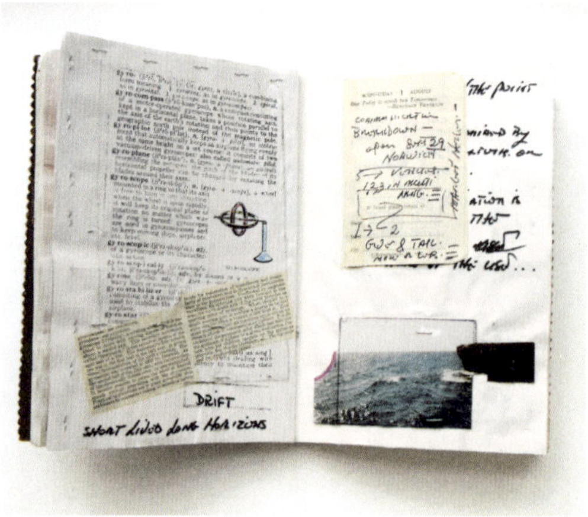

Sketchbook, 2003–4
Skizzenbuch, 2003/04

Tatsächlich sind die Dinge bei Weiner »in plain sight«, vor aller Augen offenbar. In den frühen Skizzenbüchern wird ein Blick auf die Sprache deutlich, der etwas wahrnimmt, was einer auf die Immaterialität des Textes ausgerichteten Lektüre entgeht. Weiner achtet darauf, wie die Worte platziert sind, in welche Konstellationen sie treten. Er untersucht nicht konkrete Inhalte, sondern das ihnen zugrunde liegende Verhältnis der Dinge zur Welt und wie diese selbst zueinander auf Papier ins Verhältnis gesetzt sind. Diese Lektüre ist ebenfalls übertragbar auf Weiners gesamtes Werk. Es geht hier nicht um die Darstellung historischer, gesellschaftlicher Situationen, sondern um die Darstellung dessen, was ihnen zugrunde liegt, und dabei geht es nicht um die Suche nach Ideen, sondern um das Aufzeigen des Gebrauchs und der Funktion des Materials, der Dinge. Selten ist dabei der aktuelle Bezug so konkret wie in den Arbeiten **THE SOUNDS MADE OF TREES MADE TO FALL | DAS KRACHEN VON ZU FALL GEBRACHTEN BÄUMEN** und **MATTER SO SHAKEN TO ITS CORE TO LEAD TO A CHANGE IN INHERENT FORM TO THE EXTENT OF BRINGING ABOUT A CHANGE IN THE DESTINY OF THE MATERIAL | MATERIE DERART BIS IN DEN KERN ERSCHÜTTERT DASS ES ZU EINER VERÄNDERUNG DER INHÄRENTEN FORM FÜHRT IN DEM AUSMASS DASS ES EINE ÄNDERUNG IM SCHICKSAL DES**

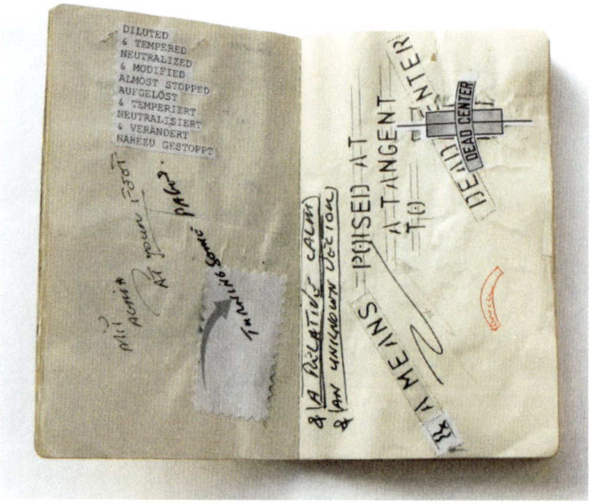

Sketchbook, 2007
Skizzenbuch, 2007

In his orientation towards nature and the "matter of fact," Weiner reveals a great proximity to the questions and concerns of physics. He is interested in the immanent laws governing material, like "dead center," "dead weight," or technical devices like the gyroscope. In an interview with Wolfgang Zinggl, Weiner says that his art is "actually a public science."[36] This can be seen in his drawings, which make use of the graphic symbols for electric circuits: the three variables in the flow of electric current—voltage, current, and resistance—are distinguishing characteristics of Weiner's works. What is underestimated above all is the stubborn insistence, the internal rage that serves as a motor for Weiner's artistic work, which is concealed by his outer amiability. "All art is made from anger" (Alle Kunst ist aus Zorn gemacht).[37] This anger is occasionally expressed in interviews. These are the moments about which, for example, the *New York Times* writes, "Mr. Weiner's actual way of describing this, evoking his years on the docks, can't be printed in this newspaper."[38] The rectangle, used in Europe as a symbol to depict resistance in electric current, is an element used by Weiner both as an empty space as well as a framing device for individual words. It is centrally anchored in Weiner's cover design for this book, along with the arrow, read as a symbol for electric current, pointing to the circle, as a source of energy. As Weiner once said to Dieter Schwarz, "I'm interested in paradigms, I'm interested in signage."[39]

Weiner's observation of the use of language is also reflected in his recourse to figures of speech, to book titles, film titles, and song titles in his works: **EARTH TO EARTH ASHES TO ASHES DUST TO DUST, AS FAR AS THE EYE CAN SEE, AS LONG AS IT LASTS, A CHIP**

MATERIALS BEWIRKT. Letztere hatte ihre Premiere 2003 im Essener Kunstverein Ruhr und wurde 2005 auf der Biennale Venedig zentral auf der Fassade des italienischen Pavillons gezeigt.

In seiner Orientierung auf die Natur und das, was man im Englischen als »matter of fact« bezeichnet, zeigt Weiner eine große Nähe zu den Fragen der Physik. Ihn interessieren die Eigengesetzlichkeiten von Material wie »Totpunkt«, »Totgewicht« oder technische Geräte wie das Gyroskop. Im Interview mit Wolfgang Zinggl sagt Weiner, seine Kunst sei »eigentlich eine öffentliche Naturwissenschaft«.[36] Das kann man bis in seine Zeichnungen verfolgen, die vor allem die grafischen Symbole der elektrischen Schaltungen übernehmen: Die drei Variablen im Fließen von elektrischem Strom – Spannung, Stromstärke und Widerstand – benennen entscheidende Charakteristika der Arbeiten von Weiner. Unterschätzt wird vor allem das hartnäckige Beharren, der innerliche Zorn als Motor für Weiners künstlerisches Schaffen, der sich hinter seiner äußerlichen Liebenswürdigkeit verbirgt. »All art is made from anger« (Alle Kunst ist aus Zorn gemacht).[37] Dieser Zorn schafft sich gelegentlich in Interviews Raum. Das sind dann die Momente, die eine *New York Times* mit den Worten festhält: »Die Ausdrucksweise, in der Mr. Weiner dies heute beschreibt, lässt an seine Zeit in den Docks denken und ist nicht geeignet, in dieser Zeitung wiedergegeben zu werden.«[38] Das Rechteck, in Europa Symbol für den Widerstand in der Darstellung des Stromkreislaufs, ist ein von Weiner als Leerraum und als Umgrenzung einzelner Wörter eingesetztes Element, das zentral in Weiners Covergestaltung des vorliegenden Buchs verankert ist, ebenso wie der Richtungspfeil als Symbol des Stromflusses und der Kreis als Energiequelle.

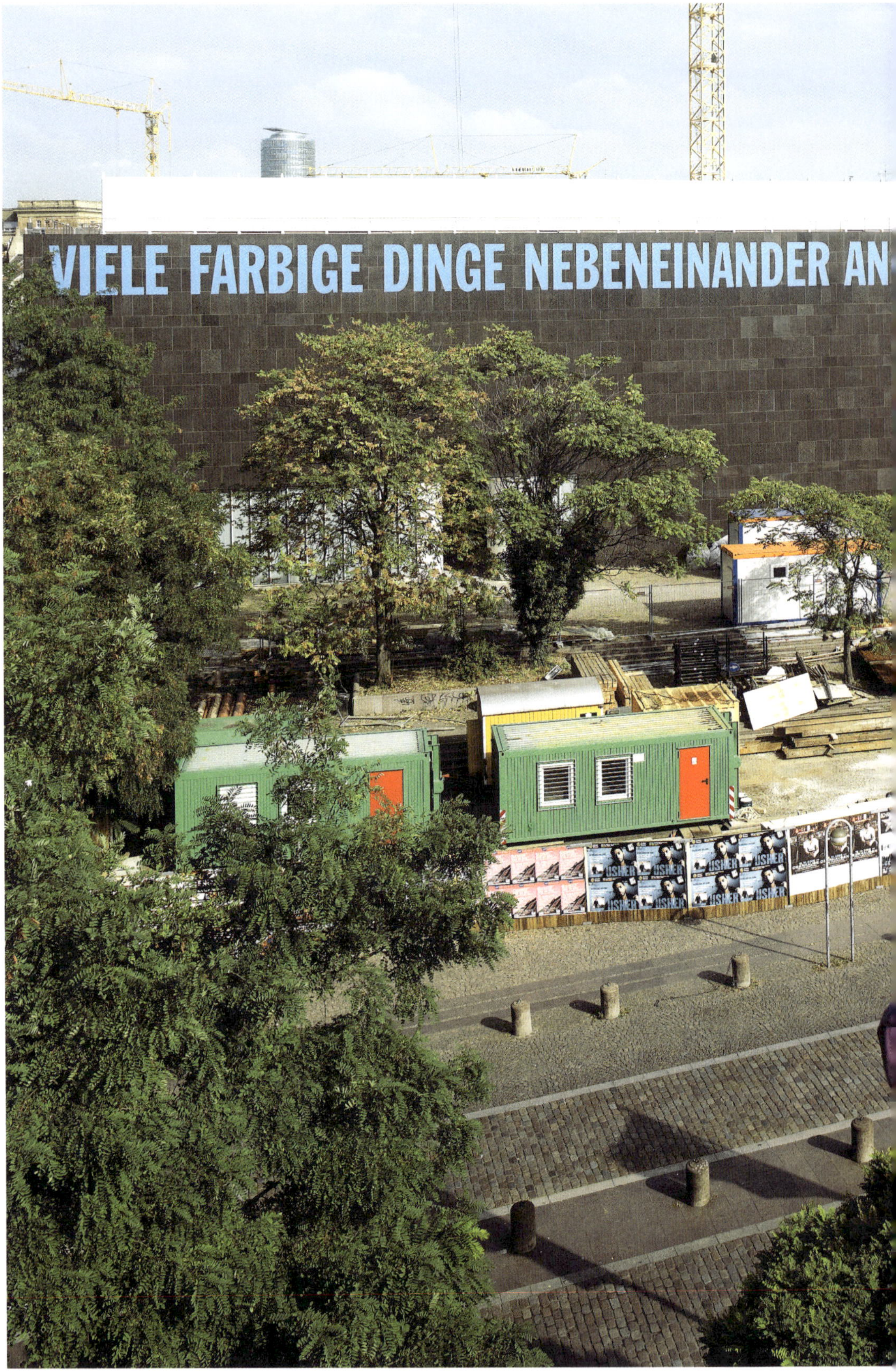
VIELE FARBIGE DINGE NEBENEINANDER AN
USHER

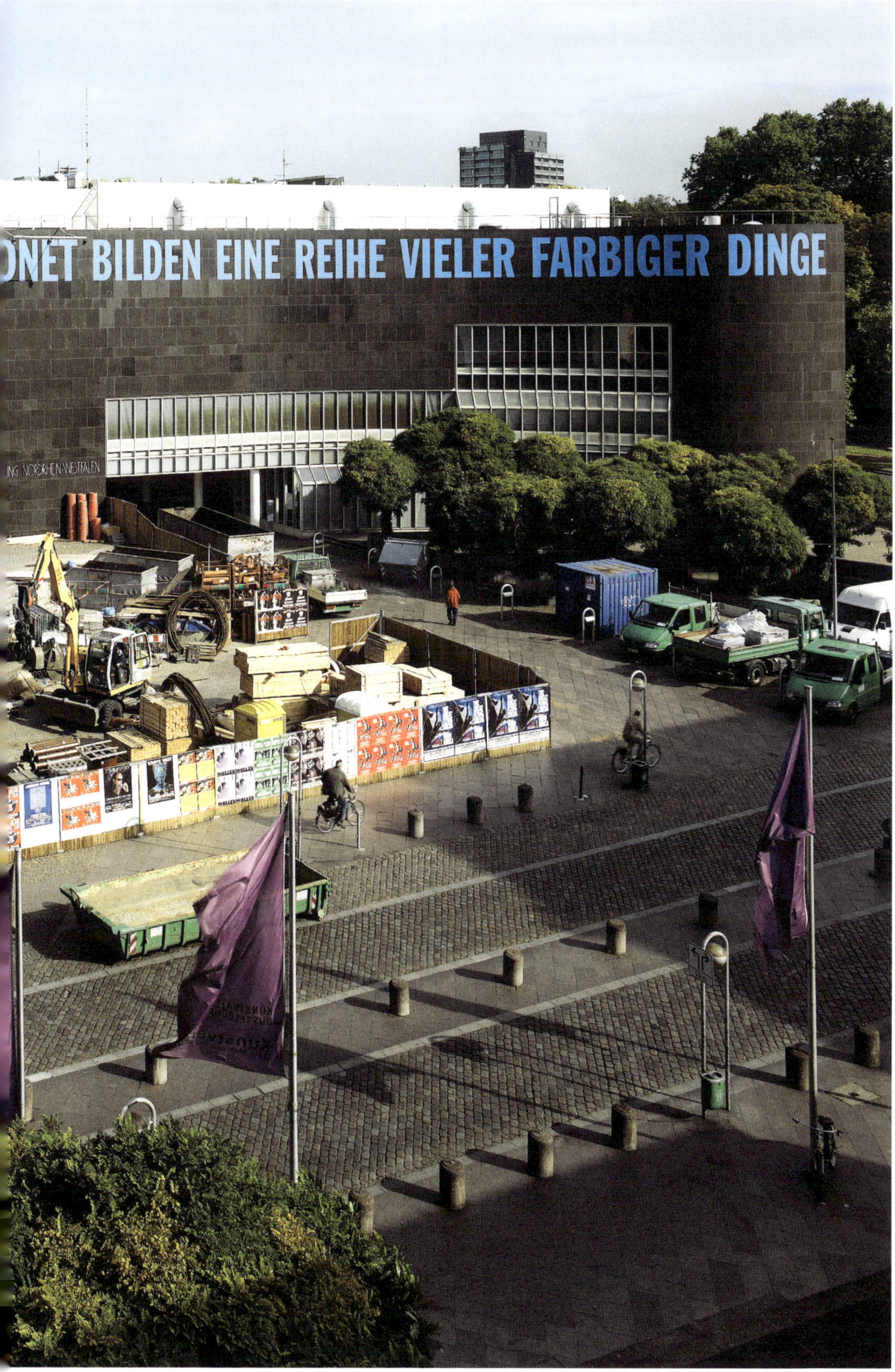
ONET BILDEN EINE REIHE VIELER FARBIGER DINGE

TAKEN OFF AN OLD BLOCK, IN PLAIN SIGHT, CATCH AS CATCH CAN, GONE WITH THE WIND, and **THEN THERE WERE NONE,** as well as in his exhibition titles: *Books Do Furnish a Room, Rosebud, Written on the Wind,* and *Rites of Passage.*[40] Early seventies works are interesting in this context. Weiner takes unspectacular word assemblages from daily language that are to be understood literally, in works such as **OVER THE EDGE, AROUND THE BEND, BESIDE ITSELF, STRUNG OUT.** Roberta Smith refers to a "strong erotic undercurrent, something that is more explicit in Mr. Weiner's films."[41] Kathryn Chiong shows this in an exemplary fashion in looking at one of his simple early works, **TO AND FRO. FRO AND TO. AND TO AND FRO. AND FRO AND TO. | HIN UND HER. HER UND HIN. UND HIN UND HER. UND HER UND HIN.**, which is used in Weiner's first film *A First Quarter* (1973) in a variety of contexts, and she refers to the political subtext of **CRATERED . . . TRENCH . . . SHOTGUN BLAST** against the backdrop of the Vietnam War.[42] "The nice thing about using language is that you don't have to subjugate your own personality to make an objective piece of work. The work itself is objective in its relationship of one material to another, but you know what things stand for."[43]

The reason that the beholder feels a sense of freedom contemplating Weiner's work can be attributed to the fact that Weiner does not make himself the subject: "I am not content."[44] This wordplay is an expression of a fundamental dissatisfaction with the state of society from an American socialist perspective and as an active dialectical materialist. But at the same time, the statement—with the final word being read according to the reader's mood—signifies the decided removal of the artist himself as the subject of his art; as Ferdinand Schmatz freely

Gegenüber Dieter Schwarz äußert Weiner: »Ich interessiere mich für Paradigmen, ich interessiere mich für Zeichensysteme.«[39]

Weiners Beobachtung des Sprachgebrauchs zeigt sich auch im Rekurs auf Redewendungen, Buch-, Film- und Songtitel in seinen Arbeiten: **ERDE ZU ERDE ASCHE ZU ASCHE STAUB ZU STAUB, SO WEIT DAS AUGE REICHT, AS LONG AS IT LASTS, A CHIP TAKEN OFF AN OLD BLOCK, IN PLAIN SIGHT, CATCH AS CATCH CAN, GONE WITH THE WIND** und **THEN THERE WERE NONE** ebenso wie in seinen Ausstellungstiteln *Books Do Furnish a Room, Rosebud, Written on the Wind* und *Rites of Passage.*[40] Interessant sind in diesem Zusammenhang die frühen Arbeiten aus den 1970er-Jahren. Weiner entnimmt dem täglichen Sprachgebrauch unscheinbare Wortfügungen wie **OVER THE EDGE** (durchgedreht), **AROUND THE BEND** (verrückt), **BESIDE ITSELF** (außer sich), **STRUNG OUT** (zugedröhnt). Sie sind jedoch wörtlich zu verstehen und daher übersetzt mit **ÜBER DEN RAND, UM DIE BIEGUNG HERUM, NEBEN SICH, AUSGESPANNT.** Roberta Smith verweist auf »einen starken erotischen Unterton in Weiners Arbeiten, etwas, das in Mr. Weiners Filmen noch deutlicher zum Tragen kommt«.[41] Exemplarisch zeigt Kathryn Chiong dies an einer seiner einfachen frühen Arbeiten – **TO AND FRO. FRO AND TO. AND TO AND FRO. AND FRO AND TO. | HIN UND HER. HER UND HIN. UND HIN UND HER. UND HER UND HIN.** –, die in Weiners erstem Film *A First Quarter* (1973) in verschiedenen Kontexte verwendet wird. Und sie verweist auch auf den politischen Subtext von **CRATERED ... TRENCH ... SHOTGUN BLAST** vor dem Hintergrund des Vietnam-Kriegs.[42] »Das Schöne, wenn man mit Sprache arbeitet, ist, daß man nicht seine eigene Persönlichkeit unterdrücken muß, um eine objektive Arbeit zu machen. Die Arbeit selbst ist objektiv in ihrer Beziehung von einem Material zu einem anderen, aber man weiß, wofür etwas steht.«[43]

Previous page:
***As Far As The Eye Can See*, installation at K20 Kunstsammlung Nordrhein-Westfalen, Düsseldorf, 2008, Annick and Anton Herbert Collection**
Vorherige Seite:
As Far as the Eye Can See, K20 Kunstsammlung Nordrhein-Westfalen, Düsseldorf, 2008, Sammlung Annick und Anton Herbert

translates, "Der Künstler ist weg. Die Kunst ist der Weg."[45] Weiner's statement "your personal enlightenment or your personal angst is not a fit subject for art"[46] makes clear that the rejection of an artist's ego as the subject of art can by no means be considered part of the postmodern concept of the death of the author. Nothing could be more foreign to Weiner than the disappearance of the author behind the sliding chains of signifiers without reference. His writings are the expression of a neutral, scholarly perspective of observation that Walter Benjamin also claims for himself as "masculine writing."[47] Weiner's works are always descriptions. There might be a preference of a certain person for certain colors in choosing their clothing, for instance in the work **WITH A TOUCH OF PINK WITH A BIT OF VIOLET WITH A HINT OF GREEN | MIT EINEM HAUCH VON ROSA MIT EINEM BISSCHEN VIOLETT MIT EINER SPUR VON GRÜN**, made for his gallerist Dorothee Fischer. Or his interest in the draping of fabric, as in **CHANGED FIRST TO CONTAIN A GESTURE THEN TO FOLLOW A CURVE & THEN TO SUPPORT A FOLD EACH TRANSITION ACQUIRING A NEED OF ITS OWN FULL CIRCLE | GEÄNDERT ZUERST UM EINE GESTE ZU ERLANGEN DANN EINE KURVE ZU VERFOLGEN & DANN EINE FALTE ZU STÜTZEN JEDER DIESER ÜBERGÄNGE ERWIRBT DIE NOTWENDIGKEIT SEINES VOLLEN KREISES**. These concrete observations can be condensed to the following programmatic statement: "Art per se must be a rendering of that gesture that fold that curve that helps us to realize we are now not then."[48]

"I am not content" is a double entendre[49] that reflects a spectrum of Weiner's convictions in making reference to his work: his typography committed to a strict objectivity, his recourse to empirical reality, the lack of a subject when setting participles, and the rejection of narration

Der Grund für die Freiheit, die der Betrachter in der Tat angesichts von Weiners Arbeiten empfindet, kann auf die Tatsache zurückgeführt werden, dass Weiner seine Person nicht zum Gegenstand macht: »I am not content.«[44] Das Wortspiel ist Ausdruck eines grundsätzlichen Missbehagens an dem Zustand der Gesellschaft aus der Perspektive eines amerikanischen Sozialisten und aktiven dialektischen Materialisten: »Ich bin nicht zufrieden.« Gleichzeitig signalisiert das Statement den dezidierten Entzug des Künstlers selbst als Gegenstand seiner Kunst, von Ferdinand Schmatz frei übersetzt mit: »Der Künstler ist weg, die Kunst ist der Weg.«[45] Weiners Aussage, »die persönliche Erleuchtung oder die persönlichen Ängste [...] sind kein angemessenes Thema der Kunst«,[46] macht deutlich, dass die Ablehnung des Künstler-Egos als Gegenstand der Kunst in keiner Weise in das postmoderne Konzept vom Tod des Autors einzuordnen ist. Nichts wäre Weiner so fremd wie das Verschwinden des Autors hinter dem Gleiten von Signifikantenketten ohne Referenz. Seine Schreibweise ist Ausdruck einer neutralen, wissenschaftlichen Beobachterperspektive, die auch Walter Benjamin für sich als »männliches Schreiben« beansprucht.[47] Weiners Arbeiten sind immer Beschreibungen. Das kann die Vorliebe eines Menschen für bestimmte Farben bei der Wahl der Kleidung sein, beispielsweise **WITH A TOUCH OF PINK WITH A BIT OF VIOLET WITH A HINT OF GREEN | MIT EINEM HAUCH VON ROSA MIT EINEM BISSCHEN VIOLETT MIT EINER SPUR VON GRÜN**, eine Arbeit für seine Galeristin Dorothee Fischer. Oder sein Interesse an dem Drapieren von Stoff: **CHANGED FIRST TO CONTAIN A GESTURE THEN TO FOLLOW A CURVE & THEN TO SUPPORT A FOLD EACH TRANSITION ACQUIRING A NEED OF ITS OWN FULL CIRCLE | GEÄNDERT ZUERST UM EINE GESTE ZU ERLANGEN DANN EINE KURVE ZU VERFOLGEN & DANN EINE FALTE ZU STÜTZEN JEDER DIESER ÜBERGÄNGE ERWIRBT DIE** by denying any concrete situational embedding; often not even an object is mentioned. And yet it is hard to find another artist so present in the public art sphere[50] whose personifications are of such interest to art critics. Be it his voice (as Randy Kennedy describes it, his "smoke-deepened basso-profundo"[51]), his beard ("trademark flowing Moses beard"[52]), his humor, the bright red color of the jacket, the brand of his cigarettes ("The Discreet Charm of the Gauloisie"[53]), his cigarette rolling (that provoked David Colman to coin the metaphor, "His art is for those who like to roll their own"), the whiskey, the amiability, the easygoing character, the impatience, as well as his generosity and modesty. God, godfather, head of Conceptual Art, founding guru (Grace Glueck[54]), beatnik: the chain of names is long and speaks for the interest and the spontaneous sympathy that the artist inspires.

Working with language always means "living in quotations" (Max Frisch). Literary theory negotiates this aspect with the concept of "intertexuality": "citation, citation de la citation, citation de la citation de la citation."[55] In her poetological analysis of Gottfried Keller's *Romeo und Julia auf dem Dorfe*, which in terms of the sensuality of the terminology employed is much closer to Weiner's art, Eva Geulen describes the phenomenon of the appropriation of a tradition, and with it the phenomenon of nomadic language that is important here. Geulen places the idea of "being unclaimed," taken from the novel itself, in relation to the juridical term of *res nullius*, "nobody's property." In Keller's novel, the two main protagonists come into conflict over matters of borders and property. Over long passages, Keller describes this "unclaimed field" between

NOTWENDIGKEIT SEINES VOLLEN KREISES. Diese konkreten Beobachtungen können sich zu der programmatischen Aussage verdichten: **ART PER SE MUST BE A RENDERING OF THAT GESTURE THAT FOLD THAT CURVE THAT HELPS US TO REALIZE WE ARE NOW NOT THEN**.[48]

»I am not content«, spiegelt in seiner Doppeldeutigkeit[49] ein Spektrum von Weiners Überzeugungen, das sich in jeder Entscheidung hinsichtlich seiner künstlerischen Arbeit nachvollziehen lässt: Von der einer strengen Sachlichkeit verpflichteten Typografie, dem Rekurs auf die empirische Realität über das Fehlen eines Subjekts im Setzen der Partizipien bis zur Verweigerung einer Narration im Entzug einer konkreten situativen Einbettung, oft ist noch nicht einmal ein Objekt benannt. Und dennoch gibt es kaum einen Künstler, der in der Kunstöffentlichkeit so präsent ist[50] und dessen Eigenschaften und Vorlieben so im Interesse der Kunstkritiker stehen. Seien es seine Stimme, die Randy Kennedy mit »tiefster Raucherbass«[51] beschreibt, sein »unverwechselbarer, wallender Moses-Bart«,[52] sein Humor, die knallrote Farbe der Jacke, die Marke seiner Zigaretten (»Der diskrete Charme der Gauloisie«), deren Drehen aus losem Tabak David Colman zur Metapher gereichte: »[…] seine Kunst ist für die, die gerne selber drehen«,[53] der Whiskey, die Liebenswürdigkeit, die Gelassenheit, die Ungeduld ebenso wie seine Großzügigkeit und Bescheidenheit. Gott, Gottvater, Oberhaupt der Concept Art, Founding guru (Grace Glueck),[54] Beatnik – die Kette der Namen ist lang und spricht für das Interesse und die spontane Sympathie, die der Künstler weckt.

Mit Sprache arbeiten bedeutet immer ein »Leben im Zitat« (Max Frisch), literaturtheoretisch verhandelt unter dem Begriff der Intertextualität:

the fields of the increasingly antagonistic farmers. More and more it turns into a stone wall (stonewall), for both farmers constantly expand their own field by plowing ever more furrows on the middle field, and the stones are thrown onto the remaining strip, which gets narrower and narrower. Just as the farmers take hold of the unclaimed ground, Keller's novel also takes possession of its literary predecessors.[56] "This raises the question of the 'property' on which the narrative positions itself, and the question of the stones with which it asserts its own sphere against predecessors or competitors. As we know, the narrative owns neither the property nor the stones; *Romeo und Julia auf dem Dorfe* is unclaimed property."[57]

Lacking concrete narrative, the question of subject matter in Weiner's art is superfluous, and

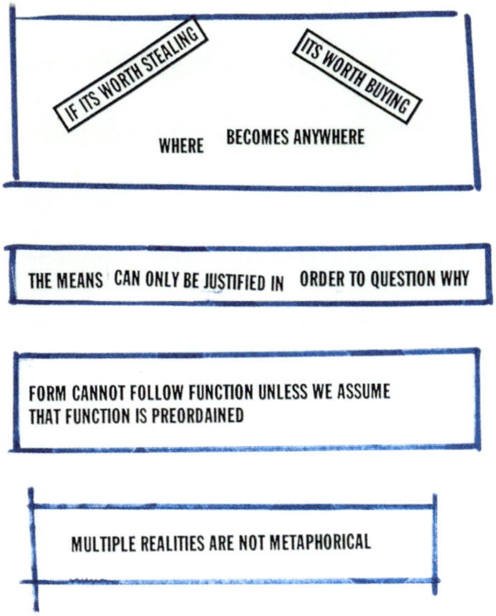

Working drawing for the opera *The Society Architect Ponders the Golden Gate Bridge*, one of 26 collages, 2000
Arbeitszeichnung für die Oper *The Society Architect Ponders the Golden Gate Bridge*, eine von insgesamt 26 Collagen, 2000

»citation, citation de la citation, citation de la citation de la citation«.[55] In der Sinnlichkeit der Terminologie näher an Weiners Kunst fasst Eva Geulen in ihrer poetologischen Analyse von Gottfried Kellers *Romeo und Julia auf dem Dorfe* das Phänomen der Aneignung einer Stofftradition und damit auch das entscheidende Phänomen der nomadisierenden Sprache, das hier von Bedeutung ist. Geulen setzt den der Novelle entliehenen Begriff der Herrenlosigkeit mit dem juristischen Terminus der Res nullius, der »herrenlosen Dinge«, in Bezug. In Kellers Novelle geraten die Protagonisten in einen Streit über die Frage nach Grenzen und Besitz. Über lange Passagen erzählt Keller von diesem »herrenlosen Acker« zwischen den Feldern der zunehmend verfeindeten Bauern. Immer mehr türmt er sich zum Steinwall, da beide Bauern ihre Felder um immer wieder neue Furchen aus dem mittleren Acker erweitern und die Steine auf den immer schmaler werdenden Reststreifen werfen. So wie sich die Bauern des herrenlosen Guts bemächtigen, so bemächtigt sich auch Kellers Novelle seiner literarischen Vorgänger.[56] »Damit ist die Frage nach dem ›Grund und Boden‹ (137) gestellt, auf dem die Erzählung sich eingerichtet hat, und nach den Steinen, mit denen sie ihre Sphäre gegen Vorgänger oder Konkurrenten behauptet. Bekanntlich gehören ihr weder Grund noch Steine, bei ›Romeo und Julia auf dem Dorfe‹ handelt es sich um herrenloses Gut.«[57]

Aufgrund des Fehlens einer Narration erübrigt sich für Weiners Kunst die Frage nach dem Stofflichen, und dennoch stellt sich die Frage nach dem »Grund und Boden« in verschärfter Form. Der Künstler arbeitet mit »herrenlosem Gut«, mit Sprache, die ihren Weg in das Leben, in die Kultur gefunden hat und von ihm erneut in die Kultur, in das Leben yet the question of property remains. The artist works with "unclaimed things," language that found its way into life, and culture, and which is reintroduced into culture, into life: **THINGS THEMSELVES ON TOP OF OTHER THINGS ON TOP OF SOMETHING ELSE NOW & THEN | DINGE SELBER AUF ANDEREN DINGEN AUF ETWAS ANDEREM JETZT & DANN.** Language-based works are also such "unclaimed things." Anyone can take them home, without paying for them, a behavior that Weiner comments upon in **IF ITS WORTH STEALING ITS WORTH BUYING.**[58] In a visually complex etching, Weiner returns to this subject. It emerges in the context of the exhibition of two works by Weiner in 1995 at Galerie Dorothea van der Koelen in Mainz. The exhibition title *Vorstellungsrealitäten* ("Realities of Imagination") is a quote taken from the etching. The works intersect words in English and German in a parallel configuration **SALT/SALZ** or **FIRE/FEUER** with **WATER/WASSER, WITH/MIT, WITHOUT/OHNE,** and **SAND/SAND.** The etching abstracts the works from verbal language with boxes in orange and red but keeps the graphic features, so that the relationship between the elements is retained. Weiner operates similarly in other works with empty parentheses, which in Frege's concept of "unsaturated expressions" symbolized with parentheses might have a background in the philosophy of language.[59] Lawrence Weiner refers to them as an "editorial introduction."[60] Beneath the drawing is the German neologism *Vorstellungsrealitäten,* and added to this seemingly paradoxical concept is the text of a sign that can be seen in shops all over the United States: **YOU BREAK IT YOU BOUGHT IT.** Tradition has it that if a customer breaks an object in a shop, it is considered purchased; that is, the customer bears responsibility for it by handling it—like Weiner's art, which can be taken home in the mind.

eingebracht wird: **DINGE SELBER AUF ANDEREN DINGEN AUF ETWAS ANDEREM JETZT & DANN**. Sprachbasierte Arbeiten sind auch solche herrenlosen Dinge. Jeder kann sie mit nach Hause nehmen, ohne sie zu bezahlen, ein Verhalten, das Weiner mit **IF ITS WORTH STEALING ITS WORTH BUYING** kommentiert.[58] In einer visuell vielschichtig angelegten Radierung kommt Weiner auch auf dieses Thema zu sprechen. Sie entstand 1995 im Zusammenhang mit der Ausstellung zweier Arbeiten Weiners in der Galerie Dorothea van der Koelen, Mainz. Der Ausstellungstitel *Vorstellungsrealitäten* ist ein Zitat aus der Radierung. Die Arbeiten verschränken in einer parallelen Konfiguration Wörter in der englischen und deutschen Sprache **SALT/SALZ** beziehungsweise **FIRE/FEUER** mit **WATER/WASSER, WITH/MIT, WITHOUT/OHNE** und **SAND/SAND**. Mit Kästen in Orange und Rot abstrahiert die Radierung von der verbalen Sprache der Arbeiten, behält aber deren Grafik bei, sodass die Beziehung zwischen den Elementen beibehalten wird. Ähnlich operiert Weiner in anderen Arbeiten mit leeren Klammern, die in Freges Konzept der mit Klammern symbolisierten »ungesättigten« Ausdrücke einen sprachphilosophischen Hintergrund haben mögen.[59] Lawrence Weiner bezeichnet sie als »editorische Vorbemerkung«.[60] Der Zeichnung ist der deutschsprachige Neologismus »Vorstellungsrealitäten« unterlegt und diesem scheinbar paradoxen Begriff der Text eines Hinweisschildes hinzugefügt, das man in Läden überall in den USA finden kann: **YOU BREAK IT YOU BOUGHT IT**. Was man zerbricht, wird als gekauft betrachtet, das heißt, man trägt die Verantwortung, wenn man damit umgeht – wie Weiners Kunst, die man im Kopf nach Hause tragen kann.

»Buying Art You Can't Take Home« betitelte die *Newsweek* 2011 einen Artikel über Sammler von

In 2011, *Newsweek* published an article about collectors of Conceptual Art entitled "Buying Art You Can't Take Home."[61] The article was illustrated with a photograph of that year's Art Basel showing a work by Lawrence Weiner. Weiner's art in fact cannot be taken home as an "object" per se. It requires no insurance, no storage; there is no "original." The question remains: what does one acquire when purchasing "a Weiner"? The very question is misguided. Weiner's statement of intent from 1968 infers that one does not just purchase a work, but takes on responsibility for it. This is stated in a letter received from Weiner. The owner is free to have the work installed as he or she sees fit. Collectors often arrange for the installation according to their needs and desires, be it hand painted, stenciled, put up in vinyl, etc., and at times install it themselves. Works where a drawing is an integral element have a digital or analog model to work from. The collector's responsibility for the work means more than the freedom to decide where it is shown, or in which cultural context it is embedded. The taking on of responsibility becomes an engagement with the significance of the work, as any public or private location—not just a museum—can be its destination.

The question "Who are you sleeping with?," which the art magazine *Monopol* asks an owner of an artwork every month, is, as Weiner might

Konzeptkunst und zeigte ein Foto von der Art Basel desselben Jahres mit einer Arbeit von Lawrence Weiner.[61] Als »Ware« lässt sich Weiners Kunst tatsächlich nicht nach Hause tragen. Sie erfordert keine Versicherung, kein Depot, es gibt kein Original. So bleibt die Frage, was man erwirbt, wenn man einen »Weiner« kauft. Schon die Frage ist falsch gestellt. Aus Weiners *Statement of Intent (Absichtserklärung)* geht hervor, dass man keine Arbeit kauft, sondern die Verantwortung dafür übernimmt. Das steht in einem Schreiben, das man von Weiner erhält. Und damit ist der Käufer frei, die Arbeit so auszuführen, wie er es für angemessen hält. Oft veranlassen die Sammler die Ausführung der Arbeiten nach ihren Vorstellungen, ob handgemalt, mit Schablonen aufgebracht oder in Vinyl, gelegentlich führen sie sie auch selbst aus. Arbeiten, bei denen eine Zeichnung integraler Bestandteil ist, haben eine digitale oder analoge Vorlage. Die Verantwortung des Sammlers für die Arbeit bedeutet die freie Entscheidung darüber, an welchem Ort sie gezeigt, in welchem kulturellen Kontext sie eingebettet wird. Allein das verlangt dem Besitzer eine intensive Auseinandersetzung mit der Bedeutung der Arbeit ab, da nicht nur das Museum, sondern jeder öffentliche Kontext möglich ist.

Die Frage »Mit wem schlafen Sie?«, von der Kunstzeitschrift *Monopol* jeden Monat einem anderen Kunstbesitzer gestellt, gilt ganz im Sinne Weiners nicht dem Eigentum, sie gilt dem Gebrauch der

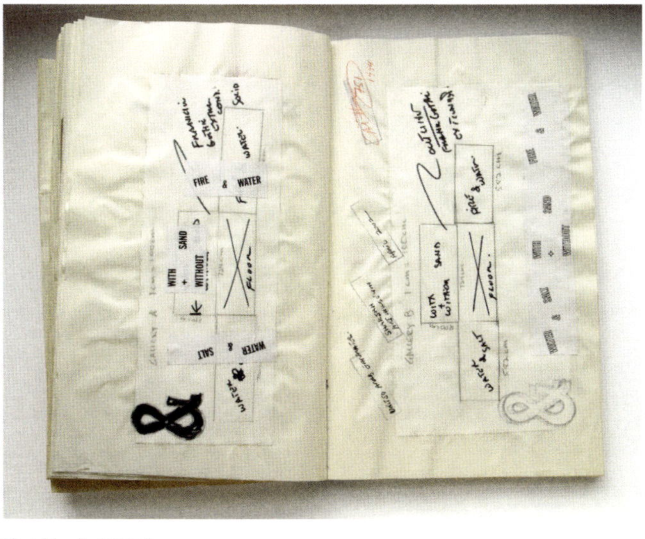

Sketchbook, 2001–2
Skizzenbuch, 2001/02

Following page:
VORSTELLUNGSREALITÄTEN / YOU BREAK IT YOU BOUGHT IT, print edition, Frankfurter Kunstverein, 1994–95, Private collection
Nächste Seite:
VORSTELLUNGSREALITÄTEN / YOU BREAK IT YOU BOUGHT IT, Jahresgabe, Frankfurter Kunstverein, 1994/95, Privatsammlung

VORSTE
REALIT
YOU
BRE
&
YOU
BOU

LLUNGS
TEN

AK IT
&
GHT IT ×

26/60 Liv (94)

agree with, not a question of property, but about the use of art in everyday life. With his work *N. Schmidt*, artist Gregor Schneider raised a monument to a collector,[62] an expression of respect for an individual whose passion for art and its integration into his life are unique. When Mr. Schmidt installed Weiner's works on the exterior of his home in the surroundings of large-scale sculptures by Carl Andre, Bruce Nauman, Richard Long, and Sol LeWitt, he placed Weiner with his peers, among them, Minimalist sculptors, while grasping the sculptural meaning of Weiner's work.

Kunst im täglichen Leben. Der Künstler Gregor Schneider setzte mit seiner Arbeit *N. Schmidt*[62] einem Sammler ein Denkmal – Ausdruck der Wertschätzung eines Menschen, dessen Leidenschaft für die Kunst und ihre Integration in sein Leben einzigartig sind. Wenn dieser Sammler Weiners Arbeiten im Außenbereich seines Hauses im Kontext großer Skulpturen von Carl Andre, Bruce Nauman, Richard Long und Sol LeWitt zeigt, und Weiner mit seinen Künstlerkollegen, darunter minimalistische Bildhauer, versammelt, trifft er wie kaum ein anderer die skulpturale Bedeutung seiner Arbeiten.

TENSION ENOUGH TO HOLD A STONE ABOVE THE RHINE | SPANNUNG GENUG EINEN STEIN ZU HALTEN ÜBER DEM RHEIN is written on a brick. It is an edition that is thematically concerned with sculpture and architecture and it has a place in the daily life of Stefanie Jansen, head of exhibition management at Kunstsammlung NRW in Düsseldorf. The brick plays with Mies van der Rohe's famous quotation, "Architecture starts when you carefully put two bricks together," and refers to Weiner's installation at Villa Haus Esters, a home designed by Mies van der Rohe and now converted into a museum.

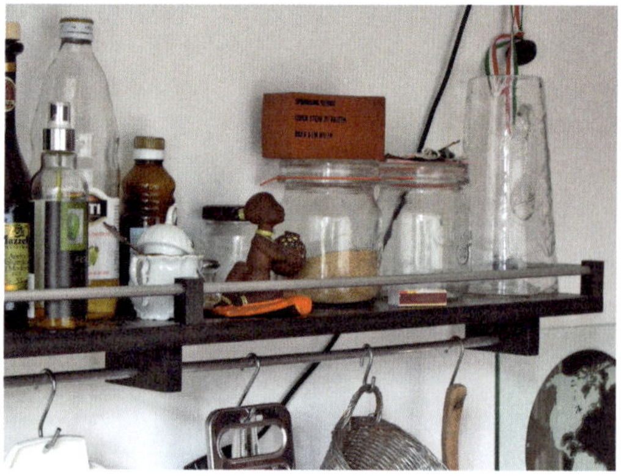

Brick edition, fundraiser for the renovation of Haus Esters, Krefeld, 1999, Stefanie Jansen Collection
Ziegelstein, Edition, zugunsten der Renovierung von Haus Esters, Krefeld, 1999, Sammlung Stefanie Jansen

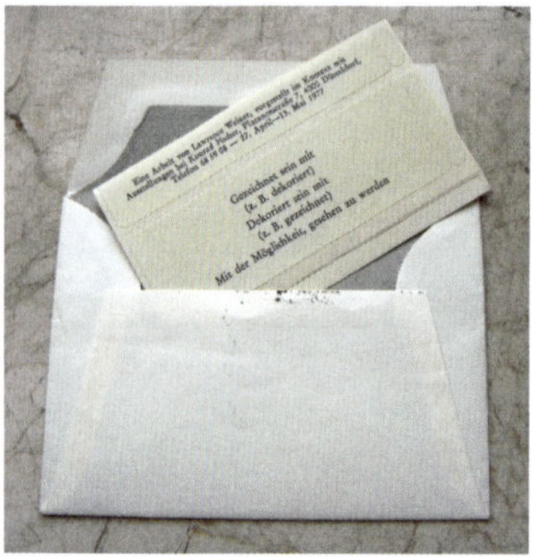

Announcement sticker, Konrad Fischer Galerie, Düsseldorf, 1977, N. Schmidt Collection
Ankündigungsetikett, Konrad Fischer Galerie, Düsseldorf, 1977, Sammlung N. Schmidt

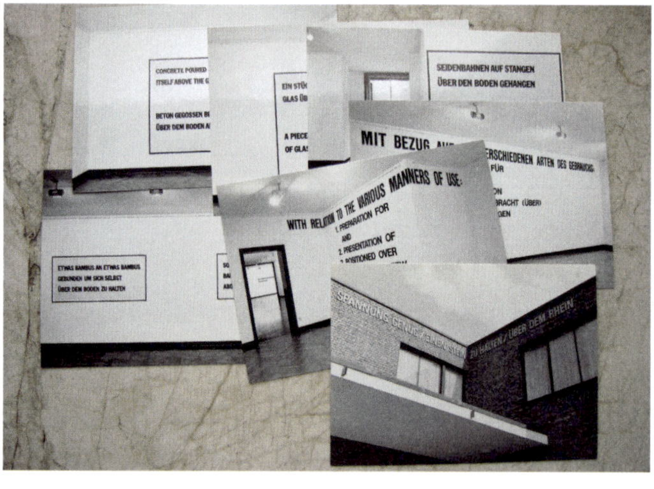

Exhibition postcards, *Altered to Suit*, Museum Haus Esters, Krefeld, 1988, N. Schmidt Collection
Ausstellungspostkarten, *Passend gemacht*, Museum Haus Esters, Krefeld, 1988, Sammlung N. Schmidt

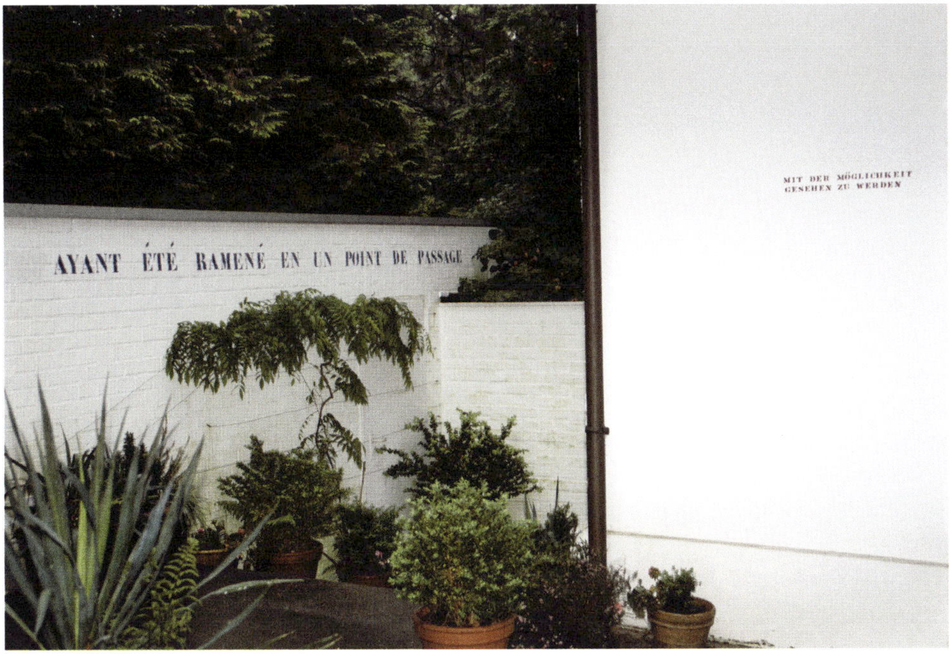

Installation view, 2011, N. Schmidt Collection
Installationsansicht, 2011, Sammlung N. Schmidt

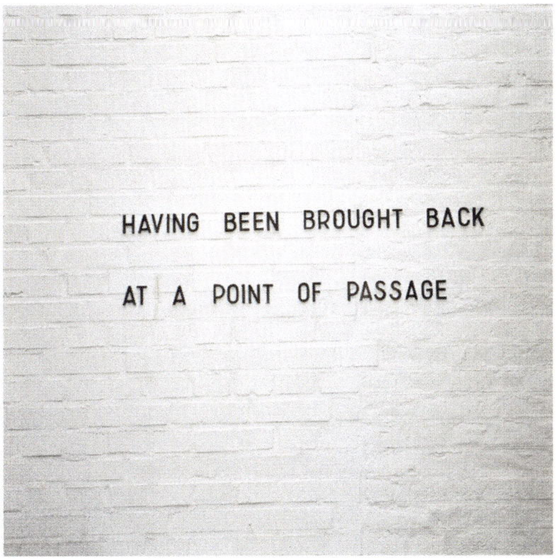

Installation view, 2011, N. Schmidt Collection
Installationsansicht, 2011, Sammlung N. Schmidt

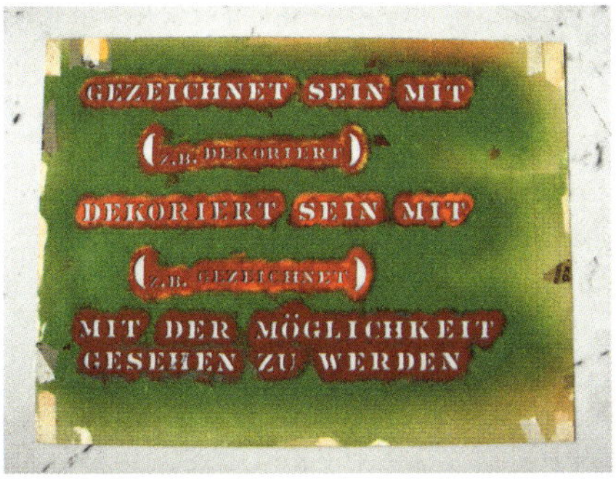

Original installation stencil, N. Schmidt Collection
Original-Installationsschablone, Sammlung N. Schmidt

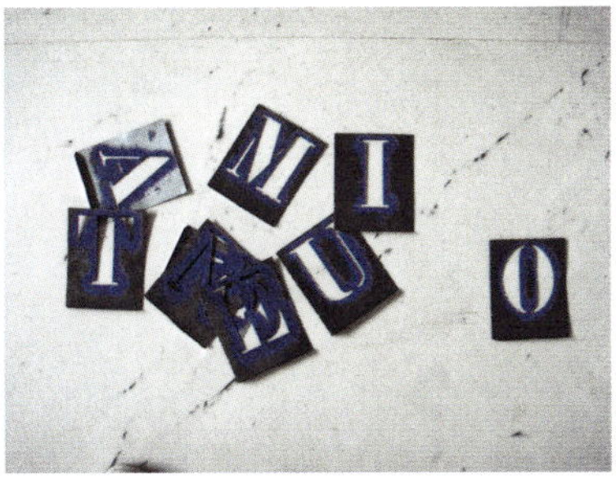

Installation stencil, N. Schmidt Collection
Installationsschablone, Sammlung N. Schmidt

Just over nine meters long, the work is applied in respectfully muted gray (plastic) letters that span diagonally above the corner entranceway to the Krefeld residence.

A work by Weiner has accompanied Peter Kogler since his conversion of a former locksmith's atelier into a large studio in Vienna's Third District; Weiner, a friend of the artist for many years, placed the work at Kogler's disposal. Applied to the wall in Kogler's studio, one could assume it is an integral work. Considered by Weiner an aphorism, that is a drawn aphorism that operates as an equivalent to speech, it is not catalogued in his works. For the title and cover of this publication Weiner has continued to work with this particular aphorism, isolating individual elements for one issuance, and bringing them together again in another. After returning to a second sketch, which was created while making the first, "Nach bildende Kunst / After Fine Art" is now placed in a powerful vertical lineament as the title of this book, while the drawing, separated from the title by the names, sets in motion the process alluded to. This movement process is shown amplified by Weiner in the special edition designed for this book by breaking the frame.

The conductor Michael Klaar encountered a work by Weiner in 1993 at an exhibition in Vienna and acquired it immediately.[63] He felt challenged by its hermeticism. An early collector of Donald Judd's work, he likes art that is not hierarchical: "Each element is important."[64] And when Cologne collector Reiner Speck acquires a work on the subject of time,[65] one can assume it is a daily companion in his life, even without being physically present in his house.

TENSION ENOUGH TO HOLD A STONE ABOVE THE RHINE | SPANNUNG GENUG EINEN STEIN ZU HALTEN ÜBER DEM RHEIN steht auf einem Ziegelstein. Es ist eine Edition, die sich thematisch mit Skulptur und Architektur befasst und die einen Platz im täglichen Leben von Stefanie Jansen, Leiterin der Abteilung Ausstellungsmanagement der Kunstsammlung Nordrhein-Westfalen in Düsseldorf, gefunden hat. Die Edition spielt mit Mies van der Rohes berühmtem Zitat, Architektur beginne, wenn man zwei Ziegelsteine sorgfältig zusammenfüge, und bezieht sich damit auf Weiners Installation an der zum Museum umgewidmeten Villa Haus Esters von Mies van der Rohe. Mit knapp neun Metern Länge überspannt die Arbeit in respektvoll zurückhaltend grauen (Plastik-)Lettern den Eckeingang der Architektenvilla in Krefeld.

Seit Abschluss des Umbaus einer ehemaligen Schlosserei in ein weiträumiges Atelier im dritten Bezirk in Wien begleitet den Künstler Peter Kogler eine Arbeit von Weiner, die dieser ihm – in langjähriger Freundschaft verbunden – zur Verfügung stellte. Die Zeichnung auf der Wand in Koglers Atelier ist integraler Bestandteil der Arbeit und fungiert gleichrangig als Sprache. Es ist keine ins Werkverzeichnis aufgenommene Sprachskulptur, Weiner zählt die Arbeit zu den Aphorismen. Für die Titel- und Covergestaltung der vorliegenden Publikation hat Weiner an diesem Aphorismus weitergearbeitet, einzelne Elemente isoliert und sie in einer Konstellation wieder zusammengeführt. Gleichzeitig greift er auf einen weiteren im Zuge des ersten entstandenen zweisprachigen

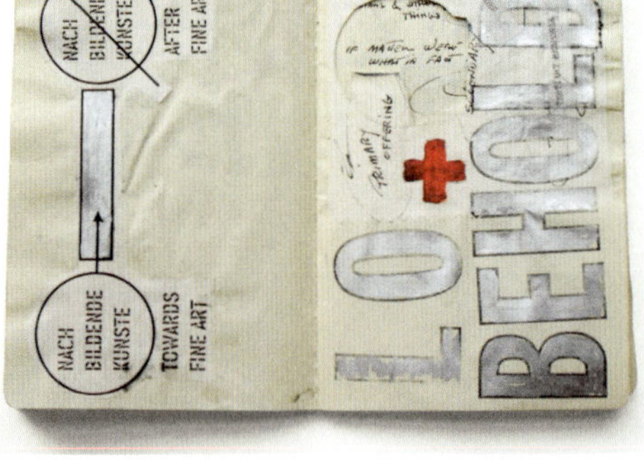

Sketchbook, 2005
Skizzenbuch, 2005

Weiner's interest is in language in every sense, be it its typographical appearance, its sound and cadence, its transiency in collective memory, or to specific lexical and grammatical structures that come to the surface when translated. The semiotician Umberto Eco places the process of translation under the sign of the "as if." In the best of cases, he argues, translation is saying "as if" the same thing with different words. In poetic texts, Eco continues, the problem of the "as if" becomes central, and occupies the entire field.[66] Weiner places emphasis—despite his fascination

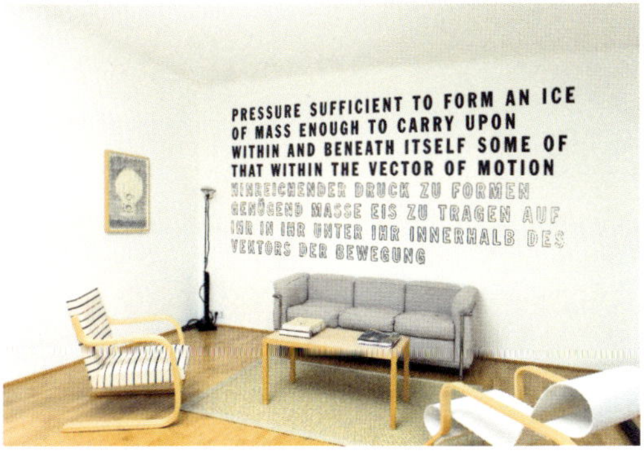

Vienna, 1993, Michael Klaar Collection
Wien, 1993, Sammlung Michael Klaar

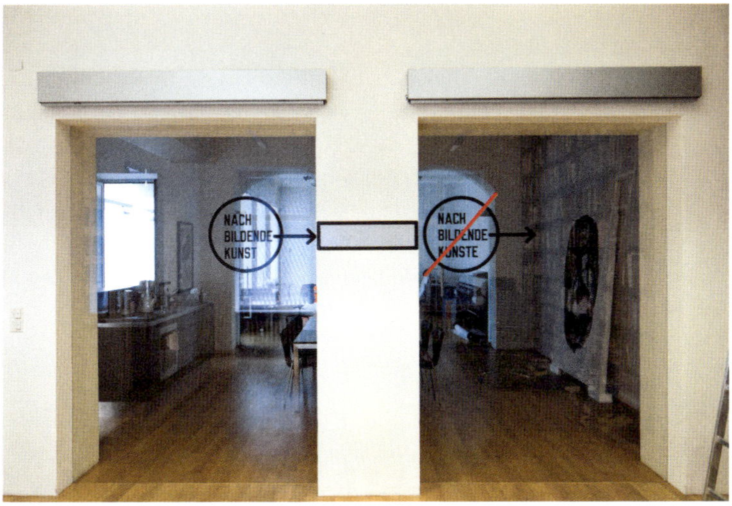

Atelier Peter Kogler, Vienna, 2008
Atelier Peter Kogler, Wien, 2008

Entwurf zurück: »Nach bildende Kunst / After Fine Art« ist nun in energischem vertikalen Lineament als Titel des Buches gesetzt, während die Zeichnung, durch die Namen vom Titel getrennt, den angesprochenen Prozess in Gang setzt. Diesen Prozess der Bewegung verstärkt Weiner in der für das Buch entworfenen Sonderedition durch das Aufbrechen des Rahmens.

Der Dirigent Michael Klaar traf 1993 während einer Ausstellung in Wien auf eine Arbeit Weiners und erwarb sie spontan.[63] Ihn forderte ihre Hermetik heraus. Als früher Sammler von Arbeiten Donald Judds mag er eine Kunst, die nicht hierarchisch ist: »Jedes Element ist wichtig.«[64] Und wenn der Kölner Sammler Reiner Speck eine Arbeit von Weiner zum Thema Zeit erwirbt,[65] kann man davon ausgehen, dass sie auch ohne physische Präsenz in seinem Haus ein täglicher Begleiter seines Lebens ist.

Weiners Interesse gilt Sprache in jeglicher Hinsicht, sei es ihr typografisches Erscheinungsbild, ihr Klang und Rhythmus, ihr Nomadisieren im kollektiven Gedächtnis oder ihre spezifischen lexikalischen und grammatischen Strukturen, die vor allem bei der Übersetzung zum Tragen kommen. Der Semiotiker Umberto Eco stellt Übersetzungsprozesse »unter das Zeichen eines *Quasi*. Im besten Fall sagt man beim Übersetzen *quasi* dasselbe mit anderen Worten.« In poetischen Texten rückt, so Eco, »das Problem dieses *Quasi* ins Zentrum und besetzt das gesamte Feld«.[66] Weiner legt den Schwerpunkt – trotz with the sensual aspects of text—on the propositional content of statements. Connotations and transferences in the sense of metaphors are to be supplied by the beholder or reader; the author does not serve as the decisive authority. The conviction of basic translatability that Weiner shares with translation studies and its practice is situated in the expressive reference to the material, a prerequisite especially seen in light of his recurrent amendment "language + the materials referred to" when required in catalogues and by museum registrars to state the materials used to make the work. One of his quintessential works of expanded paradigm, translated into many languages, confirms this simple 1969 statement: **A TRANSLATION FROM ONE LANGUAGE TO ANOTHER | EINE ÜBERSETZUNG VON EINER SPRACHE IN DIE ANDERE.** In its bilingualism, the work demonstrates that a transfer has taken place, from one language to the other, and it facilitates additional transfers to other media, such as drawing, spoken in film, video, or in a song, i.e. "re-constructed."[67]

The discretionary latitude in terms of translation already begins with the conjugation of weak verbs in English—for example, the 1971 work

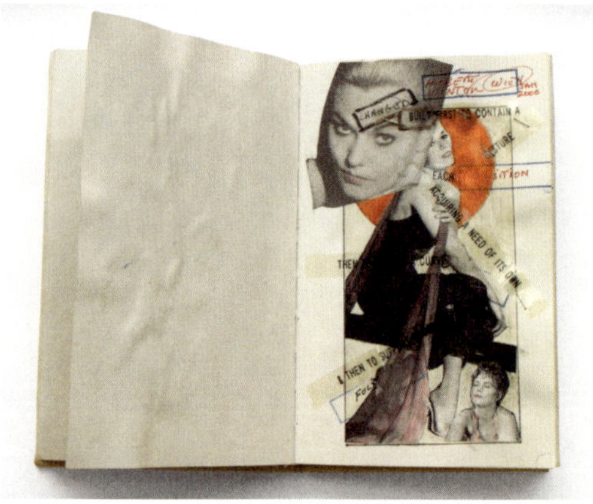

Sketchbook, 1999–2001
Skizzenbuch, 1999–2001

seiner Faszination für die Sinnlichkeit von Texten – auf den propositionalen Gehalt der Aussagen. Konnotationen und Übertragungen im Sinne von Metaphern sind vom Betrachter oder Leser einzubringen, der Autor fungiert nicht als Entscheidungsinstanz. Die Überzeugung von einer grundsätzlichen Übersetzbarkeit, die Weiner mit Translatologie und Übersetzungspraxis teilt, gründet in der ausdrücklichen Referenz auf die Materialien, eine Voraussetzung, auf die jede Arbeit durch den Zusatz »language + the materials referred to« (Sprache + die benannten Materialien) zurückgeführt wird, wenn Kataloge oder Museumsarchivare verlangen, die Materialien anzugeben, die zur Herstellung der Arbeit verwendet wurden. Eines seiner paradigmatischen, in viele Sprachen übersetzten Statements von 1969 konstatiert die schlichte Aussage **A TRANSLATION FROM ONE LANGUAGE TO ANOTHER | EINE ÜBERSETZUNG VON EINER SPRACHE IN DIE ANDERE**. In der Zweisprachigkeit führt die Arbeit selbst vor, dass eine Übertragung stattgefunden hat, von einer Sprache in die andere, und sie ermöglicht weitere Übertragungsprozesse in andere Medien wie beispielsweise in eine Zeichnung, in gesprochene Sprache, in Film, Video, oder einen Song, eine »Re-Konstruktion«.[67]

Die Ermessensspielräume bei der Übersetzung beginnen schon bei der Flexion der schwachen Verben im Englischen, **FLOWED** (1971) etwa, das unentschieden zwischen Präteritum und Partizip Perfekt steht. Entgegen der Dominanz von Partizipien bei Weiner ist es in *Specific & General Works* mit dem Präteritum übersetzt: **FLOSS SANFT**.[68] Die *Jahresgabe* 1972 des Kunstvereins Münster dagegen

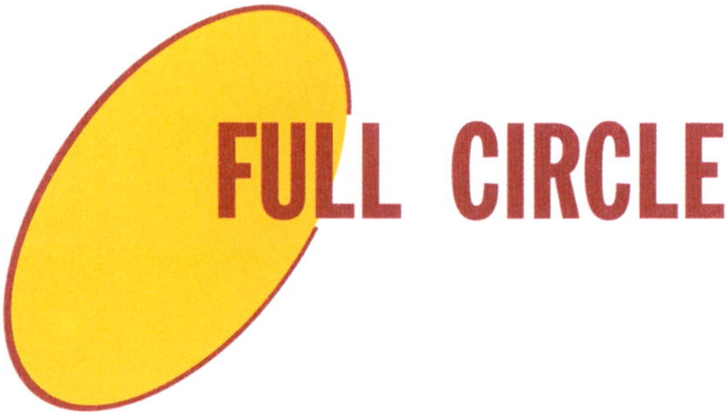

Exhibition announcement, *Full Circle*, Galerie Hubert Winter, Vienna, 2000
Ausstellungsankündigung, Full Circle, Galerie Hubert Winter, Wien, 2000

FLOWED—that stand undecided between the preterit and the perfect participle. Contrary to the dominance of the participle in Weiner, the verb has been translated in *Specific & General Works* with the preterit, **FLOSS SANFT**,[68] while the Kunstverein Münster edition from 1972 also makes use of the participle, **SANFT GEFLOSSEN**. The more Weiner makes language itself the material of his works and engages with idiomatic phrases and self-referential looping, the more open the translation proves to be. This is illustrated by the increasing variation in the translations used. **FULL CIRCLE**, for example, is translated as **VOLLE RUNDUNG** and **OF ITS FULL CIRCLE** with **SEINES VOLLEN KREISES**. At the exhibition *Full Circle*,[69] ellipses are on view; the design of the invitation is an ellipse with open ends that is penetrated by the title of the exhibition. Weiner writes "more of an open-ended ellipse" in his Documenta 13 *100 Notes—100 Thoughts* notebook, 2011. The idiomatic turn of phrase "to come full circle" indicates, for example, at the end of a lecture wanting to return to the point of departure, but at the same time having gone beyond it, being one step ahead. A philosophically charged and controversial concept such as "hermeneutic circle" is avoided by Weiner, just as he avoids all humanities jargon, which is always the expression of a certain theoretical formation and a certain historical standpoint, a perspective that cannot be reconciled with an oeuvre that is based on observation and the here and now. The image of an open-ended ellipse, in contrast, remains, and Weiner trusts in the legibility of the visible when he depicts the meaning of this figure of thought graphically. *Learn to Read Art* was the title of a 1995 exhibition of his books at the New York Public Library; *Books Do Furnish a Room / Kunst ist lesbar* was the title of

verwendet das Partizip: **SANFT GEFLOSSEN**. Je mehr Weiner Sprache selbst zum Material seiner Arbeiten macht und sich auf idiomatische Wendungen und selbstreferenzielle Schleifen einlässt, desto offener erweist sich die Übersetzung. Das zeichnet sich in der zunehmenden Varianz der Übersetzungen ab. **FULL CIRCLE** etwa wird mit **VOLLE RUNDUNG** und **OF ITS FULL CIRCLE** mit **SEINES VOLLEN KREISES** übersetzt. In der Ausstellung *Full Circle*[69] sind Ellipsen zu sehen, in der grafischen Darstellung auf der Einladungskarte ist es eine Ellipse mit offenen Enden, in die der Ausstellungstitel eindringt. »More of an open ended ellipse«, schreibt Weiner 2011 in seinem *dOCUMENTA (13) Notebook*. Die idiomatische Wendung »to come full circle« signalisiert etwa zum Abschluss eines Vortrags, an den Ausgangspunkt zurückkehren zu wollen, ihn aber gleichzeitig bereits überwunden zu haben und einen Schritt weiter gekommen zu sein. Einen philosophisch aufgeladenen und kontrovers diskutierten Begriff wie beispielsweise »hermeneutischer Zirkel« vermeidet Weiner wie grundsätzlich alle geisteswissenschaftlichen Fachtermini, die zwangsläufig immer auch Ausdruck einer bestimmten Theoriebildung und eines bestimmten historischen Standorts sind – eine Perspektive, die mit einem auf Beobachtung und dem Hier und Jetzt beruhenden Werk unvereinbar ist. Das Bild der »open-ended ellipse« dagegen steht, und Weiner vertraut auf die Lesbarkeit des Sichtbaren, wenn er die Bedeutung dieser Denkfigur grafisch darstellt. *Learn to Read Art / Lerne Kunst zu lesen* war 1995 der Titel der Ausstellung seiner Bücher in der New York Public Library, *Kunst ist lesbar / Books Do Furnish a Room* einer früheren, ähnlichen Ausstellung 1989 im Portikus in Frankfurt a. M. Zwar beziehen sich diese Titel in erster Linie auf verbale Sprache, das Medium der Zeichnung gewinnt jedoch als gestische Form a similar, earlier show at Frankfurt's Portikus in 1989. While these titles refer first and foremost to verbal language, in Weiner's language works the use of forms increasingly gains significance as a gestural form of communication. It can be illustrative, as in **TAKEN TO AS DEEP AS THE SEA CAN BE | MITGENOMMEN BIS ZUR TIEFSTEN STELLE DES MEERES**, or it can bestow certain configurations with a greater universality than is possible through language, as in the etching **VORSTELLUNGSREALITÄTEN**.

Lawrence Weiner's numerous sketches and notes from his sketchbooks are less a site of conception than a site of registering decisions made for installations, editions, posters, prints, and are comparable to the manuscript of a writer before printing: details of the exhibition site, color, typeface, size, and placement of the works are sketched. These sketchbooks show Lawrence Weiner as an artist who draws, writes, and collages with great pleasure and intensity, regardless of whether he uses remnants of fabric, packaging paper, writing or graph paper, in calendars, notebooks, or books. He works with anything, be it a concoction of his own color, a common felt-tip pen and pencils, watercolor, lacquer, or marker, and collages cut from an old encyclopedia, works typed on self-adhesive labels, printouts, photographs, postcards, and found paper items.

PUT ASIDE OR PUT AWAY | AUFGESCHOBEN ODER AUFGEHOBEN is an ingenious translation, but at the price of losing the literal level of meaning. Can consequences be deduced from this for the translation of Weiner's language works? For example, the refusal to use idiomatic phrases in translation allows a concrete material reference to move to the background in favor of emphasizing the poetic function of

der Kommunikation in Weiners Spracharbeiten zunehmend an Bedeutung. Es kann illustrativ sein wie **TAKEN TO AS DEEP AS THE SEA CAN BE | MITGENOMMEN BIS ZUR TIEFSTEN STELLE DES MEERES** oder bestimmten Konfigurationen eine noch größere Allgemeinheit verleihen, als dies über die Sprache möglich ist, wie in der Radierung **VORSTELLUNGSREALITÄTEN**.

Lawrence Weiners zahlreiche Skizzen und Notizen aus seinen Skizzenbüchern, die er auf seinen Reisen als Werktagebuch mit sich führt, sind weniger Ort der Konzeption als Ort des Notats der getroffenen Entscheidungen für die Installationen, Editionen, Plakate, Drucke und dem Manuskript eines Autors vor der Drucklegung vergleichbar: Skizziert sind Details des Ausstellungsorts, Farbe, Schrifttype, Größe, Platzierung der Arbeiten. Diese Skizzenbücher zeigen Lawrence Weiner als Künstler, der mit großer Lust und Intensität zeichnet, schreibt und collagiert, egal ob auf Stoffresten, Pack-, Schreib- oder Rechenpapier, in Kalendern, Schreibheften oder Büchern. Er arbeitet mit allem, sei es mit einer Mischung seiner eigenen Farben, mit gewöhnlichen Filzstiften und Bleistiften, Aquarell-, Lackfarbe oder Edding und aus alten Enzyklopädien ausgeschnittene Collagen, Klebeetiketten mit auf der Schreibmaschine getippten Spracharbeiten, Ausdrucken von Computerdateien, Fotos, Postkarten und Fundstücken aus Papier.

PUT ASIDE OR PUT AWAY | AUFGESCHOBEN ODER AUFGEHOBEN ist eine kongeniale Übersetzung, jedoch um den Preis des Verzichts der wortwörtlichen Bedeutungsebene, das Beiseite- oder Weglegen eines Gegenstands. Lassen sich daraus Konsequenzen für die Übersetzung der Spracharbeiten Weiners ableiten? Beispielsweise der Verzicht auf idiomatische Wendungen beim Übersetzen, die den konkreten language. Following Thomas Kling, who placed the phenomenon of intertextuality at the center of his literary work and explored the sediment of literary traditions with *Sondagen* (sondage or test excavation),[70] writer and translator Stefan Weidner, in dismissing the question of translatability as nonsensical, combines the question of the translatability of literary texts with the model of literature that is understood as fundamentally intertextual:

> In the actual, naively literary sense of translation, better literature is never translatable. But if we leave this idealized conception of translation aside, and replace it with a close, intertextual dependence, by a narrow relationship of influence between two writers, naturally only in one direction (one of whom is then named translator), translation is then based on a so-to-speak medieval, premodern concept of translation, and the translator is not understood as a copyist, but as a writer, the exasperating fundamental discussion of translatability is made superfluous.[71]

According to Weidner, a translation "tends invariably . . . to claim to be a translation, and thus claims to be accessing something else."[72] In line with this reasoning, it is logical to think that Weiner might consider each translation a new work, as the beholder-cum-translator-cum-author accesses that something else.[73] And in so doing, it is up to the translator to articulate his or her understanding of a sentence in the translation and to activate a certain level of significance, or to choose an open, general translation that leaves space for later readers. A work *en route* with its variety of translators—there are far more

Materialbezug zugunsten der Betonung der poetischen Funktion der Sprache in den Hintergrund treten lassen? Im Sinne Thomas Klings, der das Phänomen der Intertextualität ins Zentrum seines literarischen Schaffens gestellt hat und den Sedimenten des literarisch Tradierten mit *Sondagen* (Probeschnitte) – so der Titel eines Gedichtbands[70] – nachgeht, verbindet auch der Schriftsteller und Übersetzer Stefan Weidner die Frage nach der Übersetzbarkeit von literarischen Texten mit dem Modell einer als grundsätzlich intertextuell verstandenen Literatur, wenn er schon allein die Frage nach Übersetzbarkeit als »unsinnig« abtut:

> Im eigentlichen, naiv wörtlichen Sinn von Übersetzung ist bessere Literatur nie übersetzbar. Lässt man diese idealisierte Vorstellung vom Übersetzen hingegen fallen und ersetzt sie durch eine nahe, intertextuelle Abhängigkeit, durch ein enges, freilich nur in einer Richtung wirksames Beeinflussungsverhältnis zweier Autoren (von denen der eine dann »Übersetzer« genannt wird), legt man sozusagen einen »mittelalterlichen«, vorneuzeitlichen Begriff von Übersetzung zugrunde und begreift den Übersetzer nicht als Kopierer, sondern als Autor, erübrigt sich die leidige Grundsatzdiskussion um Übersetzbarkeit.[71]

Nach Weidner ist eine Übersetzung »tendenziell immer [...] Behauptung einer Übersetzung und damit Behauptung eines Zugangs zu etwas Anderem«.[72] Dann ist es nur folgerichtig, wenn Weiner jede Übersetzung als eine neue Arbeit betrachten könnte, als den Zugang, den ein Rezipient qua Übersetzer / Autor zu seiner Arbeit gefunden hat.[73] Und so steht es dem Übersetzer frei, in der Übersetzung sein Verständnis eines Satzes zu artikulieren than one hundred different sources—can only be reflected in a fundamental openness vis-à-vis the translations.

Weiner's tolerance, however, should be relativized. It must be seen against the backdrop of presenting his translated works together with the English. In this way, the act of translation as such remains transparent, thus revisable, and free of the arbitrary. Due to the broad linguistic abilities that Weiner has acquired over the years, in the end he retains control over the translations that, as a rule, are discussed extensively, and in many of which he himself is directly involved. His fascination with a single article in German distinguishing between salt water and fresh water led to one his of most famous works **AN DIE SEE** and **AN DEN SEE**. But the grammatical gender proves more complex than considered, for in the dative of the feminine **SEE** the supposedly masculine article *der* again comes into play. And there is thus a translation of the work that rigorously keeps the feminine form of the article that Weiner noted in his sketchbooks.[74] It follows the logic of the block-like, sculptural structure of his texts, rather than its grammar.

TO THE SEA
AN DIE SEE
ON THE SEA
AUF DIE SEE
FROM THE SEA
VON DIE SEE
AT THE SEA
IN DIE SEE
BORDERING THE SEA
GRENZEND AN DIE SEE

und eine bestimmte Bedeutungsebene zu aktivieren oder eine offene, allgemeine Übersetzung zu wählen, die den nachfolgenden Rezipienten einen eigenen Spielraum lässt. Ein Werk en route mit seiner Vielfalt an Übersetzern – es sind weit über hundert verschiedene Quellen – kann nur in einer grundsätzlichen Offenheit gegenüber den Übersetzungen gespiegelt werden.

Weiners Toleranz ist jedoch zu relativieren. Sie muss vor dem Hintergrund gesehen werden, dass er seine übersetzten Arbeiten zusammen mit dem englischen Text präsentiert. Auf diese Weise bleibt der Übersetzungsvorgang als solcher immer transparent, damit revidierbar und der Beliebigkeit entzogen. Wegen der breiten Sprachkenntnisse, die Weiner in all den Jahren erworben hat, behält er letztlich die Kontrolle über die Übersetzungen, die in der Regel intensiv diskutiert werden, an vielen

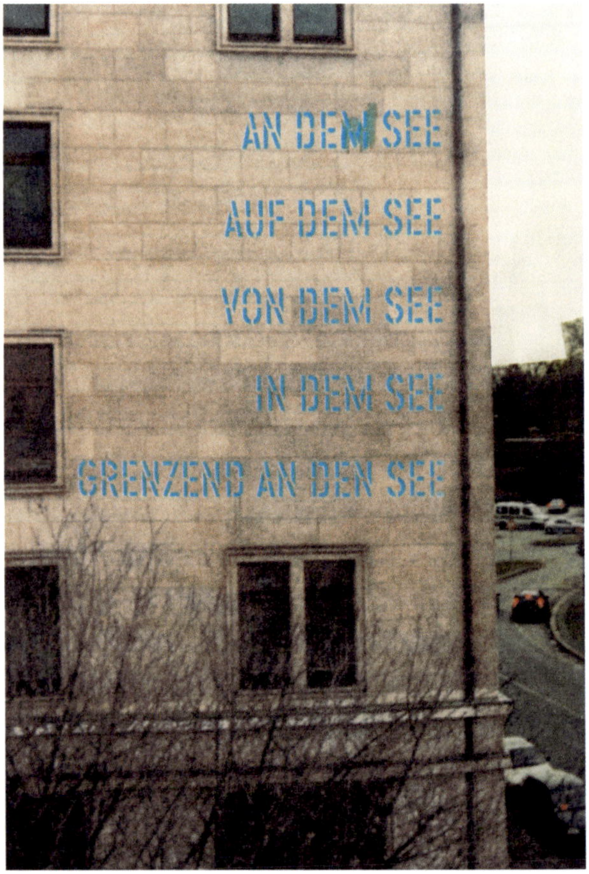

HWWA, Neuer Jungfernstieg, Hamburg, 2004, photo from Sketchbook, 2004–5
HWWA, Neuer Jungfernstieg, Hamburg, 2004, Foto aus dem Skizzenbuch, 2004/05

The quite complicated forms of the German definite article (*der, die, das*) in contrast to the unchanging English "the" lead to numerous variations of these works. For instance, the work **TO THE LAKE** consists of only three words but requires—in order to be correct—the translation to be in the accusative. Dative and accusative alternate in different presentations of the work, which can be seen in the handwritten addition to a photograph from Hamburg. In 50 *Arbeiten von Lawrence Weiner* (Münster, 1972), only the work **TO THE SEA** is included, and is translated as **ZUR SEE**, whereby the play with the feminine and masculine article, unrecognizable when the work is seen in isolation, is abandoned in favor of the connotation *zur See fahren,* "to go to the sea." A later exhibition at Vienna's BAWAG Foundation in 2006 is dedicated to the wealth of forms of the German articles *der, die, das.* In the German translation, again by Ferdinand Schmatz, the English article "the" is represented by XXX, leaving the beholder a choice of gender, case, and number.

Weiner's block-like approach to language, comparable to the stamp printing of the typography, also reflects his widely discussed translation from the English to mark his Berlin Guggenheim exhibition in 2000 **NACH ALLES | AFTER ALL**. Here, Weiner ignores all declinations of the pronoun unknown to English. When he translates **AFTER ALL** with **NACH ALLES**, he avoids the leveling idiomatic phrase *nach allem,* which can no longer transport the enormity

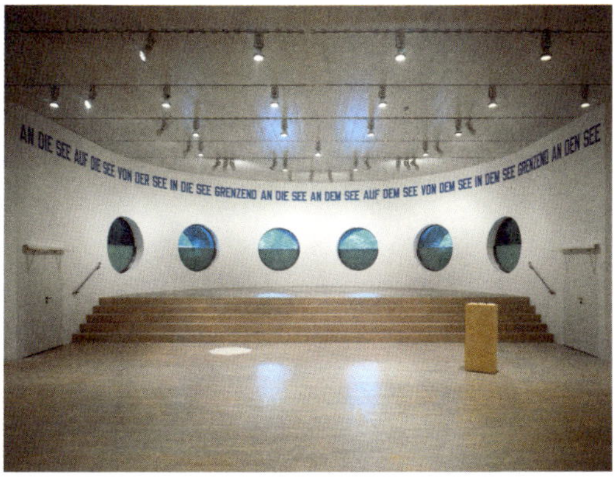

As *Far as the Eye Can See*, K21 Kunstsammlung Nordrhein-Westfalen, Düsseldorf, 2008
As Far as the Eye Can See, K21 Kunstsammlung Nordrhein-Westfalen, Düsseldorf, 2008

ist er selbst direkt beteiligt. So führt seine Verwunderung darüber, dass ein Artikel im Deutschen über Salz- und Süßwasser entscheidet, zu einer seiner bekanntesten Arbeiten **AN DIE SEE** und **AN DEN SEE**. Doch das grammatische Genus erweist sich als vertrackter als gedacht, denn im Dativ kommt bei der weiblichen See der vermeintlich männliche Artikel »der« ins Spiel. Und so gibt es eine streng die weibliche Form des Artikels bewahrende Übersetzung der Arbeit, die Weiner in seinen Skizzenbüchern notiert hat.[74] Sie folgt der Logik einer blockartigen, skulpturalen Struktur seiner Texte statt ihrer Grammatik.

TO THE SEA
AN DIE SEE
ON THE SEA
AUF DIE SEE
FROM THE SEA
VON DIE SEE
AT THE SEA
IN DIE SEE
BORDERING THE SEA
GRENZEND AN DIE SEE

Die im Gegensatz zum unveränderlichen englischen »the« recht komplexen Formen des bestimmten Artikels im Deutschen führt zu zahlreichen Varianten dieser jeweils nur aus drei Wörtern bestehenden Arbeiten. **TO THE LAKE** erfordert in der Übersetzung korrekterweise den Akkusativ. Dativ und Akkusativ wechseln jedoch in den verschiedenen Präsentationen, was in der handschriftlichen Ergänzung auf dem Foto aus Hamburg dokumentiert ist. In 50 *Arbeiten von Lawrence Weiner,* Münster 1972, wird aus dem Gesamtkomplex nur die Arbeit **TO THE SEE** aufgenommen und übersetzt mit **ZUR SEE**, wodurch das in der isoliert dastehenden of a concept like *alles*. Recalling the crisp diction of this central work by Weiner, which took the insatiable passion for research and collecting of Wilhelm von Humboldt as its starting point, the title of this book also picks up on this—*Nach bildende Kunst / After Fine Art*: "It is a pity that the translation does not carry the double meaning in German of towards & away from."[75] The book's title signals Weiner's dialectical approach, which refuses the either/or of Aristotelian logic. Striving "towards fine art" means at the same time leaving art behind: "after fine art." The process of travel abstracted in the drawing as a switching of an entry sign and an exit sign plays with Weiner's understanding of art as a "signpost."[76] In the special edition print that accompanies this volume, the circle breaks open the rectangle; art is *en route* and cannot be stopped.

"En route / Auf dem Weg" is once again a central theme for Weiner in a very literal sense: along his routes through New York City's East Village and West Village, nineteen manhole covers are marked with the inscription **IN DIRECT LINE WITH THE OTHER & THE NEXT**.[77] Weiner contributed a postcard with a photograph of one of these manhole covers to the Munich *Heimweg* project. "En route" is one of many expressions used by Weiner to show being caught in constant movement. In addition, he puts his work on multiple everyday objects, like pins and stickers, handkerchiefs and caps, temporary tattoos. The work finds its way to posters, numerous artist books, and into catalogues and treatises. Behind this nomadism is the desire to embed the works in a cultural context, in the flow of life, and in this way to have an impact on a socio-cultural "configuration" that he does not accept.[78]

Arbeit ohnehin nicht erkennbare Spiel mit dem weiblichen und männlichen Artikel zugunsten der Konnotation »zur See fahren« aufgegeben wird. Dem Formenreichtum des bestimmten Artikels im Deutschen ist eine spätere Ausstellung in der Bawag Foundation, Wien, im Jahre 2006 gewidmet. Hier wird in der deutschen Übersetzung, die wieder von Ferdinand Schmatz stammt, der englische Artikel »the« durch XXX dargestellt und damit dem Betrachter die Wahl von Genus, Kasus und Numerus überlassen.

Weiners blockartig mit Sprache verfahrender Umgang, vergleichbar dem Stempeldruck in der Typografie, spiegelt auch seine vieldiskutierte Übersetzung aus dem Englischen anlässlich der Berliner Guggenheim-Ausstellung *Nach alles / After All*. Weiner ignoriert hier die dem Englischen unbekannte Beugung des Pronomens. Wenn er **AFTER ALL** mit **NACH ALLES** übersetzt, umgeht er damit die nivellierende idiomatische Wendung »nach allem«, die das Ungeheuerliche, das ein Begriff wie »alles« besagt, gar nicht mehr zu transportieren vermag. An die spröde Diktion dieser zentralen Arbeit Weiners, die den unersättlichen Forscher- und Sammlerdrang Wilhelm von Humboldts zum Ausgang nahm, schließt auch der Titel dieses Buches an: *Nach bildende Kunst / After Fine Art*. »Es ist schade, dass sich die doppelte Bedeutung von ›nach‹ als ›hin zu‹ & ›weg von‹ nicht übertragen lässt.«[75] Der Buchtitel signalisiert den der aristotelischen Logik widersprechenden dialektischen Ansatz Weiners. Das Streben nach der Kunst: »towards fine art« bedeutet zugleich, die Kunst hinter sich zu lassen: »after fine art«. Der in der Zeichnung abstrahierte Prozess des Reisens als Wechsel von Ortseingangs- und -ausgangsschild spielt auf Weiners Verständnis der Kunst als »Wegweiser«[76] an. In der Grafik

One of Weiner's earliest sketchbooks includes a handwritten note: "Ein Ausdruck hat nur im Strome des Lebens Bedeutung / An expression has meaning only in the stream of life." This aphorism from the context of Ludwig Wittgenstein's late philosophy has a particular background. In its German formulation, it cannot be found anywhere in the philosopher's partially typed and handwritten notes cut into slips of paper. We find instead: "Denn die Wörter haben eben nur im Fluß des Lebens Bedeutung."[79] The bilingual edition *Letzte Schriften / Last Writings* quotes the aphorism in yet another formulation, but refers to *Wittgenstein: A Memoir*, written by Wittgenstein's American friend Norman Malcolm.[80] This memoir, published in the United States in 1958, contains the quotation translated in the version noted by Weiner. Malcolm had invited Wittgenstein to the U.S. in 1949, two years before his death, and meticulously recorded all the

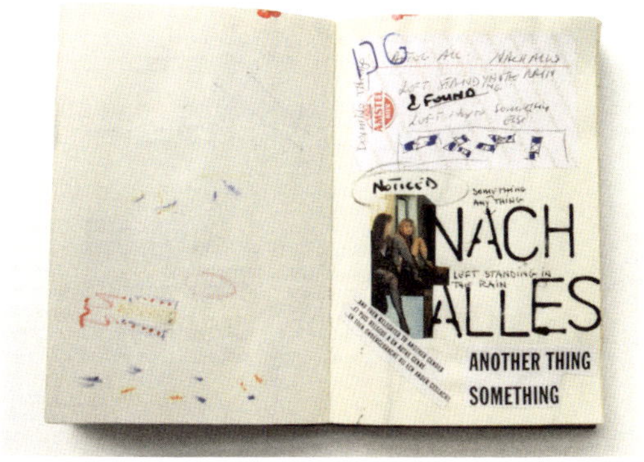

Sketchbook, 2000–1
Skizzenbuch, 2000/01

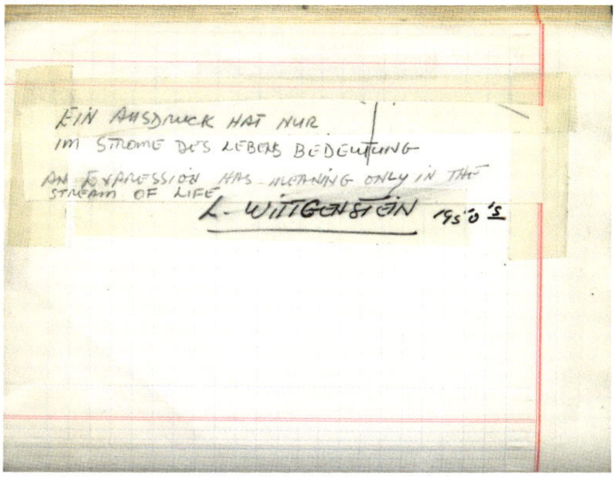

Sketchbook, 1975
Skizzenbuch, 1975

der dem Buch beigestellten Sonderedition sprengen die Kreise das Rechteck. Die Kunst ist en route und auf ihrem Weg nicht aufzuhalten.

»En route / Auf dem Weg« ist einmal im ganz wörtlichen Sinne ein zentrales Thema bei Weiner: Entlang seiner Wege durch das Village in New York City sind 19 Kanaldeckel mit der Inschrift **IN DIRECT LINE WITH THE OTHER & THE NEXT**[77] markiert. Eine Postkarte mit dem Foto eines dieser Kanaldeckel hat Weiner dem Projekt *Heimweg* in München beigesteuert. »En route« ist einer der vielen Begriffe, mit denen Weiner seine unaufhörliche Bewegung ausdrückt, entsprechend den in ständiger Wanderschaft begriffenen Arbeiten Weiners auf zahlreichen Alltagsgegenständen wie Anstecknadeln und Stickern, Taschentüchern und Mützen, temporären Tattoos. Die Arbeiten finden ihren Weg auf Poster, in zahlreiche Künstlerbücher, Kataloge und Monografien. Hinter diesem Nomadentum steht der Wunsch, die Arbeiten in einen kulturellen Kontext, in den Strom des Lebens, einzubetten und auf diese Weise auf eine gesellschaftlich-kulturelle »Konfiguration« einzuwirken, mit der er nicht einverstanden ist.[78]

In einem der ersten Skizzenbücher von Weiner findet sich ein handschriftliches Notat: »Ein Ausdruck hat nur im Strome des Lebens Bedeutung / An expression has meaning only in the stream of life«, ein Aphorismus Ludwig Wittgensteins aus dem Kontext seiner Spätphilosophie, mit dem es eine ganz eigene Bewandtnis hat. Es gibt ihn in dieser deutschsprachigen Formulierung nirgends in den teils maschinen-, teils handschriftlich überlieferten Notizen und den in Zettel zerschnittenen Typoskripten des Philosophen. Dort steht vielmehr: »Denn die Wörter haben eben nur im conversations they had held. This sentence is the only one that Malcolm included in German, providing an English translation in parentheses.

> One remark of his struck me then, as it does now, as being especially noteworthy and as summing up a good deal of his philosophy. It is "Ein Ausdruck hat nur in [*sic*] Strome des Lebens Bedeutung" (An expression has meaning only in the stream of life).[81]

In the 1959 German edition of this memoir, the English edition's bilingual presentation of the quote is absent, and the primacy of Malcolm's atypical inclusion of the German with the grammatical error, which provides clear evidence of authenticity, is corrected.[82] In a later Weiner sketchbook, the quotation is repeated and typed on self-adhesive labels of the kind that Weiner used occasionally in the seventies for exhibitions and announcements.[83] Here, Weiner retained only the German version. In an interview with Michael Gibbs held in 1982, Weiner again quotes Wittgenstein's statement, again in German.[84] In the 2008 conversation with John Slyce held at Tate Modern he again quoted it in German. In so doing, this quote in Weiner's sketchbook is not just an interesting document found in the labyrinthine paths taken by a quotation to another language of a sentence "en route": an Austrian philosopher utters the quotation in the U.S. to an American friend, who notes it in German and presents it in two languages in a memoir written in English. Lawrence Weiner must have taken the aphorism from a conversation:

> I believe it had nothing to do on my end with Malcolm's memoir on Wittgenstein. But

Fluß des Lebens Bedeutung.«[79] Die zweisprachige Ausgabe *Letzte Schriften / Last Writings* druckt den Aphorismus wieder in einer anderen Formulierung ab, verweist aber dabei auf *Wittgenstein. A Memoir,* geschrieben von Wittgensteins amerikanischem Freund Norman Malcolm.[80] In diesem 1958 in den USA veröffentlichten Erinnerungsbuch findet sich tatsächlich das Zitat in dem auch von Weiner notierten Wortlaut. Malcolm hatte Wittgenstein 1949, zwei Jahre vor dessen Tod, in die USA eingeladen und hielt alle Gespräche, die er dort mit ihm führte, mit großer Sorgfalt fest. Dieser Satz ist jedoch der einzige, den Malcolm in deutscher Sprache abdrucken ließ und dem er die englische Übersetzung nur in Klammern beistellte.

> One remark of his struck me then, as it does now, as being especially noteworthy and as summing up a good deal of his philosophy. It is ›Ein Ausdruck hat nur in [sic!] Strome des Lebens Bedeutung‹ (An expression has only meaning in the stream of life).[81]

In der 1959 erschienenen deutschen Ausgabe von *Ludwig Wittgenstein. Ein Erinnerungsbuch* fehlt die zweisprachige Wiedergabe des Zitats der englischen Ausgabe, und ist damit das für Malcolm höchst ungewöhnliche Bewahren der deutschsprachigen Formulierung nicht erkennbar; auch der Grammatikfehler, in der englischen Ausgabe ein deutlicher Beleg für die Authentizität, ist korrigiert.[82] In einem späteren Skizzenbuch Weiners

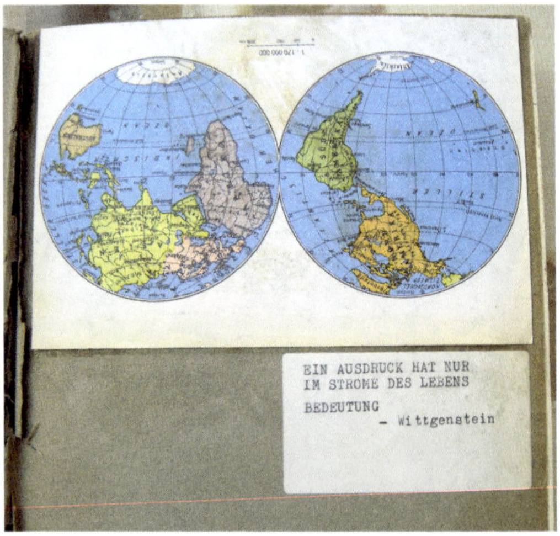

Sketchbook, 1975–78
Skizzenbuch, 1975–1978

> in 1958 I was leaving High School & very engaged in conversations with the abstract expressionists who were very engaged with conversations concerning Jaspers & Jacques Maritain & I guess somebody told me about it. I must have heard it initially in German because I still don't know the translation for Ausdruck. I always translated it as a thrown out idea only has meaning in the stream of life (an idea thrown out there . . .).[85]

The reception of a foreign language quotation illustrates once again the importance of the materiality of language. Putting aside for just a moment the content: the form, the rhythmic character of the sentence that results from the frequent repetition of unaccented syllables, should not be underestimated as a factor, albeit minor, in the attraction of this formulation, for Malcolm, who noted it in German, and for Weiner, who later seized on it. It can be seen in many of Weiner's works, for example the work shown in 1970 in Monschau in der Eifel, **SLOWLY RAISED WATER | LANGSAM GESTIEGENES WASSER**, a translation from English by Weiner himself. You need to hear Weiner when he speaks the work in German and to see the gestures that accompany his speaking in order to feel his enthusiasm about rhythm and formulation in his work. In the conversation at Tate Modern, Weiner describes the process of his work with language: "x x x x becomes x and y and y and x . . . That's my way of trying to make the work as beautiful as possible, because you want the work to be as attractive as possible to get somebody to take the trouble to basically say it out loud to themselves. And once they do you got them."[86] Weiner's interest in the German saying "Eile mit Weile" can also be seen in this

findet sich eine Wiederholung des Zitats. Es ist mit Schreibmaschine auf die selbstklebenden Etiketten geschrieben, die er in den 1970er-Jahren gelegentlich für Ausstellungen und Einladungskarten verwendete.[83] Bei diesem maschinenschriftlichen Notat hält Weiner nur die deutschsprachige Version fest. Auch in einem 1982 in englischer Sprache geführten Interview mit Michael Gibbs zitiert Weiner Wittgensteins Satz auf Deutsch,[84] ebenso 2008 in einem Gespräch mit John Slyce in der Tate Modern. Damit ist dieses Zitat in Weiners Skizzenbüchern einmal ein interessantes Dokument der verschlungenen Wege einer fremdsprachlichen Überlieferung eines Satzes »en route«: Ein österreichischer Philosoph äußert ihn in den USA gegenüber einem amerikanischen Freund, der ihn auf Deutsch notiert und in einem in englischer Sprache geschriebenen Erinnerungsbuch zweisprachig überliefert. Lawrence Weiner muss den Aphorismus selbst auch einem Gespräch entnommen haben.

> Ich glaube, das hatte bei mir nichts mit Malcolms Wittgenstein-Erinnerungen zu tun. Aber 1958 hatte ich gerade die High School absolviert & unterhielt mich häufig mit den abstrakten Expressionisten, die sich wiederum häufig über Jaspers & Jacques Maritain unterhielten & ich vermute, jemand hat mir davon erzählt. Ich muss es zuerst auf Deutsch gehört haben, denn ich weiß immer noch nicht, wie man ›Ausdruck‹ übersetzt. Ich habe es immer mit ›ein Gedanke, der ausgesprochen wurde, hat nur im Strom des Lebens Bedeutung‹ übersetzt (ein Gedanke, der dort ausgesprochen wurde […]).[85]

Die Rezeption des fremdsprachlichen Zitats verdeutlicht zum andern aber auch nochmals die Bedeutung der Materialität von Sprache. Lässt context, and it surfaces repeatedly in his sketchbooks. He translates the phrase into English as **GRACEFUL HASTE**, taking up with apparent ease the assonance and alliteration from the German phrase. In poetological terms, "graceful haste" could be read as the description of a rhythm of elegance contained in many of Weiner's works. Elegance, a word Weiner often uses, stands in conflict with the perceived "raw energy"[87] of other works.

Weiner makes Wittgenstein's aphorism into one of the most important reference points for his artistic work. By returning the metaphorical expression to its literal meaning, **IN THE STREAM** becomes part of the title of Weiner's 1995 exhibition in Valencia: "I am fascinated by rivers because of the changing stability of water."[88] In Western philosophy, the image of the river represents the first example of the dialectical principle: "Into the same rivers we step and do not step, we are and are not."[89] The current not only stands for eternal flux, but also for the necessity of form as a condition of change. Water requires a riverbed to flow, but also forms that riverbed by flowing. This dialectical relationship plays a central role in Wittgenstein's linguistic philosophy. A meaning is open, but not arbitrary in the use of the language. It is bound to a consistency, although not a rigid one, which Wittgenstein captures with the term "life form." Wittgenstein's

man für einen Moment den Inhalt beiseite: Ein nicht zu unterschätzender Faktor bei der Faszination für diese Formulierung, die Malcolm veranlasste, sie auf Deutsch zu notieren, mag ebenso für Weiner die Rhythmisierung der Sprache in diesem Satz sein, die sich durch die häufige Doppelung unbetonter Silben auszeichnet. Sie lässt sich auch in vielen Arbeiten Weiners nachweisen, zum Beispiel in der 1970 in Monschau in der Eifel gezeigten Arbeit **SLOWLY RAISED WATER | LANGSAM GESTIEGENES WASSER**, eine Übersetzung aus dem Englischen, die von Weiner selbst stammt. Man muss Weiner hören, wenn er diese Arbeit auf Deutsch spricht, man muss die Gesten sehen, die sein Sprechen begleiten, um seine Begeisterung für diesen Rhythmus und diese Formulierung zu spüren. In dem erwähnten Gespräch in der Tate Modern beschreibt Weiner den Prozess seiner Arbeit mit Sprache: »x x x x wird zu x und y und y und x. [...] Das ist meine Art zu versuchen, die Arbeit so schön wie möglich zu machen, denn man möchte, dass das Werk möglichst ansprechend ist, um jemanden dazu zu bringen, sich die Mühe zu machen, dies laut auszusprechen. Und wenn sie das tun, hat man sie gewonnen.«[86] In dem Kontext ist auch Weiners Interesse an der deutschen Redensart »Eile mit Weile« zu sehen, die immer wieder in seinen Skizzenbüchern auftaucht: Er übersetzt sie mit **GRACEFUL HASTE** ins Englische und nimmt mit einer ganz offensichtlich Leichtigkeit die Assonanz und Alliteration aus dem Deutschen auf. Will man sie poetologisch lesen, könnte man »graceful haste« als Beschreibung eines Rhythmus der Eleganz in vielen Spracharbeiten Weiners sehen, wobei Eleganz – ein Wort, das Weiner

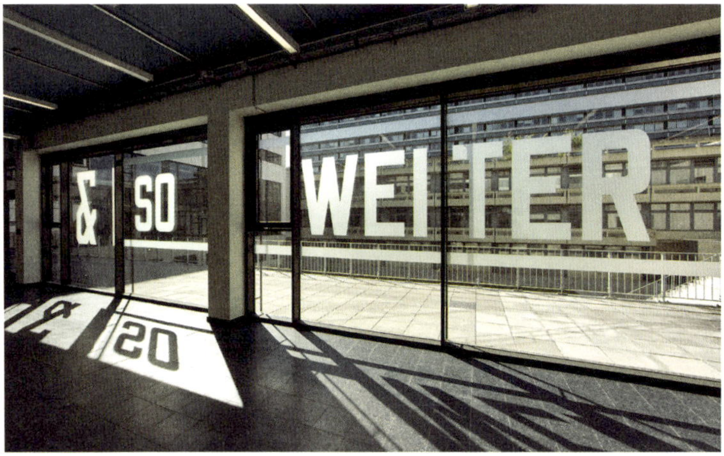

New ID building, Ruhr-Universität Bochum, 2010
Neubau ID, Ruhr-Universität Bochum, 2010

central statement from his later years, “The meaning of a word is its use in the language,” can only be seen in the context of a life form, the stream of life. The world is not, according to Markus Gabriel, “a blurry flux, that would conflict with the fact that some things are recognizable. It is much rather the case that, due to its partial recognizability, the world is much like a film, and it is allotted the proper measure of motion and stasis in order to reveal itself as intelligible and comprehensible.”[90] Weiner varies the dialectics of “motion and stasis” in countless works: **& SO WEITER …**—and so on …—is the text of a permanent installation for the new engineering building built in 2010 at Ruhr-Universität Bochum. Installed on a picture window in a hallway facing a terrace, he ends the work with three oversized dots that simulate a significant sequence in gestural language. But the text remains caught in its mirrored—i.e. obverse/converse—repetition and its framing within a rectangle; the ampersands lie at the extremities: at the beginning, at one extremity, in its customary form; at the end, at the other extremity, inverted, and thus transformed. The

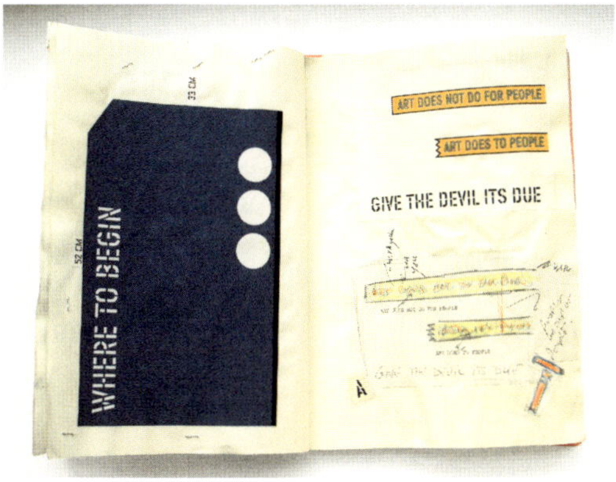

Sketchbook, 2004–5
Skizzenbuch, 2004/05

selbst häufig gebraucht – in Spannung zu der »raw energy«[87] anderer Arbeiten zu sehen ist.

Weiner macht Wittgensteins Aphorismus zu einem der wichtigsten Referenzpunkte für seine künstlerische Arbeit. Mit der Verkürzung auf **IN THE STREAM** und damit einer Rückführung des metaphorischen Ausdrucks in die Wörtlichkeit wird er 1995 Ausstellungstitel in Valencia. »Flüsse faszinieren mich wegen der veränderlichen Stabilität des Wassers.«[88] Das Bild des Flusses steht am Anfang der abendländischen Philosophie als erste Überlieferung des dialektischen Prinzips: »In die gleichen Ströme steigen wir und steigen wir nicht; wir sind es und wir sind es nicht.«[89] Der Strom steht nicht nur für die unaufhörliche Veränderung, sondern auch für die Notwendigkeit einer Form als Bedingung der Veränderung. Das Wasser braucht das Flussbett, um fließen zu können, formt es seinerseits aber durch das Fließen. Diese dialektische Beziehung spielt in Wittgensteins sprachphilosophischer Theorie eine zentrale Rolle. Eine Bedeutung ist offen, aber nicht beliebig im Gebrauch der Sprache. Sie ist an eine Beständigkeit gebunden, die aber selbst auch nicht starr ist und die Wittgenstein mit dem Begriff der »Lebensform« fasst. Wittgensteins zentraler Satz aus seiner Spätphilosophie, »Die Bedeutung eines Wortes ist sein Gebrauch in der Sprache«, ist nur im Kontext einer Lebensform zu sehen, im Strome des Lebens. Die Welt, so Markus Gabriel, ist kein »verwischter Flux. Vielmehr ist die Welt aufgrund ihrer partiellen Erkennbarkeit wie ein Film auf das richtige Maß von Stillstand und Bewegung angewiesen, um sich als intelligibel, d. h. als verstehbar zu erweisen […].«[90]

Following page:
Lawrence Weiner in his studio in New York, 2011
background: exhibition poster, EILE MIT WEILE / GRACEFUL HASTE, Galerie Mai 36, Zurich, 2010 and a draft for the collector’s edition, NACH BILDENDE KUNST / AFTER FINE ART, Hatje Cantz, 2012
Nächste Seite:
Lawrence Weiner in seinem Studio in New York, 2011
Im Hintergrund: Ausstellungplakat, EILE MIT WEILE / GRACEFUL HASTE, Galerie Mai 36, Zürich, 2010, und Entwurf für die Collector’s Edition NACH BILDENDE KUNST / AFTER FINE ART, Hatje Cantz, 2012

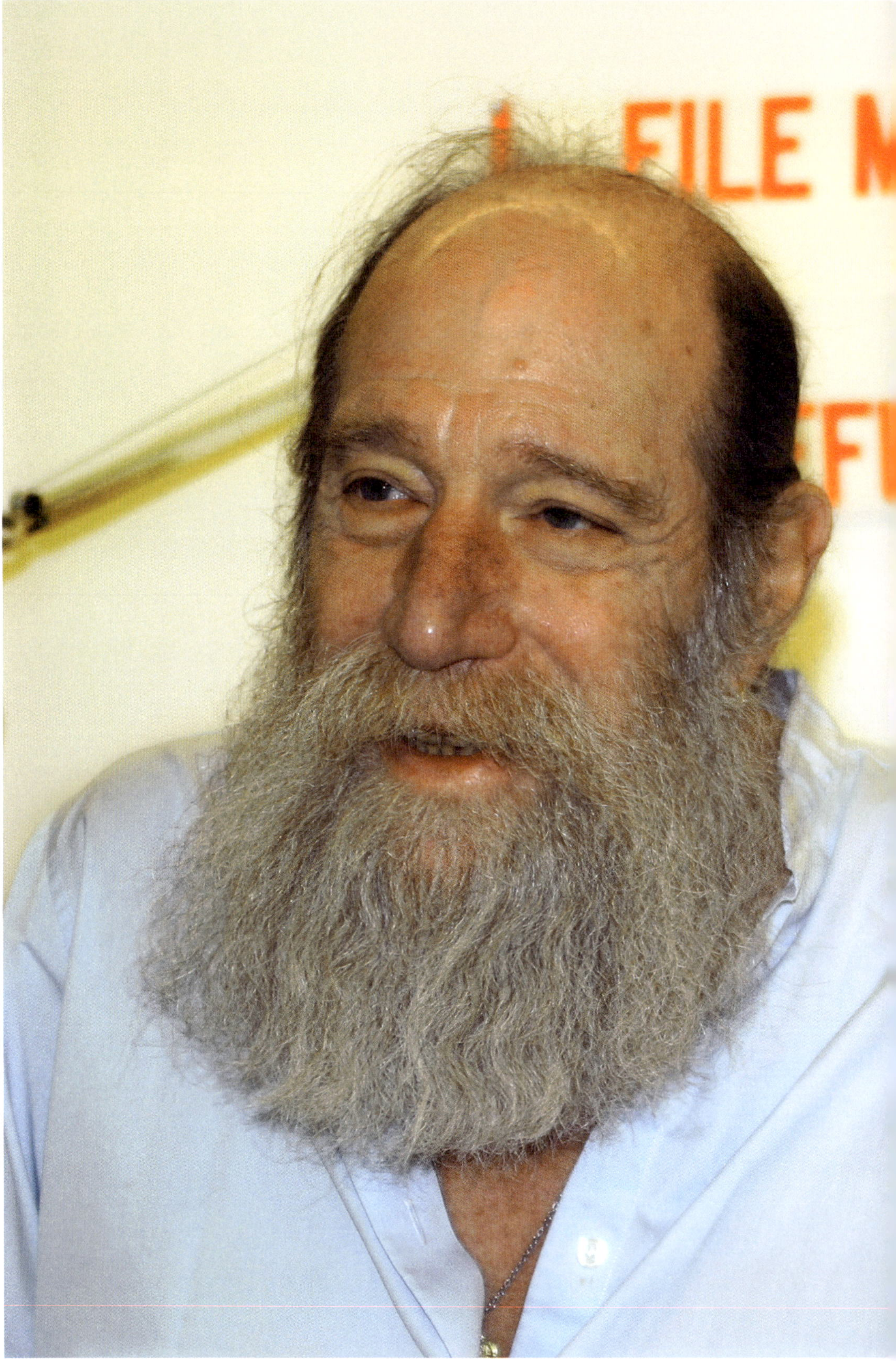

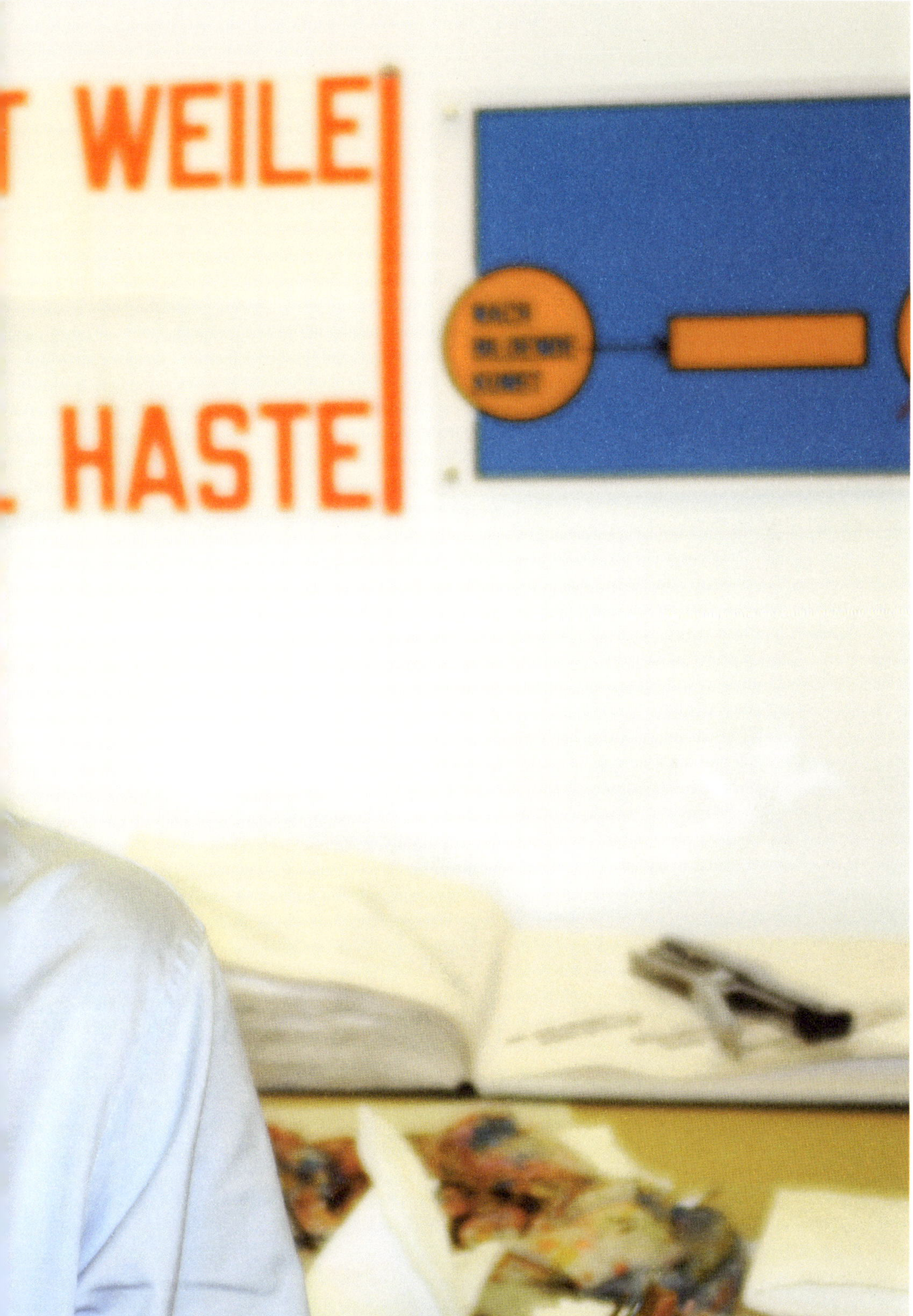
WEILE
HASTE

dialectic also inheres in the metaphor of **FULL CIRCLE**, as well as in the early works in which the points mark a stasis, a position from which a change occurs to contradict the previous state.[91]

Translation for Weiner is a multilayered process that can go from material to language and back to material in the sense of a re-construction. Allowing for the fundamental possibility that his works be materially carried out, the very attempt at translation in a literal sense, as he explored in the Bern exhibition *Works & Re-Constructions / Werke & Re-Konstruktionen* with the creation and presentation of objects described in the works, feeds the suspicion that Weiner's works are not really about that at all. His oeuvre begins with works that literally exploded bourgeois and nationalist values of the sixties and seventies. Here, even a description in which a square is cut from a carpet proves to be extremely subversive, because it is limited to "a carpet in use." The emphasis is shifted to a more philosophical social interest in the transformation of the world by humanity, by what can be attributed to the task assigned to humanity by the God of

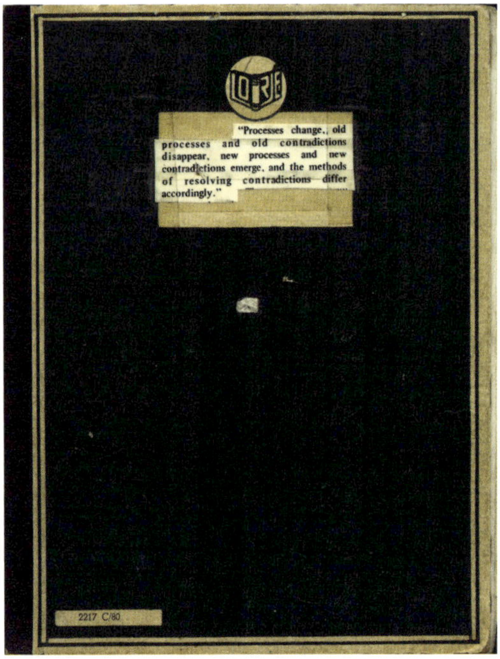

Sketchbook, 1975
Skizzenbuch, 1975

Die Dialektik von Stillstand und Bewegung variiert Weiner in zahllosen Arbeiten: **& SO WEITER ...** lautet der Text einer permanenten Installation in dem Neubau für Ingenieurswissenschaften der Universität Bochum aus dem Jahre 2010. Die Arbeit ist entlang einer geschosshohen Fensterzeile mit Zugang zu einer Terrasse ausgeführt. Sie schließt mit drei übergroßen Punkten, die als Sprachgestus eine gewichtige Schrittfolge simulieren. Der Text bleibt jedoch gefangen in seiner spiegelbildlichen Wiederholung und der Rahmung in einem Rechteck, während die Et-Zeichen an beiden Seiten außerhalb stehen, am Anfang normal zu lesen, am Schluss gespiegelt und damit verändert. Die Dialektik liegt auch der Denkfigur des **FULL CIRCLE** und den frühen Arbeiten zugrunde, in denen die Punkte jeweils einen Stillstand markieren – eine Setzung, von der aus dann wieder eine dem erreichten Status widersprechende Veränderung ausgeht.[91]

Übersetzen ist bei Weiner ein vielschichtiger Prozess, der vom Material in die Sprache und zurück zum Material im Sinne einer Re-Konstruktion gehen kann. Die grundsätzliche Möglichkeit der materiellen Ausführung seiner Arbeiten eingeräumt, leistet aber genau der Versuch dieser Übersetzung im wortwörtlichen Sinne, wie er in der Berner Ausstellung *Konstruktion & Re-Konstruktion* mit der Herstellung und Präsentation der in den Spracharbeiten beschriebenen Objekten erprobt wurde, dem Verdacht Vorschub, dass es darum in Weiners Arbeiten tatsächlich nicht geht. Am Anfang stehen seine bürgerliche und nationalistische Wertvorstellungen im wortwörtlichen Sinne sprengenden Arbeiten aus den 1960er- und 1970er-Jahren. In ihnen erweist sich selbst eine Beschreibung, in der ein Quadrat aus einem the Old Testament or to what Marx, to whom Weiner refers to as "a hard-core American socialist,"[92] conceives under the term "labor." "Labor," or "work," in its comprehensive anthropological sense is ultimately a central term in Weiner's oeuvre—reinforcing the "put in place"—that targets not only its sculptural dimension but also the change in social conditions in a fundamental sense. "The economic structure should take into account the fact that each object that is produced, even a stone carried from point A to point B, has entailed human endeavor and human labor."[93]

A Swedish clothing company titles the catalogue for their design line for the spring and summer 2011 collections "Work," presenting "great utilitarian styles that simply work." Straight forms, oversized garments, and zippers define the look. The materials: linen, drill, cotton, waxed, washed, shrunken, crinkled, knitted, ribbed. In the catalogue—matte paper rhythmically interweaved with selectively placed glossy sheets—people and professions are presented, including Vivian Westwood's personal assistant, the speech artist behind the voice saying "Stand clear of the closing doors" in the London Underground, a book designer, a baker, and a film projectionist. The message: the individual is not defined by their appearance, but by their labor, their approach to things. There appear sentences like, "At the end of the day, it's all about yeast, flour, water and salt." Or, "We run the film very quickly through our fingers and you need to detect minute little tears or ridges. It's very much about the sense of touch."[94]

Weiner keeps a close eye on fashion, for he believes that it represents an important mode of

Teppich geschnitten wird, als äußerst subversiv, da sie »einem Teppich in Gebrauch« vorbehalten ist. Der Schwerpunkt verschiebt sich auf ein eher philosophisch-gesellschaftliches Interesse an der Veränderung der Welt durch den Menschen, durch das, was man auf den alttestamentarischen Auftrag Gottes an die Menschen zurückführen mag oder was Marx, auf den sich Weiner als »a hard-core American socialist«[92] beruft, unter den Begriff der Arbeit fasst. Arbeit in ihrer umfassenden anthropologischen Bedeutung ist letztlich der Zentralbegriff in Weiners Œuvre, steht hinter dem »Put in place«, das eben nicht nur auf dessen skulpturale Dimension zielt, sondern die Veränderung der gesellschaftlichen Situation in einem fundamentalen Sinn. »Die ökonomische Struktur sollte berücksichtigen, daß jeder Gegenstand, der produziert wird, selbst ein Stein, der von Punkt A nach Punkt B gebracht wird, menschliche Anstrengung und menschliche Arbeit erfordert hat.«[93]

Mit »Work« betitelt ein schwedischer Modekonzern den Katalog der Frühjahrs- und Sommerkollektion 2011 für seine Designlinie. Präsentiert wird »tolle funktionale Mode, die einfach alles mitmacht«. Gerade Formen, Oversize, Reißverschlüsse bestimmen das Erscheinungsbild. Die Materialien: Leinen, Drillich, Baumwolle, imprägniert, vorgewaschen, gekrumpft, gecrinkelt, gewirkt, gerippt. In dem Katalog – viel mattes Papier im Rhythmus mit gezielt eingesetztem Glanzpapier – werden Menschen und Berufe vorgestellt, darunter die persönliche Assistentin von Vivian Westwood, die Sprechkünstlerin hinter der Stimme des »Stand clear of the closing doors« in der Londoner U-Bahn, ein Buchgestalter, ein Bäcker und eine Filmvorführerin. Die Botschaft: Der Mensch definiert sich nicht über sein Aussehen, sondern über

presentation beside art. And if, as Elena Esposito suggests, fashion is a "formal principle" that "responds to structural problems of modernity" by succeeding in '"making shared points of reference and bonds possible in a field where each move appears contingent and thus possible in a different way,"[95] this fashion catalogue articulates the "needs and desires" for tactility, materiality, and an immediacy in approaching simple things as an expression of their valuation, a longing that Lawrence Weiner's works also deal with and to which younger artists in particular react.[96] Weiner does not see the artist as outside society, but as part of it, and his task is to integrate "a gesture of simple, normal labor"[97] into the realm of culture. His invitation to Documenta 13, forty years after his first participation at Documenta, is symptomatic here. There is a need for a theory of things and their significance in our culture, something unfortunately overlooked by modern social theory and semiotics. What becomes increasingly clear is, as Hartmut Böhme and Johannes Endres put it, "Things as the condition of the possibility of our selves."[98] For Weiner's oeuvre, this concerns a sociopolitical understanding of culture from the very beginning. Ultimately, the insistent reference to things ("language + the materials referred to") is the background for his strict refusal of a metaphorical use of language: *A STONE IS A STONE*,[99] an article whereby Weiner shows he is quite aware of the irreducibility of metaphor in language and art, and, with the choice of terms with manifold readings, explores its limits.

Ann Goldstein, who provided an overview of Weiner's works in the catalogue of the American retrospective held in Los Angeles and New York,

seine Arbeit, seinen Umgang mit den Dingen. Es erscheinen Sätze wie: »Schlussendlich dreht sich alles um Hefe, Mehl, Wasser und Salz.« Oder: »Wir lassen den Film ganz schnell durch die Finger gleiten, und dabei muss man winzige Risse oder Furchen aufspüren. Es geht vor allem um den Tastsinn.«[94]

Mode wird von Weiner sehr genau beobachtet, da sie für ihn neben der Kunst einen wichtigen Präsentationsmodus darstellt. Und wenn Mode als »Formprinzip« (Elena Esposito) Antwort auf »Strukturprobleme der Moderne« gibt, zum Beispiel »gemeinsame Bezugspunkte und Verbindlichkeiten möglich zu machen in einem Feld, wo jeder Zug im radikalen Sinne als kontingent und mithin als auch anders möglich erscheint«,[95] so artikuliert dieser Modekatalog das Bedürfnis nach Taktilität, Materialität, nach einer Unmittelbarkeit im Umgang mit einfachen Dingen als Ausdruck ihrer Wertschätzung – eine Sehnsucht, von der auch Lawrence Weiners Arbeiten handeln und auf die gerade junge Künstler reagieren.[96] Weiner sieht den Künstler nicht außerhalb der Gesellschaft, sondern als Teil von ihr, und seine Aufgabe ist es, »eine Geste von einfacher, normaler Arbeit«[97] in die Kultur einzubringen. Seine Einladung zur *dOCUMENTA (13)*, vierzig Jahre nach seiner ersten documenta-Teilnahme, ist symptomatisch. Es gibt ein Bedürfnis nach einer Theorie der Dinge und ihrer Bedeutung in unserer Kultur, das von den Gesellschafts- und Zeichentheorien vernachlässigt wurde. »Dinge als Be-dingung der Möglichkeit unserer selbst«,[98] so Hartmut Böhme und Johannes Endres, rücken in den Fokus. Für Weiners Œuvre gilt das von Anfang an in einem gesellschaftlich-politischen Verständnis von Kultur. Nicht zuletzt ist die beharrliche Referenz auf and the following year in Düsseldorf, sums up in her concluding sentence: "The relationship of human beings to objects remain at the core of Weiner's practice."[100] The verb "remain" indicates that this has been Weiner's artistic intention from the very start. *Statements,* as his first publication of work was titled in 1968, refers not to statement in the sense of a pronouncement, but in terms of an invoice, or, in more literal terms, an acknowledgement of existence, i.e. it has to be there in order for it to be accounted for, as Lawrence Weiner explains in a 1990 interview with Phyllis Rosenzweig:

> When you get your American Express bill, it says "statement enclosed." It tells you that you drank fourteen tequilas, you did this, you did that. That's all Statements ever was. It told you how many pieces of stone were moved and where.[101]

Inseparably linked to the anthropological concept of labor, the moving of stones, is the question of human needs and desires, an aspect one must be conscious of when considerations of the philosophy of language and/or art theoretical considerations come into play—for which Weiner's sparse works provide almost inexhaustible material and make up the main part of the secondary literature.

> Concerning the NYC *Manhole Covers,* I was asked by a television station why I'm doing such a calm work since I've been known since my youth as an aggressive civil rights activist involved in all sorts of things. In fact, it's not, for its implications are quite intense! . . . I don't see a need for a new concept of morality,

die Dinge (»language + the materials referred to«) der Hintergrund für die strikte Verweigerung eines metaphorischen Gebrauchs der Sprache in seinen Arbeiten: **A *STONE* IS A *STONE* | EIN *STEIN* IST EIN *STEIN*,**[99] wobei sich Weiner durchaus der Nichthintergehbarkeit der Metapher in der Sprache und der Kunst bewusst ist und in der Wahl mehrfach codierter Begriffe ihre Grenzen ausreizt.

Ann Goldstein, die in dem Katalog der amerikanischen Retrospektiven in Los Angeles und New York einen Überblick über Weiners Arbeiten gibt, fasst in ihrem Schlussabsatz zusammen: »Die Beziehung des Menschen zu den Dingen bleibt das zentrale Thema von Weiners Schaffen.«[100] Das Verb »bleiben« signalisiert, dass dies von Beginn an das künstlerische Anliegen Weiners ist. Statements, wie die erste Veröffentlichung seiner Werke 1968 betitelt war, bedeutet nicht »Feststellung« im Sinne einer dezidierten Äußerung, sondern bezieht sich auf eine Abrechnung oder in einem wörtlicheren Sinn auf eine Bestätigung der Existenz, etwas muss da sein, um abgrechnet zu werden, wie Lawrence Weiner 1990 im Interview mit Phyllis Rosenzweig erläutert:

> Wenn man die Rechnung von American Express bekommt, steht auf dem Umschlag: »Statements enclosed«. Und sie sagt einem, daß man vierzehn Tequilas getrunken hat, daß man dies getan hat, daß man das getan hat. Genau das ist *Statements* gewesen. Es sagte, wie viele Steine bewegt wurden und wohin.[101]

Mit dem anthropologischen Begriff der Arbeit, dem Bewegen von Steinen, untrennbar verbunden ist die Frage nach den menschlichen Bedürfnissen – ein Aspekt, dessen man sich bewusst sein muss,

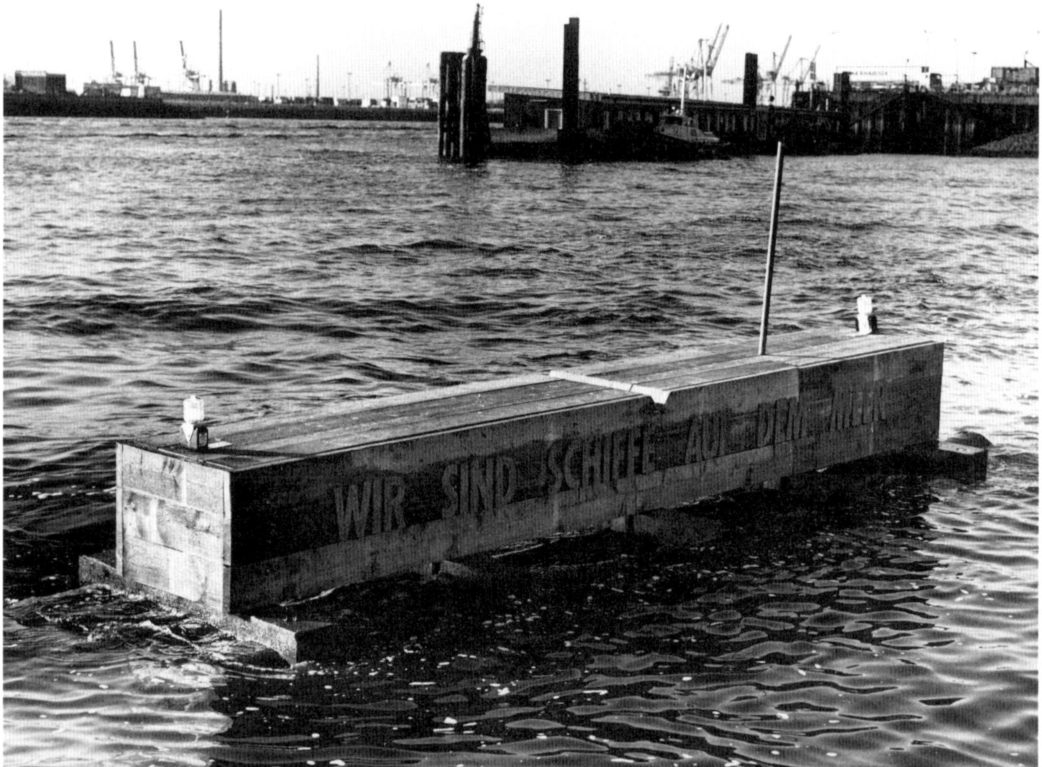

***Hamburg Projekt*, Port of Hamburg, 1989**
Hamburg Projekt, Hamburger Hafen, 1989

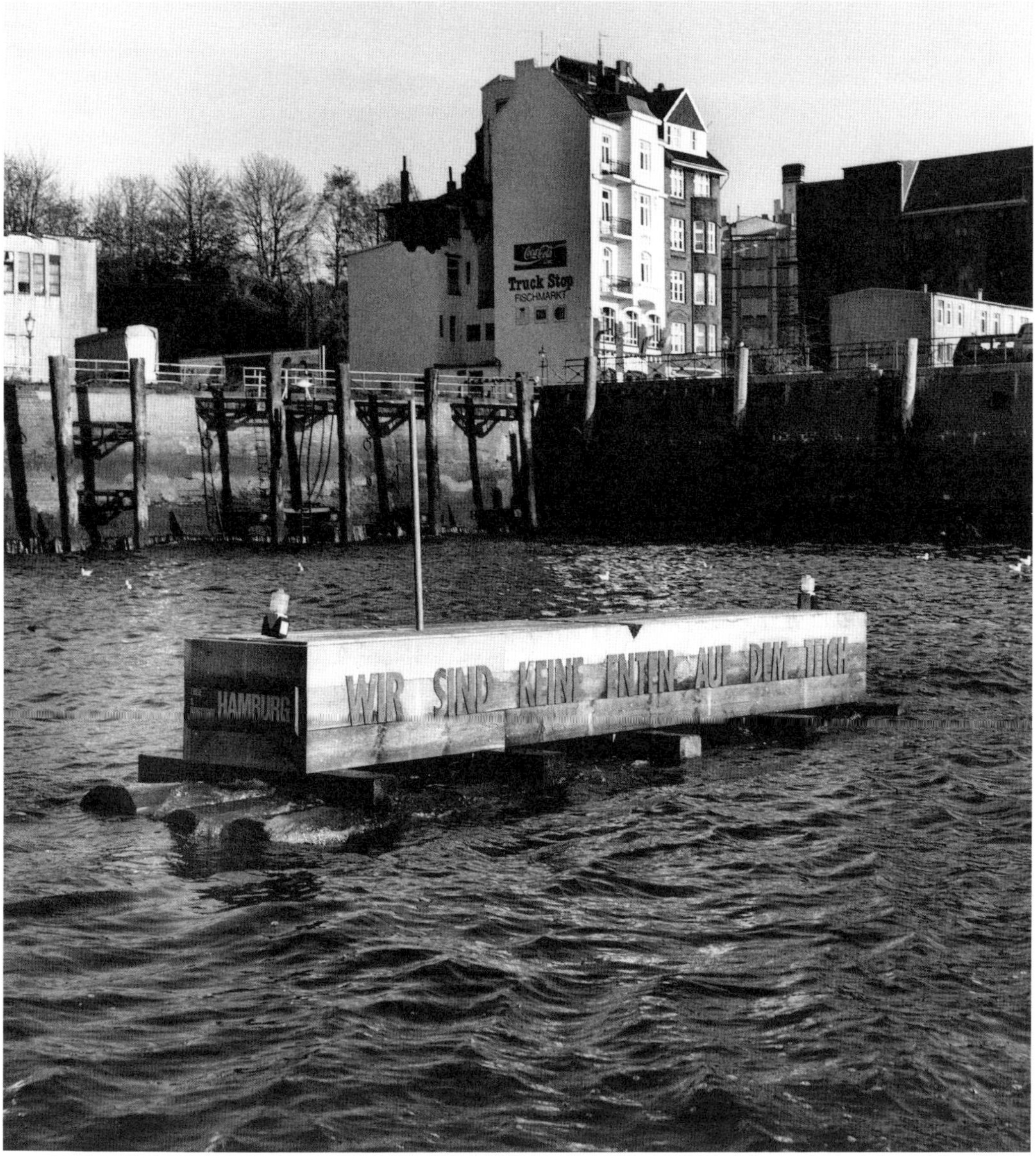

***Hamburg Projekt*, Port of Hamburg, 1989**

Hamburg Projekt, Hamburger Hafen, 1989

for changing the basic morality of American working class socialism—which essentially means that everybody has a right to food, education, a place to live, health care, and a public library. That's about what I expect from a society. That's perhaps my only *idée fixe.*[102]

Even if the works can be created and reconstructed, this only makes sense to the extent that this allows us to learn something about humanity's handling of the world and learn to respect the "dignity of the object."[103] Through his works' fundamental openness that allows for personal association, Weiner addresses the decisive moment when people "realize that there is an existential relationship they could make. But that's when they need it. And then perhaps they'll find it."[104]

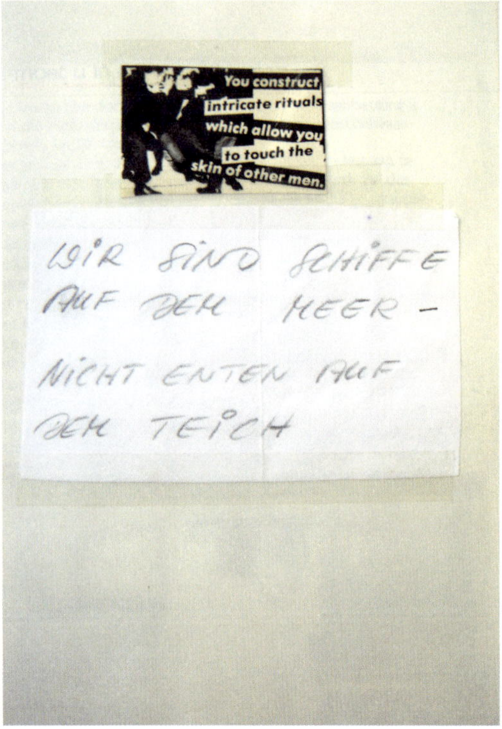

Sketchbook, 1975–78
Skizzenbuch, 1975–1978

wenn sprachphilosophische oder kunsttheoretische Überlegungen ins Spiel kommen –, für die Weiners karge Arbeiten nahezu unerschöpfliches Material liefern und die den Hauptteil der Sekundärliteratur ausmachen.

Im Zusammenhang mit den NYC *Manhole Covers* wurde ich vom Fernsehen gefragt, wie es kommt, dass ich nun eine so ruhige Arbeit mache, da ich doch seit meiner Jugend als aggressiver Bürgerrechtler – in dies und jenes verwickelt – bekannt sei. In Wirklichkeit ist die Arbeit natürlich nicht zurückhaltend, denn ihre Implikationen sind ziemlich heftig. […] Ich sehe keinen Bedarf nach einem neuen moralischen Konzept, nach einer Veränderung der grundlegenden Moral des amerikanischen Arbeiterklasse-Sozialismus – der im Wesentlichen besagt, dass alle ein Recht haben auf Nahrung, auf Bildung, auf ein Zuhause, auf Gesundheitsfürsorge und auf eine öffentliche Bibliothek. Das ist ungefähr das, was ich von einer Gesellschaft erwarte. Das ist möglicherweise auch meine einzige idée fixe.[102]

Und auch wenn sich die Arbeiten ausführen, rekonstruieren lassen, macht das nur insofern Sinn, als man dabei etwas über den Umgang des Menschen mit der Welt erfährt und die »Würde des Gegenstands«[103] respektieren lernt. Mit der prinzipiellen Offenheit, die alle persönlichen Assoziationen, die Menschen damit verbinden, berücksichtigt, spricht Weiner den entscheidenden Moment an, in dem die Menschen »realisieren, dass es da auch noch eine existenzielle Beziehung gibt, die sie aufbauen können. Aber dies geschieht erst dann, wenn sie ihrer auch bedürfen – und dann, vielleicht, werden sie sie finden.«[104]

**WE ARE SHIPS AT SEA
NOT DUCKS ON A POND**

**WIR SIND SCHIFFE AUF DEM MEER
WIR SIND KEINE ENTEN AUF DEM TEICH**

Weiner's aphorism deals with the existential significance of movement and thus the significance of change in his understanding of art as "Nach bildende Kunst." The two brief sentences became famous far beyond the German-speaking world by way of their prominent placement on two pontoons in the Port of Hamburg in 1989. I will leave the interpretation to Michel Foucault:

> Brothels and colonies are two extreme types of heterotopia, and if we think, after all, that the boat is a floating piece of space, a place without a place, that exists by itself, that is closed in on itself and at the same time is given over to the infinity of the sea and that, from port to port, from tack to tack, from brothel to brothel, it goes as far as the colonies in search of the most precious treasures they conceal in their gardens, you will understand why the boat has not only been for our civilization, from the sixteenth century until the present, the great instrument of economic development (I have not been speaking of that today), but has been simultaneously the greatest reserve of the imagination. The ship is the heterotopia par excellence. In civilizations without boats, dreams dry up, espionage takes the place of adventure, and the police take the place of pirates.[105]

In 2007, Lawrence Weiner returned to this aphorism. Now he brings it inside, writing it in front

**WE ARE SHIPS AT SEA
NOT DUCKS ON A POND**

**WIR SIND SCHIFFE AUF DEM MEER
WIR SIND KEINE ENTEN AUF DEM TEICH**

Weiners Aphorismus aus dem Jahre 1989 gilt der existenziellen Bedeutung der Bewegung und damit der Veränderung in seinem Verständnis von Kunst als »Nach bildende Kunst«. Die beiden kurzen Sätze wurden 1989 durch die prominente Platzierung auf zwei Pontons im Hamburger Hafen über den deutschsprachigen Raum hinaus berühmt. Ich überlasse die Interpretation Michel Foucault:

> Bordelle und Kolonien sind zwei extreme Typen der Heterotopie, und wenn man daran denkt, dass das Schiff ein schaukelndes Stück Raum ist, ein Ort ohne Ort, der aus sich selber lebt, der in sich geschlossen ist und gleichzeitig dem Unendlichen des Meeres ausgeliefert ist und der, von Hafen zu Hafen, von Ladung zu Ladung, von Bordell zu Bordell, bis zu den Kolonien suchen fährt, was sie an Kostbarstem in ihren Gärten bergen, dann versteht man, warum das Schiff für unsere Zivilisation vom 16. Jahrhundert bis in unsere Tage nicht nur das größte Instrument der wirtschaftlichen Entwicklung gewesen ist (nicht davon spreche ich heute), sondern auch das größte Imaginationsarsenal. Das Schiff, das ist die Heterotopie schlechthin. In den Zivilisationen ohne Schiff versiegen die Träume, die Spionage ersetzt das Abenteuer und die Polizei die Freibeuter.[105]

2007 greift Lawrence Weiner auf diesen Aphorismus zurück. Jetzt verlagert er ihn in den Innenraum und schreibt ihn vor die Buchhandlung von of the Walter König Bookstore in Munich's Haus der Kunst. Maybe it would say that the book is an extreme form of heterotopia, a floating piece of space, a place without a place.

WE REMAIN SHIPS AT SEA
NOT AT ALL DUCKS ON A POND
SAIL ON

WIR BLEIBEN SCHIFFE AUF DEM MEER
ÜBERHAUPT NICHT ENTEN AUF EINEM TEICH
SAIL ON

Walther König im Haus der Kunst in München. Vielleicht sagt er, dass auch das Buch ein extremer Typ von Heterotopie ist, ein schaukelndes Stück Raum, ein Ort ohne Ort.

WE REMAIN SHIPS AT SEA
NOT AT ALL DUCKS ON A POND
SAIL ON

WIR BLEIBEN SCHIFFE AUF DEM MEER
ÜBERHAUPT NICHT ENTEN AUF EINEM TEICH
SAIL ON

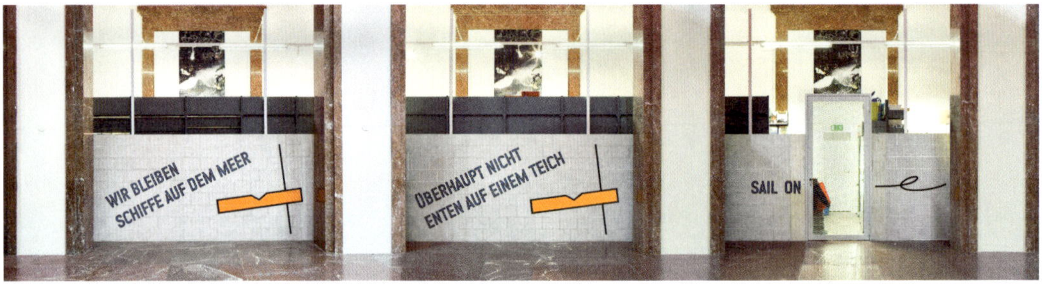

Walther König Bookstore, Haus der Kunst, Munich, 2007
Buchhandlung Walther König, Haus der Kunst, München, 2007

1 Water Benjamin, "One-Way Street," in *One-Way Street and Other Writings*, trans. Edmund Jephcott (London, 1979), p. 63; originally published in German as *Einbahnstrasse* in 1928, and reprinted (in a different typography, ignoring Benjamin's preference for sans serif) in *Gesammelte Schriften*, vol. 4.1, ed. Tillman Rexroth and Hermann Schweppenhäuser (Frankfurt am Main, 1972).

2 Gérard Genette, *Paratexts: Thresholds of Interpretation*, trans. Jane E. Lewin (Cambridge, UK, 1997), p. 1; originally published in French in 1987 as *Seuils*.

3 Ibid. Genette focuses on the medium of the book. Considering the threshold function that Genette attributes to paratexts (whereby "materiality" is something to which Genette devotes comparatively little attention), when "materiality" is mentioned in this essay, the status of a threshold and thus its relevance for the constitution of meaning remain in view.

4 *Artist Series: Lawrence Weiner*, interviewed by Debbie Millman, directed and edited by Hillman Curtis, 4:51 min., http://hillmancurtis.com/artist-series/lawrence-weiner/ (accessed August 20, 2011).

5 Benjamin 1979 (see note 1), pp. 45, 102, 70.

6 Christopher Knight, "A Treatise on Time, in Stencil," *Los Angeles Times*, April 15, 2005.

7 "A Conversation with Judith Hoffberg on Books" (2002), in *Having Been Said: Writings & Interviews of Lawrence Weiner, 1968–2003*, ed. Gerti Fietzek and Gregor Stemmrich (Ostfildern-Ruit, 2004), p. 416.

8 See Weiner's first book *Statements* (New York, 1968). "Typeset in the sans serif Royal Typewriter face using upper and lowercase letters, each statement is presented solely in language, without illustration, punctuation, or numbering. The twelve specific statements and twelve general statements each appear on the right-hand page of the book, followed at the end by two blank pages. The statements are not only materially presented in language, but also 'built' in their typeset form, which gives them an object status—each statement is formatted into narrow columns, many of which are broken mid-word." Ann Goldstein, "If It Looks Like a Duck and It Walks Like a Duck, It Is Probably a Duck," in *Lawrence Weiner: As Far as the Eye Can See* (New York, 2007), p. 123.

9 When it comes to distinguishing a language work understood as sculpture from Conceptual Art, whether or not the label represents an important factor in the reception of Weiner's artistic oeuvre is a different matter. This art form, treated as highly intellectual, appears in many reviews as something like a good address that offers a stage for a work that is "giddily elevated" from the street. Brooks Adams, "Weiner's Werkstätte," *Parkett* 42 (1994), p. 31; and from here returning the question of art's sublimity to the audience.

10 A book can be a stage as much as a building can: MANY COLORED OBJECTS PLACED SIDE BY SIDE TO FORM A ROW OF MANY COLORED OBJECTS / VIELE FARBIGE DINGE NEBENEINANDER ANGEORDNET BILDEN EINE REIHE VIELER FARBIGER DINGE was printed on the banderole of the Documenta 7 catalogue in 1982, and the work was also installed by sign painters along the architrave of the Fridericianum in Kassel during the show. The retrospective of Weiner's works presented in Düsseldorf referred to this outstanding presentation by installing this work on the elegant curved black wall of K20 Kunstsammlung Nordrhein-Westfalen, leaving it to the beholder to decide if this work was referring to objects in the surroundings or to objects of art.

11 Lawrence Weiner, *If In Fact There Is a Context: 100 Notes, 100 Thoughts* (Ostfildern, 2011), unpaginated.

12 "Early Work: Interview by Lynn Gumpert" (1982), in Fietzek / Stemmrich 2004 (see note 7), p. 122.

13 Hofberg 2002 (see note 7), p. 133.

14 For Weiner's exhibitions at Konrad Fischer, see *Ausstellungen bei Konrad Fischer, Düsseldorf, Oktober 1967–Oktober 1992* (Bielefeld, 1993); and *Ausstellungen bei Konrad Fischer/ Galerie Konrad Fischer, Düsseldorf, November 1992–Oktober 2007* (Trieste, 2007).

15 Weiner executed the work at the request of the collector, but neither the cut-out hole left in the carpet nor the cut square is the artwork; the artwork consists solely of the language sculpture. This corresponds to Weiner's Statement of Intent,

1 Walter Benjamin, *Einbahnstraße*, Berlin 1928, S. 28 f., wieder abgedr. in: ders., *Gesammelte Schriften*, Bd. 4.1, hrsg. von Rolf Tiedemann und Hermann Schweppenhäuser, Frankfurt a. M. 1972, jedoch in anderer Typografie.

2 Gérard Genette, *Paratexte. Das Buch vom Beiwerk des Buches*, Frankfurt a. M. 2003, S. 9. Der französische Originaltitel lautet *Seuils* (Schwellen).

3 Ebd. Genette konzentriert sich auf das Medium Buch. Entsprechend der Schwellenfunktion, die Genette den Paratexten zuschreibt (wobei »Materialität« ein bei Genette vergleichsweise kurz abgehandelter Aspekt ist), bleiben immer der Status einer Schwelle und damit die Relevanz für die Konstitution von Bedeutung im Blick, wenn im Folgenden von »Materialität« des Textes die Rede ist.

4 Engl. Original s. Hillman Curtis (Hrsg.), *Artist Series. Lawrence Weiner*, interviewt von Debbie Millman, o. J., http://hillmancurtis.com/artist-series/lawrence-weiner/ (20.8.2011).

5 Benjamin 1928 (s. Anm. 1), S. 7, 80, 39.

6 Engl. Original s. Christopher Knight, »A Treatise on Time, in Stencil«, in: *Los Angeles Times*, 15.4.2005.

7 Vgl. »Ein Gespräch mit Judith Hoffberg über Bücher«, in: Gerti Fietzek und Gregor Stemmrich (Hrsg.), *Gefragt und Gesagt. Schriften & Interviews von Lawrence Weiner 1968–2003*, Ostfildern-Ruit 2004, S. 450–457.

8 Vgl. das erste Buch *Statements*, New York 1968: »Die in Groß- und Kleinbuchstaben in Typewriter Royal Sans Serif gesetzten Statements wurden ausschließlich in Textform, ohne Illustrationen, Interpunktion oder Nummerierung präsentiert. Die zwölf Specific und die zwölf General Statements sind jeweils einzeln auf der rechten Buchseite abgedruckt. Danach folgen zwei leere Seiten. Die Statements werden nicht nur materiell in Sprache präsentiert, sondern auch in ihrer gesetzten Form ›gebaut‹, was ihnen den Status von Objekten verleiht – jedes Statement ist als schmale Kolumne formatiert, wobei die Zeilen häufig mitten im Wort umbrochen sind.« Engl. Original s. Ann Goldstein, »If It Looks Like a Duck and It Walks Like a Duck, It Is Probably a Duck", in: *As Far as the Eye Can See. Lawrence Weiner 1960–2007*, hrsg. von Donna M. De Salvo und Ann Goldstein, Ausst.-Kat The Museum of Contemporary Art, Los Angeles; Whitney Museum of American Art, New York; New Haven und London 2007, S. 122 f.

9 Eine andere Frage im Zusammenhang mit der Abgrenzung einer als Skulptur verstandenen Spracharbeit von der Concept Art ist, ob ihr Label nicht dennoch einen wichtigen Faktor in der Rezeption von Weiners künstlerischem Schaffen darstellt. Diese als hochintellektuell gehandelte Kunstrichtung erscheint in vielen Rezensionen als gute Adresse, die einem Werk von der Straße eine Bühne bietet, sich in »schwindelnde Erhabenheit« (Brooks Adams, »Weiners Werkstätte«, in: Parkett, 42, 1994, S. 26) zu katapultieren und von dort aus die Frage nach dem Erhabenen in der Kunst wieder ins Publikum zurückzuwerfen.

10 Ein Buch kann ebenso eine Bühne sein wie ein Gebäude: MANY COLORED OBJECTS PLACED SIDE BY SIDE TO FORM A ROW OF MANY COLORED OBJECTS / VIELE FARBIGE DINGE NEBENEINANDER ANGEORDNET BILDEN EINE REIHE VIELER FARBIGER DINGE war 1982 auf die Banderole des Katalogs der *Documenta 7* gedruckt worden. Die Arbeit war außerdem für die Dauer der Ausstellung auf den Architrav der Kunsthalle Fridericianum in Kassel gemalt worden. Weiners Düsseldorfer Retrospektive verwies auf diese herausragende Präsentation durch die Installation dieses Werkes auf der elegant geschwungenen schwarzen Wand der Kunstsammlung Nordrhein-Westfalen. Die Entscheidung, ob sich die Arbeit auf Dinge der Umgebung oder auf Kunstwerke bezog, wurde dem Betrachter überlassen.

11 Lawrence Weiner, *If in Fact There is a Context (100 Notes – 100 Thoughts / 100 Notizen – 100 Gedanken*, 8), Ostfildern 2011, o. S.

12 »Frühe Arbeiten. Interview von Lynn Gumpert« (1982), in: Fietzek / Stemmrich 2004 (wie Anm. 7), S. 129–140, hier S. 133.

13 Fietzek / Stemmrich 2004 (wie Anm. 7), S. 133.

14 Zu Weiners Ausstellungen in der Konrad Fischer Galerie s. *Ausstellungen bei Konrad Fischer, Düsseldorf, Oktober 1967–Oktober 1992*, Bielefeld 1993, und *Ausstellungen bei Konrad Fischer / Konrad Fischer Galerie, Düsseldorf, November 1992–Oktober 2007*, Trieste 2007.

published in early 1969, that typically accompanies exhibitions and publications and that is presented in this book in the form of an installation photograph from the Düsseldorf retrospective on pp. 4/5.

16 Reiner Speck, "A Sculpture for Cologne," in Lawrence Weiner: *To Build a Square in the Rhineland / Ein Quadrat im Rheinland Bauen* (Cologne, 1995).

17 Lawrence Weiner, "Sketchbook" (May 1995–January 1996).

18 See Udo Weilacher, "Hyperrealistische Schocktherapie: Adriaan Geuze," in *Zwischen Landschaftsarchitektur und Landart* (Basel, 1996), pp. 229–44; and Adriaan Geuze, "Acceleration Darwin," in Gerriet Smienk, ed., *Nederlandse Landschapsarchitectuur: Tussen traditie en experiment* (Amsterdam, 1993).

19 Marja Bloem, "How You Know Is Not What You Know," in *Lawrence Weiner: Works from the Beginning of the Sixties towards the End of the Eighties*, ed. Marja Bloem, exh. cat. Stedelijk Museum (Amsterdam, 1988), p. 58.

20 The work was commissioned by the city of Zurich, and was installed at Bellevue (BALL BEARINGS OR ROUND STONES MADE TO ROLL OUTSIDE OF WHAT THERE IS), at Limmatplatz (KUGELLAGER ODER RUNDE STEINE ZUM ROLLEN GEBRACHT AUSSERHALB WAS IST), and at Helvetiaplatz (CUSCINETTI A SFERA O CIOTTOLI LEVIGATI FATTI ROTOLARE AL DI FUORI DA CIÒ CHE È).

21 See Elisabeth Leiss, *Sprachphilosophie* (Berlin, 2009).

22 Gottlob Frege, "On Sense and Reference," trans. Max Black, in *Translations from the Philosophical Writings of Gottlob Frege*, ed. Peter Geach and Max Black (Oxford, 1952), pp. 56–78; originally published in German in 1892 as "Über Sinn und Bedeutung."

23 Ibid., p. 57.

24 Ferdinand Schmatz, "The Author Is Away, Art Is a Way," in *In the Still of the Night / Im Frieden der Nacht* (Vienna, 1991), p. 37.

25 The two poets Durs Grünbein and Joachim Sartorius and the translator Karin Graf immediately felt the challenge of Weiner's work at Cologne Cathedral. Alongside the official publication, an alternative publication with a new translation was also published: *To Build a Square in the Rhineland / Ein Viereck anlegen im Rheinland*.

26 "Art without Space" (1969), in Fietzek / Stemmrich 2004 (see note 7), p. 32.

27 "Mondrian or Volendam" (1985), in Fietzek / Stemmrich 2004 (see note 7), p. 158.

28 "Lawrence Weiner: Talking Art," in conversation with John Slyce, Tate Modern, February 2, 2008, http://channel.tate.org.uk/media/27241487001 (accessed August 20, 2011).

29 Christoph Schenker, "Lawrence Weiner: Kugellager oder runde Steine," in *Kunst und Öffentlichkeit: Kritische Praxis der Kunst im Stadtraum Zürich* (Zurich, 2007), p. 136.

30 Hubert Winter in conversation with the author, Vienna, 2011.

31 Andreas Mailath-Pokorny, Vienna's Commissioner of Culture, quoted in the *Wiener Zeitung*, June 24, 2005.

32 See Lawrence Weiner, *Specific & General Works*, ed. Le Nouveau Musée, Institut d'Art Contemporain (Villeurbanne, 1993).

33 In Düsseldorf, Weiner presented DICHT BEI in German along with the English version of his work, while in the English version of another work—PUSHED FORWARD CLOSE BY PUSHED ASIDE CLOSE BY WITH GRACEFUL HASTE—DICHT BEI is translated as CLOSE BY. See *Gyroscopically Speaking*, Marian Goodman Gallery, New York, 2011.

34 Gallery description, *Through The Warp*, Regina Rex, New York, May 28, 2011–June 19, 2011, http://www.reginarex.org/exhibition.asp?exid=466&img=1202 (accessed August 3, 2011).

35 *Monopol* 9 (2010), p. 30.

36 Wolfgang Zinggl, "Kunst als Penicillin: Gespräch mit Lawrence Weiner," *Falter* 41 (1991).

37 Fietzek / Stemmrich 2004 (see note 7), pp. 170, 301.

38 Randy Kennedy, "Language as Sculpture, Words as Clay," *The New York Times*, October 21, 2007.

39 "Interview by Dieter Schwarz" (1989), in Fietzek / Stemmrich 2004 (see note 7), p. 195.

40 All these titles can be easily found by doing a search on the Internet. Let me mention here the publishing history of Agatha Christie's novel. Originally published in 1939 as *Ten Little Niggers* in the UK, it was published a year later with the

15 Auf Wunsch des Sammlers führte Weiner diese Arbeit aus. Aber weder der Ausschnitt aus dem Teppich ist das Kunstwerk noch das herausgeschnittene Quadrat, sondern allein die Sprachskulptur. Das entspricht Weiners Anfang 1969 veröffentlichter Absichtserklärung, die alle Ausstellungen und Publikationen begleitet und im vorliegenden Buch durch ein Installationsfoto aus der Düsseldorfer Retrospektive auf S. 4/5 präsentiert wird.

16 Reiner Speck, »Eine Skulptur für Köln«, in: *To Build a Square in the Rhineland / Ein Quadrat im Rheinland bauen. Lawrence Weiner*, hrsg. von der Gesellschaft für Moderne Kunst am Museum Ludwig Köln anlässlich der Verleihung des 2. Wolfgang-Hahn-Preises an Lawrence Weiner am 8. November 1995, Köln 1995, o. S.

17 Lawrence Weiner, *Sketchbook May 95 – Jan 96*, Moved Pictures Archive, New York.

18 Vgl. Udo Weilacher, »Hyperrealistische Schocktherapie – Adriaan Geuze«, in: ders., *Zwischen Landschaftsarchitektur und Landart*, Basel 1996, und Adriaan Geuze, »Accelerating Darwin«, in: Gerrit Smienk (Hrsg.), *Nederlandse Landschapsarchitectuur. Tussen traditie en experiment*, Amsterdam 1993.

19 Vgl. Marja Bloem, »How You Know Is Not What You Know«, in: *Lawrence Weiner*, Ausst.-Kat. Stedelijk Museum, Amsterdam 1988, S. 58.

20 Die Arbeit wurde auf dem Bellevue (BALL BEARINGS OR ROUND STONES MADE TO ROLL OUTSIDE OF WHAT THERE IS), dem Limmatplatz (KUGELLAGER ODER RUNDE STEINE ZUM ROLLEN GEBRACHT AUSSERHALB WAS IST) und dem Helvetiaplatz (CUSCINETTI A SFERA O CIOTTOLI LEVIGATI FATTI ROTOLARE AL DI FUORI DA CIÒ CHE È) installiert.

21 Vgl. Elisabeth Leiss, *Sprachphilosophie*, Berlin 2009.

22 Vgl. Gottlob Frege, »Über Sinn und Bedeutung«, in: *Zeitschrift für Philosophie und philosophische Kritik*, NF 100, 1892, S. 29.

23 Ebd., S. 26.

24 Ferdinand Schmatz, »Der Autor ist weg, die Kunst ist der Weg«, in: *In the Still of the Night / Im Frieden der Nacht*, hrsg. von den Wiener Festwochen im Rahmen der Ausstellung *Topografie I*, Festraum, Wien 1991, S. 36 f.

25 Gleich zwei Dichter und eine Übersetzerin, Karin Graf, Durs Grünbein und Joachim Sartorius, fühlten sich durch Weiners Arbeit am Kölner Dom herausgefordert. So erschien zur offiziellen Publikation eine weitere mit einer neuen Übersetzung: *To Build a Square in the Rhineland / 1) Ein Quadrat im Rheinland bauen 2) Ein Viereck anlegen im Rheinland*, Köln 2005.

26 »Kunst ohne Raum«, in: Fietzek / Stemmrich 2004 (wie Anm. 7), S. 30–35, hier S. 33.

27 »Mondrian oder Volendam«, in: Fietzek / Stemmrich 2004 (wie Anm. 7), S. 172 f., hier S. 172.

28 Engl. Original s. *Lawrence Weiner: Talking Art. Lawrence Weiner discusses his work with art historian and critic John Slyce*, 2.2.2008, http://channel.tate.org.uk/media/27241487001 (20.8.2011).

29 Vgl. Christoph Schenker, »Lawrence Weiner. Kugellager oder runde Steine«, in: ders. und Michael Hiltbrunner (Hrsg.), *Kunst und Öffentlichkeit – Kritische Praxis der Kunst im Stadtraum Zürich (Schriftenreihe des Instituts für Kunst und Medien, HGK Zürich, 2)*, Zürich 2007, S. 136.

30 Hubert Winter 2011 im Gespräch mit der Autorin.

31 Andreas Mailath-Pokorny, Kulturstadtrat Wien, in: *Wiener Zeitung*, 24.6.2005.

32 Vgl. Lawrence Weiner, *Specific & General Works*, hrsg. von Le Nouveau Musée. Institut d'Art Contemporain, Villeurbanne 1993.

33 DICHT BEI, das Weiner in Düsseldorf auch der englischen Version beistellt, wurde in der englischen Version einer weiteren Arbeit mit CLOSE BY übersetzt – PUSHED FORWARD CLOSE BY PUSHED ASIDE CLOSE BY WITH GRACEFUL HASTE. Vgl. *Gyroscopically Speaking*, Marian Goodman Gallery, New York, 2011.

34 Engl. Original s. http://www.reginarex.org/exhibition.asp?exid=466&img=1202 (3.8.2011).

35 *Monopol*, 9, 2010, S. 30.

36 Wolfgang Zinggl, »›Kunst als Penicillin‹ Gespräch mit Lawrence Weiner«, in: *Falter*, 41, 1991.

37 Fietzek / Stemmrich 2004 (wie Anm. 7), S. 184 und 326.

38 Engl. Original s. Randy Kennedy, »Language as Sculpture, Words as Clay«, in: *The New York Times*, 21.10.2007.

39 »Interview von Dieter Schwarz« (1989), in: Fietzek / Stemmrich 2004 (wie Anm. 7), S. 208–213, hier S. 211.

politically correct title *And Then There Were None*. The work by Weiner of the same title is part of a private collection in Bielefeld. See the illustration in Weiner 2007 (see note 8), p. 145.

41 Roberta Smith, "The Well-Shaped Phrase as Art," *The New York Times*, November 16, 2007.

42 See Kathryn Chiong, "Sympathy for Lawrence Weiner (One Plus One)," in Weiner 2007 (see note 8), p. 331.

43 Interview by Lynn Gumpert 1982 (see note 12), p. 123.

44 Fietzek / Stemmrich 2004 (see note 7), p. 135.

45 The published translation reads: "The author is away, art is a way." See Schmatz 1991 (see note 24), p. 26. [A perhaps more accurate translation would read: "The artist is gone. Art is the way to go."—Trans.]

46 "I Am Not Content: Interview by David Batchelor" (1989), in Fietzek / Stemmrich 2004 (see note 7), p. 188.

47 See Sebastian Marx, *Betriebsamkeit als Literatur: Prosa der Weimarer Republik zwischen Massenpresse und Buch* (Bielefeld, 2009), p. 203–7; and his reference to Benjamin: "Books and harlots can be taken to bed," Benjamin 1979 (see note 1), p. 68. See also Benjamin: "If I write better German than most writers of my generation, it is thanks largely to twenty years' observance of one little rule: Never use the word 'I,' except in letters." "Berlin Chronicle" (1932), in *Selected Writings, 1931–1934* (Cambridge, Mass., 2005).

48 Peter Gordon and Lawrence Weiner, *The Society Architect Ponders the Golden Gate Bridge, oder, Wie sie kriegen was sie nicht verdienen* (Cologne, 2000), p. 68. In her catalogue essay on the conception of Weiner's first large-scale U.S. retrospective, Donna De Salvo reflects on the tension between an emphasis on the here and now and a retrospectical look, a tension that also applies to this catalogue of works: "This 'retrospectical,' as Lawrence has referred to the project, is actually at odds with the structure of his practice since 1968, which is grounded in the present moment, so that each time a work is presented it is manifest anew." Weiner 2007 (see note 8), p. 42.

49 See Interview with David Batchelor 1989 (see note 46), p. 188.

50 See Lawrence Weiner, "The reason one makes art is to start a conversation," quoted in the companion publication to *As Far as the Eye Can See*, K21 Kunstsammlung Nordrhein-Westfalen (Düsseldorf, 2008), p. 61.

51 Kennedy 2007 (see note 38).

52 Ibid.

53 David Colman, "The Discreet Charm of the Gauloisie," *The New York Times*, December 2, 2007.

54 Grace Glueck, "Art in Review; Lawrence Weiner," *The New York Times*, March 19, 2005.

55 Raimund Theis and Hans T. Siepe, eds., *Le plaisir de l'intertexte* (Frankfurt am Main, 1986).

56 Eva Geulen, "Habe und Bleibe in Kellers 'Romeo und Julia auf dem Dorfe,'" in *Zeitschrift für deutsche Philologie* (Sonderheft, 2010), pp. 253–63. "Nor is it clear whether Shakespeare can actually claim property rights himself, for he picked up traditions that stretched from Arthur Broke through Boccaccio back to Ovid and finally back to time immemorial" (p. 263).

57 Ibid., p. 262.

58 See Gordon / Weiner 2000 (see note 48), p. 78; see also 68–73.

59 See Gregor Stemmrich, "Lawrence Weiner: Material and Methodology," in Fietzek / Stemmrich 2004 (see note 7), p. 454.

60 "Interview by Phyllis Rosenzweig" (1990), in Fietzek / Stemmrich 2004 (see note 7), p. 236.

61 Blake Gopnik, "Buying Art You Can't Take Home," *Newsweek*, June 27, 2011.

62 Installation, 838 x 474 x 310 cm, 2001, Museum für Moderne Kunst, Frankfurt am Main.

63 PRESSURE SUFFICIENT TO FORM AN ICE OF MASS ENOUGH TO CARRY UPON WITHIN AND BENEATH ITSELF SOME OF THAT WITHIN THE VECTOR OF MOTION / HINREICHENDER DRUCK ZU FORMEN GENÜGEND MASSE EIS ZU TRAGEN AUF IHR IN IHR UNTER IHR INNERHALB DES VEKTORS DER BEWEGUNG.

64 Michael Klaar, telephone interview with the author, 2011.

65 JUST ANOTHER MOVEMENT OF THE TIDE (IMPAIRED) / NUR EINE ANDERE BEWEGUNG DER GEZEITEN (VERHINDERT).

66 Umberto Eco, *Experiences in Translation*, trans. Alastair McEwen (Toronto, 2008).

40 Alle diese Titel lassen sich leicht im Internet recherchieren. Hingewiesen sei hier nur auf die Editionsgeschichte des Krimis von Agatha Christie. 1939 unter dem Titel *Ten Little Niggers* in Großbritannien veröffentlicht, erschien er ein Jahr später in den USA politisch korrekt unter *And Then There Were None*. Die Arbeit Weiners gleichen Wortlauts befindet sich in einer Privatsammlung in Bielefeld, vgl. die Abb. in Los Angeles / New York 2007 (wie Anm. 8), S. 145.

41 Engl. Original s. Roberta Smith, »The Well-Shaped Phrase as Art«, in: *The New York Times*, 16.11.2007.

42 Vgl. Kathryn Chiong, »Sympathy for Lawrence Weiner (One Plus One)«, in: Los Angeles / New York 2007 (wie Anm. 8), S. 331.

43 »Frühe Arbeiten. Interview von Lynn Gumpert« (1982), in: Fietzek / Stemmrich 2004 (wie Anm. 7), S. 134.

44 *Artforum*, Mai 1982, abgebildet in: Fietzek / Stemmrich 2004 (wie Anm. 7), S. 144–146.

45 Schmatz 1991 (wie Anm. 24), S. 27.

46 »Ich bin nicht Inhalt. Interview von David Batchelor« (1989), in: Fietzek / Stemmrich 2004 (wie Anm. 7), S. 201–206, hier S. 203.

47 Vgl. Sebastian Marx, *Betriebsamkeit als Literatur. Prosa der Weimarer Republik zwischen Massenpresse und Buch*, Bielefeld 2009, S. 203 ff., und seinen Hinweis auf Walter Benjamin, »Bücher und Dirnen kann man ins Bett nehmen«, in: Benjamin 1928 (wie Anm. 1), S. 36. Vgl. auch Walter Benjamin, »Wenn ich ein besseres Deutsch schreibe als die meisten Schriftsteller meiner Generation, so verdanke ich das zum guten Teil der zwanzigjährigen Beobachtung einer einzigen kleinen Regel. Sie lautet: das Wort ›ich‹ nie zu gebrauchen, außer in den Briefen«, in: ders., *Gesammelte Schriften*, Bd. 6, hrsg. von Rolf Tiedemann und Hermann Schweppenhäuser, Frankfurt a. M. 1985, S. 475.

48 Peter Gordon und Lawrence Weiner, *The Society Architect Ponders the Golden Gate Bridge oder: Wie sie kriegen was sie nicht verdienen*, Köln 2000, S. 68. Donna De Salvo reflektiert in ihrem Katalogbeitrag die sich bei der Konzeption von Weiners ersten großen Retrospektive in den USA abzeichnende Spannung zwischen der Betonung auf dem Hier und Jetzt und einem von der Sache her rückwärts gewandten Blick – eine Spannung, die auch für das in dem vorliegenden Buch präsentierte Werkverzeichnis gilt: »Dieses ›Retrospectical‹, wie Lawrence das Projekt nannte, steht eigentlich im Kontrast zu dem Ansatz, den er seit 1968 verfolgt und der von einem starken Gegenwartsbezug geprägt ist, was bedeutet, dass sich ein Werk bei jeder Präsentation als neues Werk darstellt.« Engl. Original s. Los Angeles / New York 2007 (wie Anm. 8), S. 43.

49 Vgl. dazu »Ich bin nicht Inhalt. Interview von David Batchelor« (1989), in: Fietzek / Stemmrich 2004 (wie Anm. 7), S. 201–206, hier S. 203.

50 Vgl. Lawrence Weiner: »Der Grund, weshalb man ein Kunstwerk macht, ist, ein Gespräch zu beginnen«, in: *As Far as the Eye Can See*, Begleitpublikation K21 Kunstsammlung Nordrhein-Westfalen, Düsseldorf 2008, S. 61.

51 Engl. Original s. Kennedy 2007 (wie Anm. 38).

52 Engl. Original s. Kennedy 2007 (wie Anm. 38).

53 Engl. Original s. David Colman, »The Discreet Charm of the Gauloisie«, in: *The New York Times*, 2.12.2007.

54 Grace Glueck, »Art in Review. Lawrence Weiner«, in: *The New York Times*, 19.3.2005.

55 Raimund Theis und Hans T. Siepe (Hrsg.), *Le Plaisier de l'intertexte*, Frankfurt a. M. 1986, S. 277.

56 Vgl. dazu Eva Geulen, »Habe und Bleibe in Kellers ›Romeo und Julia auf dem Dorfe‹«, in: *Zeitschrift für deutsche Philologie, Sonderheft Grenzen im Raum – Grenzen in der Literatur*, 2010, S. 253–263, hier S. 263: »Und man kann auch nicht sicher sein, ob Shakespeare tatsächlich Eigentümerrechte beanspruchen kann, denn er griff seinerseits Stofftraditionen auf, die von Arthur Broke über Boccaccio bis zu Ovid und schließlich wohl ins Unvordenkliche zurückreichen.«

57 Ebd., S. 262.

58 Gordon / Weiner 2000 (wie Anm. 48), S. 78. Vgl. dort auch: »Verschiedene Medien«, S. 68 ff.

59 Vgl. Gregor Stemmrich, »Lawrence Weiner – Material und Methodologie«, in: Fietzek / Stemmrich 2004 (wie Anm. 7), S. 465–494, hier S. 493.

60 »Interview von Phyllis Rosenzweig« (1990), in: Fietzek / Stemmrich 2004 (wie Anm. 7), S. 255–257, hier S. 256.

67 See Weiner's text "A Translation from One Language to Another," *De Witte Raaf* (Brussels), no. 59 (January–February 1996); reprinted in Fietzek / Stemmrich 2004 (see note 7), pp. 344–45.

68 Weiner 1993 (see note 32).

69 Galerie Hubert Winter, Vienna, 2000.

70 Thomas Kling, *Sondagen* (Cologne, 2002).

71 Stefan Weidner, "Warum die orientalische Poesie so blumig ist," in *Aufbruch in die Vernunft* (Bonn, 2011), pp. 224–45, here p. 228.

72 Ibid, p. 229.

73 See Sabine Dylla, *Lawrence Weiner: Two Blocks / Zwei Blöcke*, exh. cat. Städtische Galerie Nordhorn (Nordhorn, 1993), n.p.

74 See also Weiner 1993 (see note 32).

75 Lawrence Weiner, e-mail to the author, November 15, 2010.

76 "Interview by Ann Temkin and John Ravenal" (1994), in Fietzek / Stemmrich 2004 (see note 7), p. 322; see also Stemmrich 2004 (see note 59), p. 449.

77 Commissioned by the Public Art Fund and realized in collaboration with Con Edison and Roman Stone in 2000, the manhole covers were installed within a strip of downtown Manhattan, between 14th Street and Houston.

78 For Weiner's comments on the function of the artist as a "culture fucker," see "Lawrence Weiner at Amsterdam: An Interview by Willoughby Sharp," in Fietzek / Stemmrich 2004 (see note 7), p. 51. During a short speech at the Denver Art Museum on June 22, 2010, to mark the presentation of a new installation, he said the following: "People make art. And yes, I make art because I'm not happy with the way the world looks at things, because I'm not happy with the configuration." "Lawrence Weiner Public Art Dedication," http://www.youtube.com/watch?v=RhXLywbBdRA (accessed October 27, 2011).

79 Ludwig Wittgenstein, *Schriften*, vol. 8 (Frankfurt am Main, 1982), pp. 334, 309: "Nur im Fluß der Gedanken und des Lebens haben die Worte Bedeutung [slip 173]."

80 Ludwig Wittgenstein, *Last Writings on the Philosophy of Psychology: Preliminary Studies for Part II of Philosophical Investigations*, vol. 1, ed. Georg H. von Wright and Heikki Nyman (Oxford, 1982), p. 118.

81 Norman Malcolm, *Ludwig Wittgenstein: A Memoir* (London, 1958), p. 93.

82 "Eine seiner Äußerungen erschien mir damals, wie heute, besonders bemerkenswert, als ein Resümee eines größeren Teils seiner Philosophie. Sie heißt: 'Ein Ausdruck hat nur im Strome des Lebens Bedeutung.' Wittgenstein meinte, dass dieser Aphorismus in einem seiner Manuskripte niedergeschrieben sei; und vielleicht war er es, doch habe ich ihn nirgends gesehen." See Norman Malcom, *Ludwig Wittgenstein: Ein Erinnerungsbuch* (Munich, 1961), p. 117.

83 As a self-quotation of his own way of working as well as an object of use, Weiner developed self-adhesive labels with the text of the exhibited work as invitations to his show at Galerie Fischer, Düsseldorf.

84 "Lawrence Weiner's 'Plowman's Lunch': Interview by Michael Gibbs" (1982), in Fietzek / Stemmrich 2004 (see note 7), p. 142.

85 Lawrence Weiner, e-mail to the author, March 19, 2011.

86 Weiner 2008 (see note 28). See also Weiner's statement, "The making of a work is . . . a passionate attempt to show enough of a form to attract," quoted in *Nau Em I Art Belong Yumi* (Brussels, 1994), n.p.

87 "Suzy Menkes zur Fashion Week, Berlin," *Focus* 27 (2011), p. 79.

88 "Interview in Preparation for the Conference: 'Art Meets Science and Spirituality in a Changing Economy'" (1989), in Fietzek / Stemmrich 2004 (see note 7), p. 204.

89 Heraclitus, *Fragments* B49a.

90 Markus Gabriel, "On Wolfram Hogrebe's Philosophical Approach," *Graduate Faculty Philosophy Journal* 31, no. 2 (2010), pp. 201–8, here p. 203.

91 On the cover of the notebook that contains the Wittgenstein aphorism is a quotation from Mao Zedong, *On Contradiction* (1937), "Processes change, old processes and old contradictions disappear, new processes and new contradictions emerge, and the methods of resolving contradictions differ accordingly."

61 Blake Gopnik, »Buying Art You Can't Take Home«, in: *Newsweek*, 27.6.2011.

62 2001, Rauminstallation, 838 x 474 x 310 cm, MMK Museum für Moderne Kunst, Frankfurt a. M.

63 PRESSURE SUFFICIENT TO FORM AN ICE OF MASS ENOUGH TO CARRY UPON WITHIN AND BENEATH ITSELF SOME OF THAT WITHIN THE VECTOR OF MOTION / HINREICHENDER DRUCK ZU FORMEN GENÜGEND MASSE EIS ZU TRAGEN AUF IHR IN IHR UNTER IHR INNERHALB DES VEKTORS DER BEWEGUNG.

64 Michael Klaar, 2011 in einem telefonischen Interview mit der Autorin.

65 JUST ANOTHER MOVEMENT OF THE TIDE (IMPAIRED) / NUR EINE ANDERE BEWEGUNG DER GEZEITEN (VERHINDERT).

66 Umberto Eco, *Quasi dasselbe mit anderen Worten. Über das Übersetzen*, München 2006, S. 328.

67 Siehe auch den in Fietzek / Stemmrich 2004 (wie Anm. 7), S. 373 f., wiederabgedr. Text Weiners.

68 Weiner 1993 (vgl. Anm. 32).

69 Galerie Hubert Winter, Wien, 2000.

70 Thomas Kling, *Sondagen*, Köln 2002.

71 Stefan Weidner, »Warum Übersetzungen altern und die orientalische Poesie so blumig ist«, in: *Aufbruch in die Vernunft*, Bonn 2011, S. 228.

72 Ebd., S. 229.

73 Vgl. *Lawrence Weiner. Zwei Blöcke / Two Blocks*, hrsg. von Sabine Dylla, Ausst.-Kat. Städtische Galerie Nordhorn, Nordhorn 1993, o. S.

74 Siehe auch Weiner 1993 (wie Anm. 32).

75 Engl. Original in einem E-Mail Lawrence Weiners an die Autorin, 15.11.2010.

76 »Interview von Ann Temkin und John Ravenal«, in: Fietzek / Stemmrich 2004 (wie Anm. 7), S. 347–350, hier S. 350. Vgl. auch Gregor Stemmrich, »Lawrence Weiner – Material und Methodologie«, in: Fietzek / Stemmrich 2004 (wie Anm. 7), S. 465–494, hier S. 487.

77 Vom Public Art Fund in Auftrag gegeben und in Zusammenarbeit mit Con Edison und Roman Stone 2000 realisiert, wurden die Kanaldeckel in dem Bereich zwischen der 14th Street und der Houston Street im Zentrum von Manhattan installiert.

78 Zur Funktion des Künstlers als »culture fucker« äußert sich Weiner 1972, vgl. »Lawrence Weiner in Amsterdam. Interview von Willoughby Sharp« (1972), in: Fietzek / Stemmrich 2004 (wie Anm. 7), S. 45–57, hier S. 54. Am 22.6.2010 sagte er in einer Rede anlässlich der Präsentation einer neuen Installation am Denver Art Museum: »Menschen machen Kunst. Und ja, ich mache Kunst, weil ich nicht damit zufrieden bin, wie die Welt die Dinge betrachtet, weil ich mit der Konfiguration nicht zufrieden bin.«

79 Ludwig Wittgenstein, *Bemerkungen über die Philosophie der Psychologie (= Schriften*, Bd. 8), Bd. 1: *Vorstudien zum zweiten Teil der Philosophischen Untersuchungen*, hrsg. von G. E. M. Anscombe und Georg Henrik von Wright, Bd. 2: *Das Innere und das Äußere*, hrsg. von Georg Henrik von Wright und Heikki Nyman, Frankfurt a. M. 1982, S. 334 und 309: »(Nur im Fluß der Gedanken und des Lebens haben die Worte Bedeutung.) [Zettel 173].«

80 Ludwig Wittgenstein, *Letzte Schriften über die Philosophie der Psychologie / Last Writings on the Philosophy of Psychology*, Bd. 1: *Vorstudien zum zweiten Teil der Philosophischen Untersuchungen / Preliminary Studies for Part II of Philosophical Investigations*, hrsg. von Georg H. von Wright und Heikki Nyman, Oxford 1982, S. 118.

81 Norman Malcolm, *Ludwig Wittgenstein. A Memoir*, London u. a. 1958, S. 93; dt. Übersetzung: *Ludwig Wittgenstein. Ein Erinnerungsbuch*, München und Wien 1961, S. 117.

82 »Eine seiner Äußerungen erschien mir damals, wie heute, besonders bemerkenswert, als ein Resümee eines größeren Teils seiner Philosophie. Sie heißt: ›Ein Ausdruck hat nur im Strome des Lebens Bedeutung.‹ Wittgenstein meinte, dass dieser Aphorismus in einem seiner Manuskripte niedergeschrieben sei; und vielleicht war er es, doch habe ich ihn nirgends gesehen.« Ebd.

83 Als Selbstzitat seiner Arbeitsweise ebenso wie als Gebrauchsgegenstand entwarf Weiner 1977 ein mit dem Text der ausgestellten Arbeit bedrucktes Klebeetikett als Einladungskarte für seine Ausstellung bei Konrad Fischer, Düsseldorf.

92 "The Only Thing That Knows Its Own Essence Is the Thing Itself: Interview by Carles Guerra" (1995), in Fietzek / Stemmrich 2004 (see note 7), p. 336.
93 Interview in Preparation 1989 (see note 88), p. 209.
94 *COS Magazine* 8, "Work" (Spring and Summer 2011), pp. 68, 82.
95 Thomas Khurana, "Elena Espositos Buch über die Paradoxien der Mode," *Texte zur Kunst* 56 (2004), p. 165.
96 See Bettina Pousttichi, "Zu Gast bei Bettina Pousttichi," *Art: Das Kunstmagazin* 11 (November 2010), p. 20. See also Marcus Neufanger, *Buch für Buch / Cover to Cover: Schaufensterausstellung der Buchhandlung Walther König* (Cologne, 2011).
97 "Lawrence Weiner at Amsterdam: Interview by Willoughby Sharp" (1971), in Fietzek / Stemmrich 2004 (see note 7), p. 48.
98 Harmut Böhme and Johannes Endres, eds., *Der Code der Leidenschaften: Fetischismus in den Künsten* (Munich, 2010).
99 Weiner 1996 (see note 67), reprinted in Fietzek / Stemmrich 2004 (see note 7), p. 345.
100 Goldstein 2007 (see note 8), p. 134.
101 Rosenzweig 1990 (see note 60), p. 237.
102 Schenker 2007 (see note 29), p. 139.
103 "I come from a tradition of great admirers of Walter Benjamin, but am particularly interested in the human being, the dignity of the object, and this really hasn't anything to do with metaphor or allegory." See "Interview by Caroline Schneider" (1994), in Fietzek / Stemmrich 2004 (see note 7), p. 324.
104 Schenker 2007 (see note 29), p. 138.
105 Michel Foucault, "Of Other Spaces," trans. Jay Miscowiec, *Diacritics* 16, no. 1 (Spring 1986), p. 27; originally published in French as "Des espace autres" in *Architecture / Mouvement / Continuité* (October 1984).

84 »Lawrence Weiner's ›Plowmans Lunch‹. Interview by Michael Gibbs«, in: Gerti Fietzek und Gregor Stemmrich (Hrsg.), *Having Been Said. Writings & Interviews of Lawrence Weiner 1968–2003*, Ostfildern-Ruit 2004, S. 141 ff., hier S. 142.
85 Engl. Original in einem E-Mail Lawrence Weiners an die Autorin, 19.3.2011.
86 Engl. Original s. *Weiner* 2008 (wie Anm. 28). Vgl. auch Weiners Aussage, eine Arbeit zu machen sei der leidenschaftliche Versuch, genug Form zu zeigen, um anzuziehen *(Nau Em I Art Belong Yumi*, Brüssel 1994, o. S.).
87 Suzy Menkes zur Fashion Week, Berlin, in: *Focus*, 27, 2011, S. 79.
88 »Interview im Vorfeld der Konferenz ›Kunst trifft Wissenschaft und Spiritualität in einer veränderten Ökonomie‹« (1990), in: Fietzek / Stemmrich 2004 (wie Anm. 7), S. 220–227, hier S. 220.
89 Heraklit, »Fragment B 49a«, zit. nach: Bruno Snell (Hrsg.), *Heraklit. Fragmente*, München 1979, S. 19.
90 Markus Gabriel, »Zum philosophischen Ansatz Wolfram Hogrebes«, in: Wolfram Hogrebe, *Die Wirklichkeit des Denkens. Vorträge der Gadamer Professur*, hrsg. von Jens Halfwasser und Markus Gabriel, Heidelberg 2007, S. 82.
91 Auf das Cover des Skizzenbuchs, in dem sich der Wittgenstein-Aphorismus befindet, ist ein Zitat aus Mao Tse Tung, *Über den Widerspruch / On Contradiction*, auf den Umschlag geklebt: »Processes change, old processes and old contradictions disappear, new processes and new contradictions emerge, and the methods of resolving contradictions differ accordingly.«
92 »Das einzige, was seine eigene Essenz kennt, ist die Sache selbst. Interview von Carles Guerra« (1995), in: Fietzek / Stemmrich 2004 (wie Anm. 7), S. 363–368, hier S. 365.
93 »Interview im Vorfeld der Konferenz ›Kunst trifft Wissenschaft und Spiritualität in einer veränderten Ökonomie‹« (1990), in: Fietzek / Stemmrich 2004 (wie Anm. 7), S. 220–227, hier S. 226.
94 Engl. Original s. *Work. COS Magazine*, hrsg. von Gert Jonkers und Jop van Bennekom in Zusammenarbeit mit COS, 8, Frühjahr / Sommer 2011, S. 68 und 82.
95 Thomas Khurana, »Elena Espositos Buch über die Paradoxien der Mode«, in: *Texte über Kunst*, 56, 2004, S. 165.
96 Vgl. Bettina Pousttichi in: *art. Kunstmagazin*, 11, 2010, S. 20, oder Marcus Neufanger, *Buch für Buch / Cover To Cover. Schaufensterausstellung der Buchhandlung Walther König*, Köln 2011.
97 »Lawrence Weiner in Amsterdam. Interview von Willoughby Sharp« (1972), in: Fietzek / Stemmrich 2004 (wie Anm. 7), S. 45–57, hier S. 50.
98 Hartmut Böhme und Johannes Endres (Hrsg.), *Der Code der Leidenschaften. Fetischismus in den Künsten*, München 2010, S. 11.
99 »Eine Übersetzung von einer Sprache in eine andere«, in: Fietzek / Stemmrich 2004 (wie Anm. 7), S. 373 f., hier S. 374.
100 Engl. Original s. Goldstein 2007 (wie Anm. 8), S. 134.
101 »Interview von Phyllis Rosenzweig« (1990), in: Fietzek / Stemmrich 2004 (wie Anm. 7), S. 255–257, hier S. 257.
102 Schenker (wie Anm. 29), S. 139.
103 »Ich komme aus einer Tradition, in der Walter Benjamin sehr geschätzt wird, aber was mich interessiert, ist vor allem der Mensch und die Würde des Gegenstands, und das hat nichts mit Metapher oder Allegorie zu tun.« »Weiner im Interview mit Caroline Schneider« (1994), in: Fietzek / Stemmrich 2004 (wie Anm. 7), S. 352–355, hier S. 352.
104 Schenker 2007 (wie Anm. 29), S. 138.
105 Michel Foucault, *Des Espaces autres*, Typoskript des gleichnamigen Vortrages am Cercle d'Etudes Architecturales, Paris, 14.3.1967 (Erstveröffentlichung: Oktober 1984); Michel Foucault, »Andere Räume«, aus dem Französischen von Michael Seitter, in: *Aisthesis. Wahrnehmung heute oder Perspektiven einer anderen Ästhetik*, hrsg. von Karlheinz Barck u. a., Leipzig 1999, S. 46.

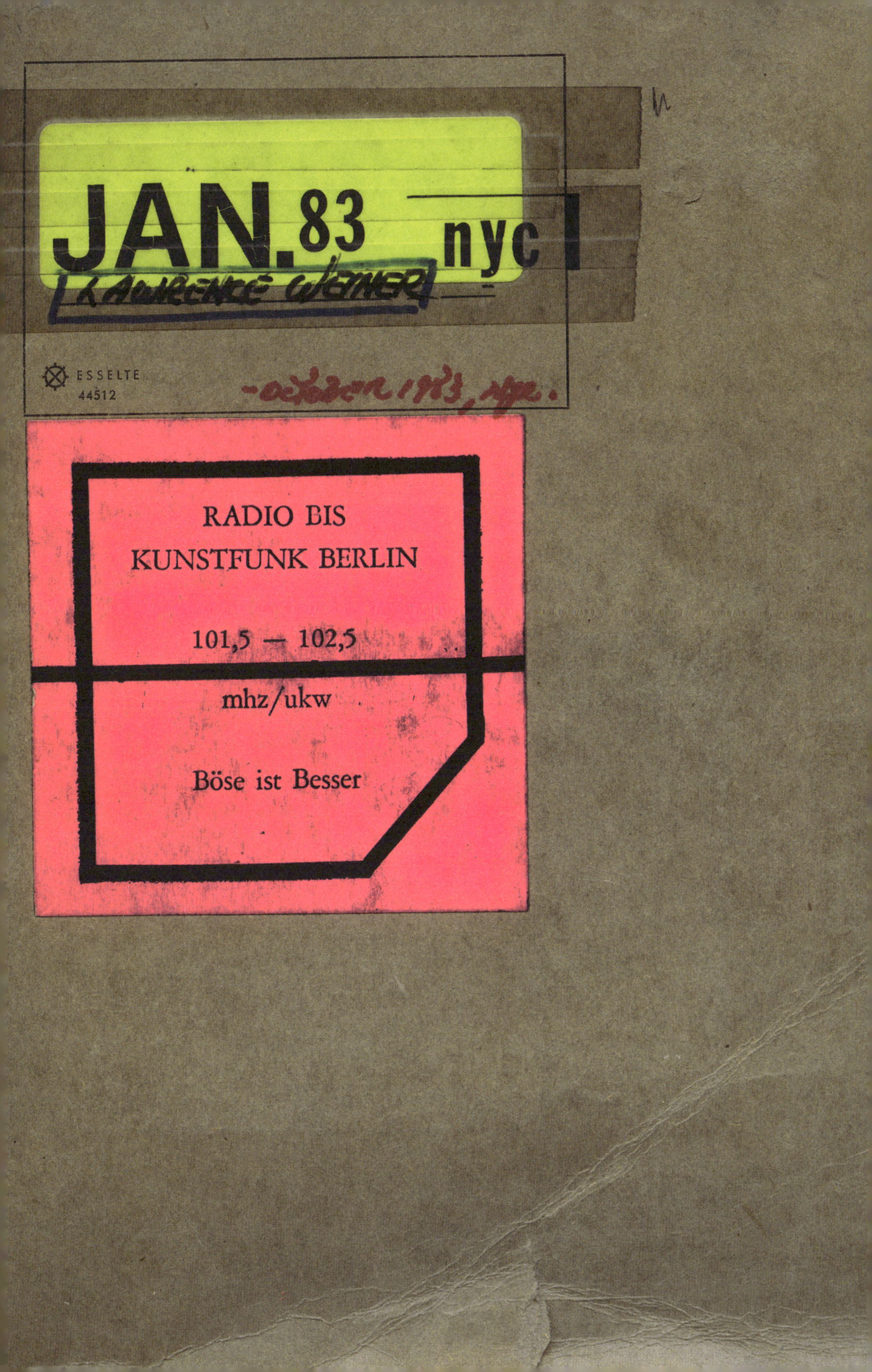
JAN. 83 nyc
LAWRENCE WEINER
ESSELTE
44512
-october 1983, nyc.
RADIO BIS
KUNSTFUNK BERLIN
101,5 — 102,5
mhz/ukw
Böse ist Besser

GENUG HIERVON ODER GENUG DAVON

GENUG HIERVON ODER GENOG DAVON

CAT. # 7
94

KUNSTHAUS BREGENZ

GENUG

THIS & THAT

DASS

ENOEG VAN DIT
F
ENOEG VAN DAT.

DIESEN

GLOSS RED
COMPUTER LETTERS.

GENUG HIERVON ODER GENUG DAVON
GENUG HIERVON ODER GENUG DAVON

RED
GLOSS

BLACK
GLOSS

RED
GLOSS

BLACK.
GLOSS

WIEN

MUSEUM FÜR ANGEWANDTE KUNST

EACH TO THEIR ABILITIES

1. THE ARTIST MAY .

2. THE WORK MAY BE FAB . .

3. THE WORK NEED NOT . . .

EACH NEED .

EACH TO THEIR NEEDS
&
EACH TO THEIR ABILITIES

JEDER NACH SEINEN BEDÜRFNISSEN
JEDER NACH SEINEN FÄHIGKEITEN

EACH BEING EQUAL & CONSISTENT
WITH THE INTENT OF THE ARTIST
THE DECISION AS TO CONDITION
RESTS WITH THE RECEIVER .
UPON THE OCCASION OF RECEIVERSHIP

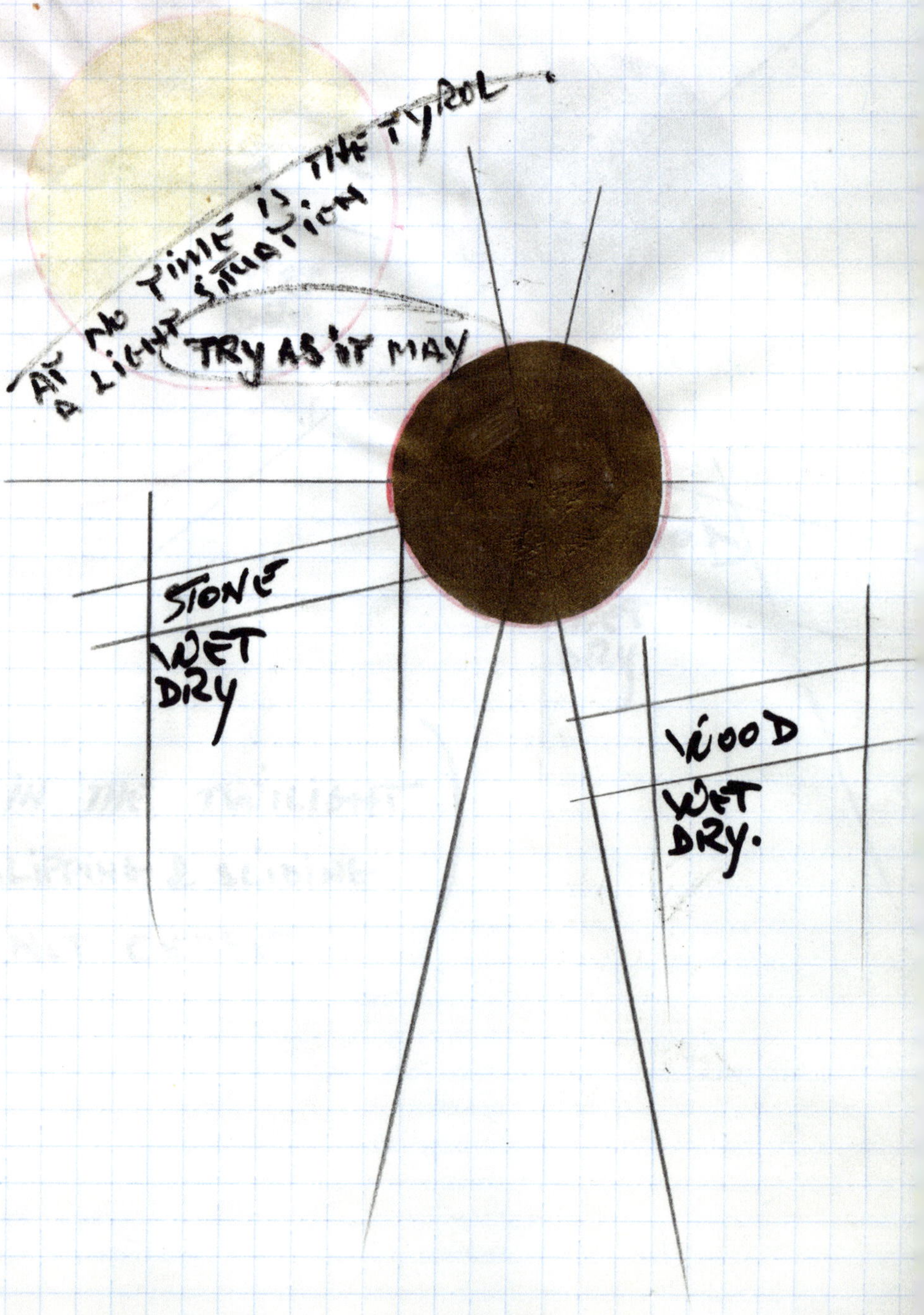
AT NO TIME IS THE TYROL
A LIGHT SITUATION
TRY AS IT MAY
STONE
WET
DRY
WOOD
WET
DRY.

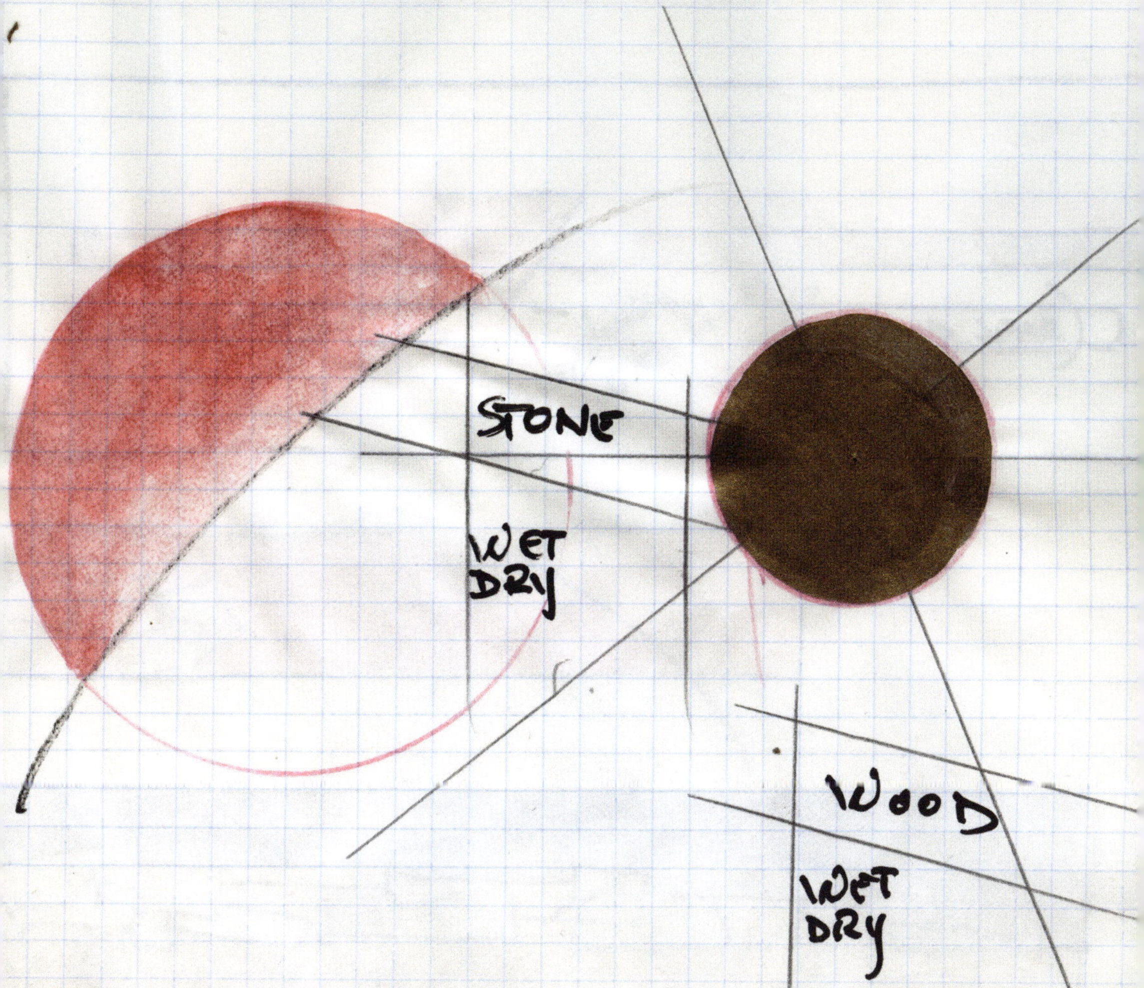

(EVEN IN THE TWILIGHT
THE SLIPPING & SLIDING
DOES NOT CEASE)

METEORITES

METEORS.

ALL THE THINGS THAT FALL OUT OF THE SKY.

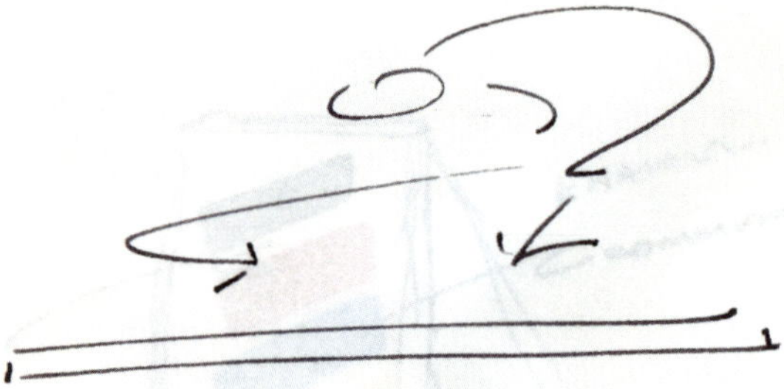

ALL THE THINGS WE THINK MUST HAVE FALLEN OUT OF THE SKY.

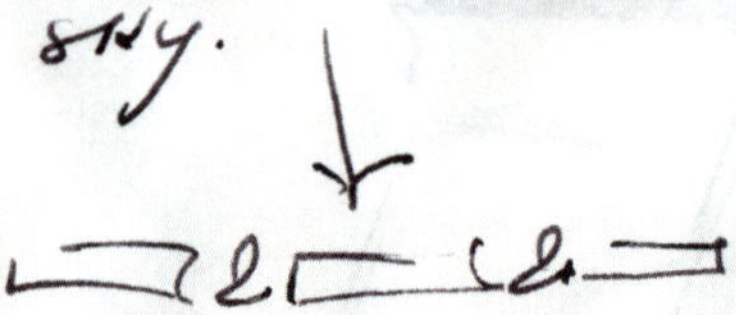

ONLY NUR BERLIN

ALL THE THINGS WE CANNOT FIND A RESEMBLANCE.

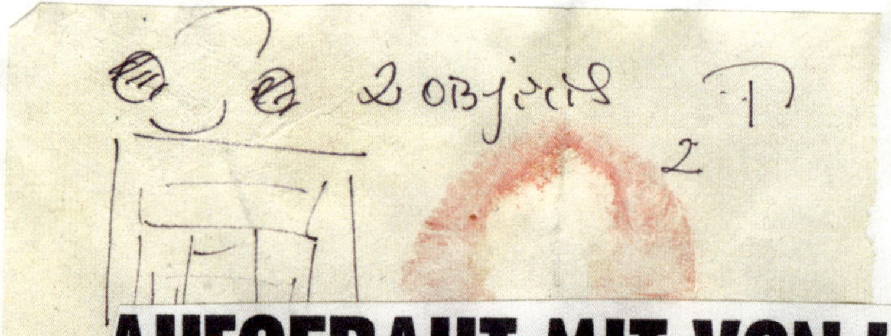

AUFGEBAUT MIT VON HIMMEL

GEFALLENEN STEINEN

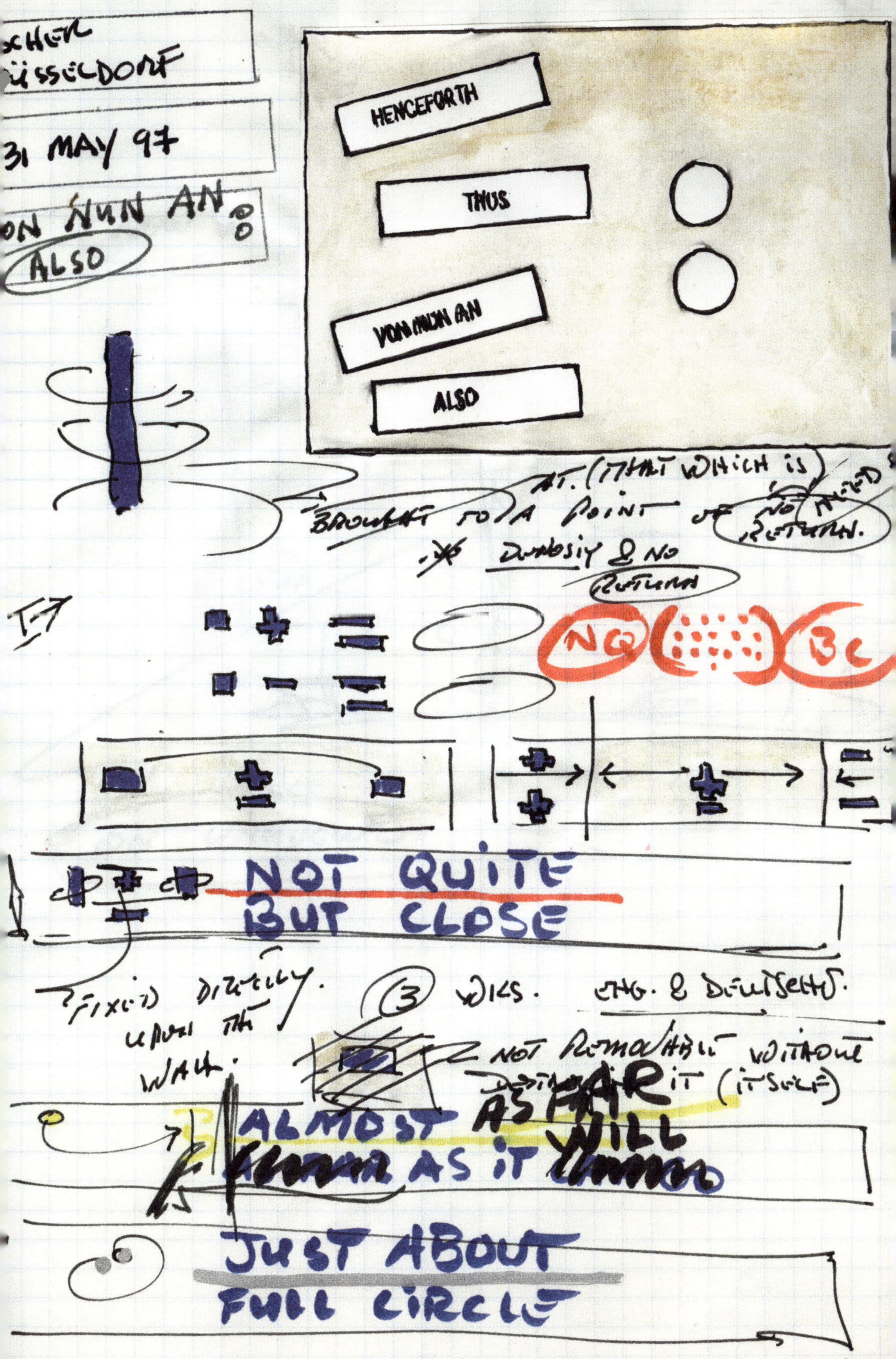
31 MAY 97
ALSO
HENCEFORTH
THUS
VON NUN AN
ALSO
NOT QUITE
BUT CLOSE
3 WKS.
NOT REMOVABLE WITHOUT
ALMOST
AS IT
WILL
JUST ABOUT
FULL CIRCLE

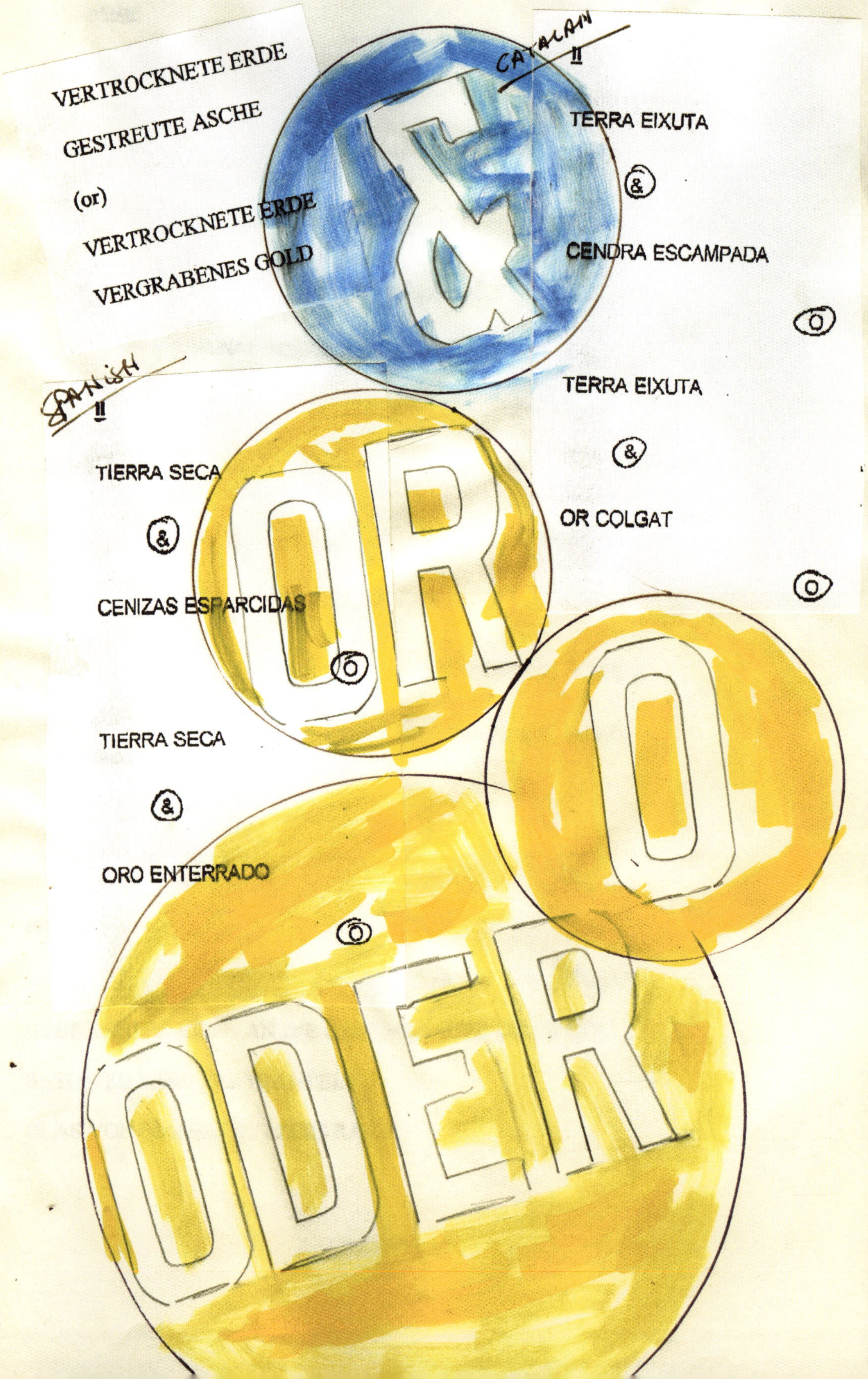
VERTROCKNETE ERDE
GESTREUTE ASCHE
(or)
VERTROCKNETE ERDE
VERGRABENES GOLD
CATALAN
II
TERRA EIXUTA
&
CENDRA ESCAMPADA
O
TERRA EIXUTA
&
OR COLGAT
O
SPANISH
II
TIERRA SECA
&
CENIZAS ESPARCIDAS
O
TIERRA SECA
&
ORO ENTERRADO
O
&
OR
O
ODER

BLOWN AWAY
UNDER CERTAIN CIRCUMSTANCES

Weggeblasen
unter gewissen Umständen

PEBBLES AND STRAW STREWN ON A
LEVEL WITH THE SURFACE OF WATER

KIESEL UND STROH GESTREUT ÜBER
DIE EBENE DER WASSER-OBERFLÄCHE

Etwas Rot gemischt mit Weiss
Etwas Blau gemischt mit Weiss
Etwas Grün gemischt mit Weiss
Etwas Violett gemischt mit Weiss
Etwas Gelb gemischt mit Weiss
(AUSSERHALB EINER GRUNDFRAGE)

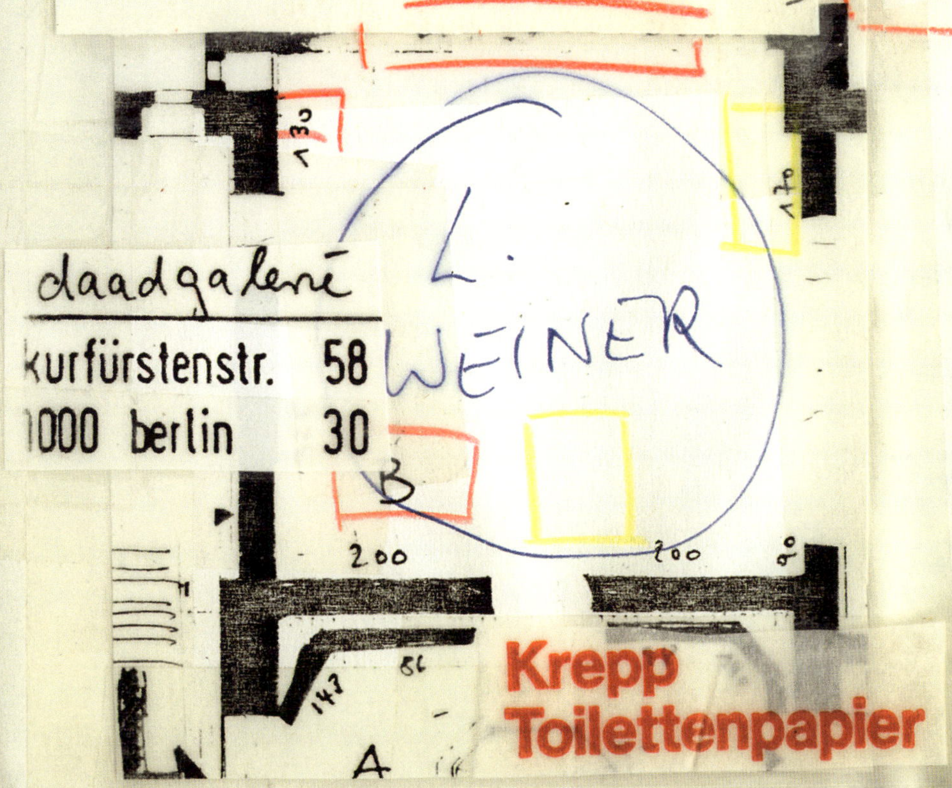

DAAD Kunstübungen Berlin

6cm – 10cm Balkon Wand

BEING WITHIN THE CONTEXT OF [A] PLACE

·

INNERHALB DES ZUSAMMENHANGES VON [EINEM] ORT SICH BEFINDEND.

BROKEN OFF / ABGEBROCHEN

BEING WITHIN THE CONTEXT OF [A] PLACE.

·

INNERHALB DES ZUSAMMENHANGES VON [EINEM] ORT SICH BEFINDEND.

im ÖFFENTLICHEN EIGENTUM ← FOR KAT. CREDIT

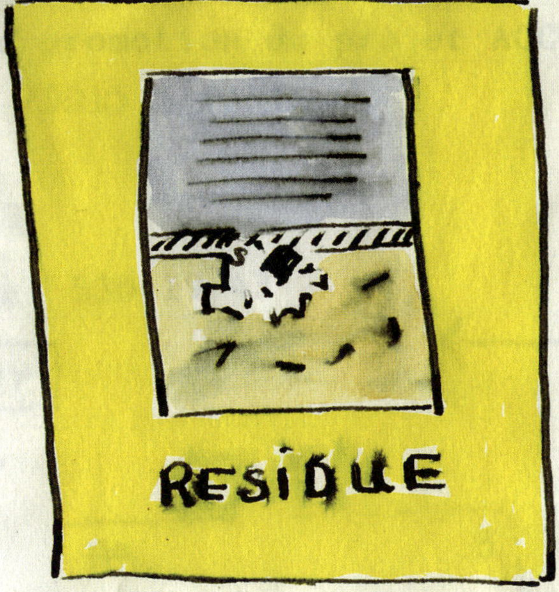

DECAYING IS ALONG THE EMBRACING OF THE INEVITABLE. (ENTROPY.)

außerhalb einer Grundfrage

PILES OF RUST - EACH LARGER THAN THE ORIGINAL PILE OF IRON

[AIR · WATER. - LESS DENSE.]

GISTEREN MENSEN

BRIGITTE MARCH

ZURÜCKGELASSEN

ZURÜCKGELASSEN AFTER THE WIND.

CAR PLATE. (SCHILD

~~NO HOLES.~~

NO MEANS OF SUPPORT.

BLACK GLOSS ON GLOSS WHT ENHAMEL.

ZURÜCK . . .

AFTER THE WIND

Miës van der Rohe, Ludwig (lōōt'vĭkh mē'ĕs vän dĕr rō'ŭ), 1886–, German-American architect, one of the BAUHAUS architects. He was an assistant to Peter Behrens, in whose office Walter Gropius and Le Corbusier had also been trained. After the First World War, Miës produced (1921) a design for an all-glass skyscraper which attracted international attention. In 1927 he was placed in charge of the Werkbund Housing Exposition at Stuttgart, for which he built a modern apartment house, and in 1929 had charge of the German section of the Barcelona International Exposition. In 1938 he became director of architecture at the Armour Institute (now the Illinois Institute of Technology) and among other projects has designed the buildings for their new campus. Miës's buildings are distinguished by their functional composition based on the lines of interior walls and the planes of floors and roof. In façades he uses great planes of glass or unobstructed wide openings. His work includes residences and workmen's dwellings. Miës became a U.S. citizen in 1944.

Krefelder Kunst

Kaiser Wilhelm

Museum Haus E

Verwaltung:
Karlsplatz 35, 41
Telefon 02151/7

KREFELD - HAUS ESTERS 88

HELOISE "A ROOM (HOUSE) OF ONES' OWN"

ART DOES FURNISH A ROOM

RED TOP yellow SKIRT
RED SHOES

LIGHT APPARATUS AS LIGHT

ARCHITECTURE WORKS

FURNITURE AS SCULPTURE.
FURNITURE AS SUPPORT

NOISE (PERIOD SPEAKERS.)

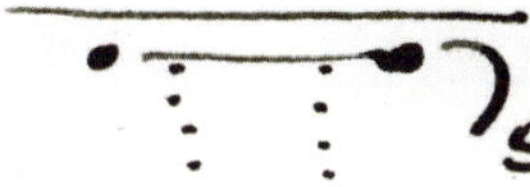

PICTURE HANGING

5cm

CAT. AS BOOK (NO SPECIFIC FORMAT)

HIGHT OF ALL RMS 2.93/95 m.

(Dr. Julian Heynen)
stellvertr. Museumsleiter

DR. GERHARD STORCK

Previous pages:
Sketchbooks, 1975–97
Vorherige Seiten:
Skizzenbücher, 1975–1997

WORKS
PRESENTED IN THE GERMAN LANGUAGE

ARBEITEN
VORGESTELLT IM DEUTSCHSPRACHIGEN RAUM

A SERIES OF STAKES SET IN THE GROUND AT REGULAR INTERVALS TO FORM A RECTANGLE 0001
TWINE STRUNG FROM STAKE TO STAKE TO DEMARK A GRID
A RECTANGLE REMOVED FROM THIS RECTANGLE

ONE QUART EXTERIOR GREEN INDUSTRIAL ENAMEL THROWN ON A BRICK WALL 0002

6 TEN PENNY COMMON STEEL NAILS DRIVEN INTO FLOOR AT INDICATED TERMINAL POINTS 0003

ONE FLUORESCEIN SEA MARKER POURED INTO THE SEA 0004

6" X 6" X 1/8" MASONITE SQUARES BRUSH PAINTED WITH INDUSTRIAL ENAMEL ALLOWED 0006
TO DRY SANDED FOR ONE MINUTE BY A FLAT FINISHING SANDER SECURED TO THE WALL
FLOOR OR CEILING BY SCREWS

GLOSS WHITE LACQUER SPRAYED FOR TWO MINUTES AT 40 lb. PRESSURE DIRECTLY 0007
UPON THE FLOOR

ONE 14 OZ. AEROSOL CAN ENAMEL SPRAYED TO CONCLUSION DIRECTLY UPON THE FLOOR 0008

TWO SHEETS OF STANDARD 8½" X 11" TYPING PAPER BONDED AT EQUAL DISTANCE 0009
FROM ON EITHER SIDE OF THE WHITE LINE OF THE LOS ANGELES FREEWAY
THE UTILIZATION OF A BROKEN DOUBLE OR OTHERWISE LINE IN NO WAY ALTERS THE INTENT

A RECTANGULAR FIELD CRATERING WITH A RECTANGLE IMPOSED 12 CHARGES EXPLODED 0011
SIMULTANEOUSLY

3 STANDARD MILLED CLEAR PINE 1" X 3" PLANKS OF ARBITRARY LENGTH WITH THE THIRD 0014
PLANK SHORTER THAN THE PRECEDING TWO GLUED TOGETHER AND SECURED TO THE WALL
AT INDICATED SCREW POINTS

EIN RECHTECK GEBILDET AUS EINER REIHE VON PFÄHLEN IN REGELMÄSSIGEN ABSTÄNDEN
IN DEN BODEN GESCHLAGEN
EIN QUADRATNETZ GEBILDET AUS VON PFAHL ZU PFAHL GESPANNTEN SEILEN
EIN QUADRAT ENTFERNT AUS DIESEM QUADRAT

EIN LITER GRÜNER HANDELSÜBLICHER AUSSENLACK AUF EINE ZIEGELWAND GEWORFEN

6 TENPENNY STAHLNÄGEL AN ANGEGEBENEN PUNKTEN IN DEN FUSSBODEN GETRIEBEN

EINE MEERWASSER LEUCHTFARBENMARKIERUNG IN DAS MEER GEGOSSEN

EINE 6 X 6 X 1/8 INCHES STARKE PRESS-SPAN-PLATTE ANGESTRICHEN MIT HANDELSÜBLICHEM LACK
GETROCKNET EINE MINUTE LANG GESCHLIFFEN MIT SCHRAUBEN AN WAND FUSSBODEN
ODER DECKE BEFESTIGT

WEISSER HOCHGLANZ LACK WÄHREND ZWEI MINUTEN MIT EINEM DRUCK VON 40 POUNDS AUF DEN
BODEN GESPRÜHT

EINE 14 OZ. AEROSOL-LACK-SPRÜHDOSE DIREKT AUF DEN FUSSBODEN AUSGESPRÜHT

ZWEI BLÄTTER NORMALES 8½ X 11 INCHES SCHREIBMASCHINEN-PAPIER IM GLEICHEN ABSTAND AUF
BEIDEN SEITEN DER WEISSEN LINIE AUF DEM LOS ANGELES FREEWAY ANGEBRACHT
DIE VERWENDUNG EINER UNTERBROCHENEN DOPPELTEN ODER ANDEREN LINIE VERÄNDERT DIE
BEDEUTUNG DES VORHABENS IN KEINER WEISE

EIN RECHTECKIGES FELD GEBILDET AUS EXPLOSIONSKRATERN DURCH ZWÖLF GLEICHZEITIG
GEZÜNDETE LADUNGEN

3 NORMALE MASCHINENGESÄGTE HELLE 1 X 3 INCHES KIEFERNBRETTER BELIEBIGER LÄNGE DAS
DRITTE BRETT KÜRZER ALS DIE VORANGEHENDEN ZUSAMMENGEKLEBT UND BEI BEZEICHNETEN
SCHRAUBPUNKTEN AN DER WAND BEFESTIGT

ONE REGULAR RECTANGULAR OBJECT PLACED ACROSS AN INTERNATIONAL BOUNDARY ALLOWED TO REST THEN TURNED TO AND TURNED UPON TO INTRUDE THE PORTION OF ONE COUNTRY INTO THE OTHER 0015

ONE PINT GLOSS WHITE LACQUER POURED DIRECTLY UPON THE FLOOR AND ALLOWED TO DRY 0016

TWO MINUTES OF SPRAY PAINT DIRECTLY UPON THE FLOOR FROM A STANDARD AEROSOL SPRAY CAN 0017

ONE SQUARE LIMESTONE SLAB OF ARBITRARY THICKNESS ONE SHEET OF BROWN WRAPPING PAPER BONDED EVEN WITH THE EDGES TO THE TOP SURFACE OF THE LIMESTONE 0018

A 36" X 36" REMOVAL TO THE LATHING OR SUPPORT WALL OF PLASTER OR WALLBOARD FROM A WALL 0021

AN AMOUNT OF BLEACH POURED UPON A RUG AND ALLOWED TO BLEACH 0024

A WALL CRATERED BY A SINGLE SHOTGUN BLAST 0026

FIRECRACKER RESIDUE OF EXPLOSIONS AT EACH CORNER OF THE EXHIBITION AREA 0027

AN OBJECT TOSSED FROM ONE COUNTRY TO ANOTHER 0028

THE RESIDUE OF A FLARE IGNITED UPON A BOUNDARY 0029

A RECTANGULAR CANVAS AND STRETCHER SUPPORT WITH A RECTANGULAR REMOVAL FROM ONE OF THE FOUR CORNERS SPRAYED WITH PAINT FOR A TIME ELAPSURE 0035

ONE QUART HEAVY GRADE MOTOR OIL POURED INTO THE GULF STREAM 0044

EIN GLEICHMÄSSIGER RECHTECKIGER GEGENSTAND AUF EINE INTERNATIONALE GRENZE GELEGT
MIT DER ERLAUBNIS DORT ZU BLEIBEN UMGEDREHT UM DEN TEIL DES EINEN LANDES
IN DAS ANDERE ZU VERLEGEN

EIN HALBER LITER GLÄNZENDER WEISSER LACK DIREKT AUF DEN FUSSBODEN AUSGEGOSSEN
GETROCKNET

FARBE AUS EINER DOSE ZWEI MINUTEN LANG AUF DEN FUSSBODEN VERSPRÜHT

EINE QUADRATISCHE KALKSTEINPLATTE BELIEBIGER STÄRKE EIN BOGEN BRAUNES PACKPAPIER
MIT DER OBEREN SEITE DES KALKSTEINS KANTENGLEICH VERBUNDEN

EIN 36 X 36 INCHES GROSSER AUSSCHNITT BIS AUF DEN GRUND DES LATTEN- ODER MAUERWERKS
AUS EINER GIPSWAND ODER WANDPLATTE

EINE MENGE BLEICHMITTEL AUF EINEN TEPPICH GEGOSSEN UND BLEICHEN GELASSEN

EINE WAND DURCH EINEN EINZIGEN SCHROTFLINTENSCHUSS MIT KRATERN ÜBERSÄT

RÜCKSTÄNDE EINES EXPLODIERTEN FEUERWERKSKÖRPERS IN JEDER ECKE DES
AUSSTELLUNGSGELÄNDES

EIN GEGENSTAND VON EINEM LAND INS ANDERE GEWORFEN

DER RÜCKSTAND EINER FACKEL DIE AUF EINER GRENZE ENTZÜNDET WURDE

EIN RECHTECK ENTFERNT AUS EINER ECKE EINER RECHTECKIGEN LEINWAND AUF KEILRAHMEN EINE
ZEITLANG MIT FARBE BESPRÜHT

EIN LITER SCHWERES MOTORÖL IN DEN GOLFSTROM GEGOSSEN

5 GALLONS WATER BASE TEMPERA PAINT POURED DIRECTLY UPON THE FLOOR AND ALLOWED TO REMAIN FOR THE DURATION OF THE EXHIBITION 0046

A 6 cm X 6 cm REMOVAL TO THE LATHING OR SUPPORT WALL OF PLASTER OR WALLBOARD FROM A WALL 0049

1000 GERMAN MARKS WORTH MEDIUM BULK MATERIAL TRANSFERRED FROM ONE COUNTRY TO ANOTHER 0051

ONE KILOGRAM OF LACQUER POURED UPON A FLOOR 0052

ONE STEEL I BEAM PLACED UPON A BOUNDARY AND ALLOWED TO REST 0053

A SQUARE REMOVAL FROM A RUG IN USE 0054

A CUP OF SEA WATER POURED UPON THE FLOOR 0055

ONE QUART ANTI FREEZE POURED UPON THE ICE LITTLE AMERICA ROSS DEPENDANCY ANTARCTICA AND ALLOWED TO REMAIN 0056
ONE QUART ANTI FREEZE POURED UPON THE ICE NORWAY STATION PRINCESS MARTHA COAST QUEEN MAUD LAND ANTARCTICA AND ALLOWED TO REMAIN

AN OBJECT SECURED UPON A BOUNDARY 0062

A TRANSLATION FROM ONE LANGUAGE TO ANOTHER 0071

AN ABRIDGEMENT OF AN ABUTMENT TO ON NEAR OR ABOUT THE ARTIC CIRCLE 0073

THE ARCTIC CIRCLE SHATTERED 0074

A GLACIER VANDALIZED 0075

20 LITER TEMPERA AUF WASSERFARBENBASIS DIREKT AUF DEN FUSSBODEN GEGOSSEN FÜR DIE DAUER DER AUSSTELLUNG

EIN 6 X 6 cm GROSSER AUSSCHNITT BIS AUF DEN GRUND DES LATTEN- ODER MAUERWERKS AUS EINER GIPSWAND ODER WANDPLATTE

MATERIAL MITTLEREN UMFANGS IM WERT VON 1000 DEUTSCHE MARK VON EINEM LAND IN EIN ANDERES GEBRACHT

EIN KILOGRAMM LACK AUF EINEN FUSSBODEN GEGOSSEN

EIN STAHL-T-TRÄGER AUF EINE GRENZE GELEGT WO ER LIEGEN BLEIBT

ENTFERNEN EINES QUADRATES AUS EINEM TEPPICH DER BENUTZT WIRD

EINE TASSE MEERWASSER AUF DEN BODEN GEGOSSEN

EIN VIERTEL FROSTSCHUTZMITTEL AUF DAS EIS IN LITTLE AMERICA ROSS DEPENDANCY ANTARKTIK GESCHÜTTET UND DORT BELASSEN
EIN VIERTEL FROSTSCHUTZMITTEL AUF DAS EIS DER NORWAY STATION PRINCESS MARTHA COAST QUEEN MAUD LAND ANTARKTIK GESCHÜTTET UND DORT BELASSEN

EIN OBJEKT GESICHERT AUF EINER GRENZE

EINE ÜBERSETZUNG AUS EINER SPRACHE IN EINE ANDERE

EINE VERKÜRZUNG DES EIN STREBEPFEILER ZUM AUF NAHE ODER UM DEN NÖRDLICHEN POLARKREIS

DER POLARKREIS ZERTRÜMMERT

EIN GLETSCHER VERWÜSTET

EINE STADT EINGEKÜSTET

EINE TURBULENZ INNERHALB EINES GEWÄSSERS HERGEFÜHRT

VERGOREN

VERSETZT

ETWAS UNTEILBARES GETEILT REDUZIERT ODER VERTEILT

DIE BESEITIGUNG EINES BODENSCHATZES

GEBRACHT

EIN DIREKTER AFFRONT AUF EINEN NATÜRLICHEN WASSERWEG

GEMALT

VERKLEINERT

ÜBERSETZT

GESTELLT

GEWORFEN

GEBROCHEN

EINE ANHÄUFUNG VON INFORMATIONEN VON HIER NACH DA GEBRACHT

EARTH TO EARTH ASHES TO ASHES DUST TO DUST 0151

SOMETHING OLD SOMETHING NEW SOMETHING BORROWED SOMETHING BLUE 0153

AND THEN THERE WERE NONE 0154

TO THE SEE 0157-0161
ON THE SEA
FROM THE SEA
AT THE SEA
BORDERING THE SEE

TO THE LAKE 0162-0166
ON THE LAKE
FROM THE LAKE
AT THE LAKE
BORDERING THE LAKE

SLOWLY RAISED WATER 0167

FLOWED GENTLY 0168

FLOWED BRISKLY 0169

A CONCISE EXPLOSION NEAR AACHEN GERMANY UPON THE COMMON BOUNDARY GERMANY BELGIUM AND THE NETHERLANDS 0185

10 lbs. MERCURY TOSSED FROM FINLAND TO SWEDEN 0188

PERHAPS WHEN REPRODUCED 0206

PERHAPS WHEN RETRANSLATED 0210

ERDE ZU ERDE ASCHE ZU ASCHE STAUB ZU STAUB

ETWAS ALTES ETWAS NEUES ETWAS ÜBERNOMMENES ETWAS BLAUES

UND DANN WAR NICHTS DA

AN DIE SEE
AUF DIE SEE
VON DER SEE
IN DIE SEE
GRENZEND AN DIE SEE

AN DEM SEE
AUF DEM SEE
VON DEM SEE
IN DEM SEE
GRENZEND AN DEN SEE

LANGSAM GESTIEGENES WASSER

SANFT GEFLOSSEN

UNGESTÜM GEFLOSSEN

EINE PRÄZISE EXPLOSION IN DER NÄHE VON AACHEN AUF DER GEMEINSAMEN GRENZE ZWISCHEN DEUTSCHLAND BELGIEN UND DEN NIEDERLANDEN

10 PFUND QUECKSILBER VON FINNLAND NACH SCHWEDEN GEWORFEN

VIELLEICHT WENN REPRODUZIERT

VIELLEICHT WENN ZURÜCKÜBERSETZT

PERHAPS AFTER BEING REDONE 0215

TOPPLED FROM ABOVE 0216

COVERED FROM THE REAR 0217

WEAKENED FROM WITHIN 0218

MOVED FROM UP FRONT 0219

TILTED FROM BELOW 0220

SHIFTED FROM THE SIDE 0221

MIDDLE OF THE ROAD 0224

LEFT OF CENTER 0225

RIGHT OF CENTER 0226

BESIDE ITSELF 0229

UNDER AND OVER. OVER AND UNDER. AND UNDER AND OVER. AND OVER AND UNDER. 0234

RISEN AND FALLEN. FALLEN AND RISEN. AND RISEN AND FALLEN. AND FALLEN AND RISEN. 0240

LIGHT AND DARK. AND DARK AND LIGHT. 0244

VIELLEICHT NACHDEM ES NEU GEMACHT WORDEN IST

VON OBEN HER GESTÜRZT

VOM RÜCKEN HER GEDECKT

VON INNEN HER GESCHWÄCHT

VON VORNE HER BEWEGT

VON UNTEN HER GEKIPPT

VON DER SEITE HER GESCHOBEN

MITTE DER STRASSE

LINKS VON DER MITTE

RECHTS VON DER MITTE

NEBEN SICH

UNTER UND ÜBER. ÜBER UND UNTER. UND UNTER UND ÜBER. UND ÜBER UND UNTER.

GESTIEGEN UND GEFALLEN. GEFALLEN UND GESTIEGEN. UND GESTIEGEN UND GEFALLEN. UND GEFALLEN UND GESTIEGEN.

HELL UND DUNKEL. UND DUNKEL UND HELL.

OVERTURNED. TURNED OVER. AND OVERTURNED. AND TURNED OVER. 0245

BROKEN OFF 0251

AFFECTED AS TO NOISE AND/OR SILENCE 0261
EFFECTED AS TO NOISE AND/OR SILENCE

CURTAILED 0264
DISENGAGED **AS TO NOISE AND/OR SILENCE**
RESTRAINED
WEAKENED
TINGED

AS IF IT WERE 0267

TO SEE AND BE SEEN 0278

TO SHOW AND TO TELL 0280

LOUDLY MADE NOISE (forte) 0282-0285
AND/OR
MODERATELY LOUDLY (mezzoforte)

SOFTLY MADE NOISE (piano)
AND/OR
MODERATELY SOFTLY (mezzopiano)

NOISE MADE VERY LOUDLY (fortissimo)
AND/OR
MODERATELY LOUDLY (mezzoforte)

NOISE MADE VERY SOFTLY (pianissimo)
AND/OR
MODERATELY SOFTLY (mezzopiano)

UMGEDREHT. DREHTE UM. UND UMGEDREHT. UND DREHTE UM.

ABGEBROCHEN (ODER) AUFGEBROCHEN

AUSGELÖST DURCH GERÄUSCH ODER STILLE
BEWIRKT DURCH GERÄUSCH ODER STILLE

EINGESCHRÄNKT
ENTSPANNT DURCH GERÄUSCH ODER STILLE
ZURÜCKGEHALTEN
GESCHWÄCHT
GETÖNT

ALS WÄRE ES

SEHEN UND GESEHEN WERDEN

ZEIGEN UND SAGEN

LAUT GEMACHTES GERÄUSCH (forte)
UND/ODER
GEMÄSSIGT LAUT (mezzoforte)

LEISE GEMACHTES GERÄUSCH (piano)
UND/ODER
GEMÄSSIGT LEISE (mezzopiano)

GERÄUSCH SEHR LAUT GEMACHT (fortissimo)
UND/ODER
GEMÄSSIGT LAUT (mezzoforte)

GERÄUSCH SEHR LEISE GEMACHT (pianissimo)
UND/ODER
GEMÄSSIGT LEISE (mezzopiano)

MADE NOISELY 0287

GREEN AS WELL AS BLUE AS WELL AS RED 0289-0293
RED AND GREEN AND BLUE MORE OR LESS
RED OVER AND ABOVE GREEN OVER AND ABOVE BLUE
RED IN RELATION TO GREEN IN RELATION TO BLUE
RED IN LIEU OF GREEN IN LIEU OF BLUE

NOT MORE NOR LESS 0295
NOT LESS NOR MORE
NOT MORE GREEN NOR LESS GREEN
NOT MORE RED NOR LESS RED
NOT MORE BLUE NOR LESS BLUE

( ) DOWN A HATCH 0300-0302
DOWN A HATCH ( )

( ) UP A TREE
UP A TREE ( )

( ) AROUND A TOWN
AROUND A TOWN ( )

GERÄUSCHVOLL GEMACHT

GRÜN WIE AUCH BLAU WIE AUCH ROT
ROT UND GRÜN UND BLAU MEHR ODER WENIGER
ROT DARÜBER HINAUS GRÜN DARÜBER HINAUS BLAU
ROT IN BEZIEHUNG ZU GRÜN IN BEZIEHUNG ZU BLAU
ROT AN STELLE VON GRÜN AN STELLE VON BLAU

WEDER MEHR NOCH WENIGER
WEDER WENIGER NOCH MEHR
WEDER MEHR GRÜN NOCH WENIGER GRÜN
WEDER MEHR ROT NOCH WENIGER ROT
WEDER MEHR BLAU NOCH WENIGER BLAU

(   ) EINE HECKE ENTLANG
EINE HECKE ENTLANG (   )

(   ) EINEN BAUM HINAUF
EINEN BAUM HINAUF (   )

(   ) UM EINE STADT HERUM
UM EINE STADT HERUM (   )

FIRE ENGULFED (DIMINISHED) EMBRACED (SMOTHERED) BY WATER (HISSING) 0303–0310
FIRE EXTINGUISHED BY MEANS OTHER THAN WATER (FIRE AND WATER MIXED)

FIRE CRAMMED (ENGORGED) GLUTTED (OVERINDULGED) WITH WOOD (CRACKLING)
FIRE FED BY OTHER THAN WOOD (ANOTHER LOG ON THE FIRE)

EARTH ENGULFED (SOAKED) EMBRACED (COVERED) BY WATER (SIGHING)
EARTH WET BY MEANS OTHER THAN WATER (ANOTHER SOAKING)

EARTH CRAMMED (PUSHED) GLUTTED (DISPLACED) WITH WOOD (CLUNKING)
EARTH ENRICHED BY OTHER THAN WOOD (ONE MORE SHOVE)

AIR ENGULFED (SMOTHERED) EMBRACED (DIMINISHED) BY EARTH (SIGHING)
AIR PUSHED BY MEANS OTHER THAN EARTH (ONE MORE SHOVE)

AIR CRAMMED (SHOVED) GLUTTED (DISPLACED) WITH WOOD (SWISHING)
AIR ENRICHED BY OTHER THAN WOOD (ONE MORE SHOVE)

WATER ENGULFED (PUSHED) EMPRACED (PUSHED) BY EARTH (WHOOSHING)
WATER PUSHED BY MEANS OTHER THAN EARTH (SHOVED ONCE MORE)

WATER CRAMMED (PUSHED) GLUTTED (PUSHED) WITH WOOD (WHOOSHING)
WATER ENRICHED BY OTHER THAN EARTH (SHOVED ONCE MORE)

... AND THEN RELEGATED TO ANOTHER GENDER 0311–0312
... AND THEN UTILISED AS TO ANOTHER GENDER

AND THEN UNTENDED AS ... 0332

FEUER EINGEHÜLLT (VERMINDERT) UMARMT (ERSTICKT) DURCH WASSER (ZISCHEND)
FEUER DURCH ETWAS ANDERES ALS WASSER GELÖSCHT (FEUER UND WASSER GEMISCHT)

VOLLGESTOPFTES FEUER (VERSCHLUNGEN) ÜBERSÄTTIGT (ÜBERVERWÖHNT) MIT HOLZ (KNISTERND)
FEUER DURCH ETWAS ANDERES ALS HOLZ GENÄHRT (EIN ANDERES SCHEIT INS FEUER)

ERDE EINGEHÜLLT (DURCHTRÄNKT) UMARMT (VERDECKT) DURCH WASSER (SEUFZEND)
ERDE DURCH ETWAS ANDERES ALS WASSER GENÄSST (NOCH EINMAL DURCHNÄSSEN)

VOLLGESTOPFTE ERDE (GESTOSSEN) ÜBERSÄTTIGT (VERSETZT) MIT HOLZ (KLAPPERND)
ERDE DURCH ETWAS ANDERES ALS HOLZ BEREICHERT (EIN STOSS MEHR)

LUFT EINGEHÜLLT (ERSTICKT) UMARMT (VERMINDERT) DURCH ERDE (SEUFZEND)
LUFT DURCH ETWAS ANDERES ALS ERDE GESTOSSEN (EIN STOSS MEHR)

VOLLGESTOPFTE LUFT (GESTOSSEN) ÜBERSÄTTIGT (VERSETZT) MIT HOLZ (SAUSEN)
LUFT DURCH ETWAS ANDERES ALS HOLZ BEREICHERT (EIN STOSS MEHR)

WASSER EINGEHÜLLT (GESTOSSEN) UMARMT (GESTOSSEN) DURCH ERDE (ZISCHEN)
WASSER DURCH ETWAS ANDERES ALS ERDE GESTOSSEN (NOCHMAL GESTOSSEN)

VOLLGESTOPFTES WASSER (GESTOSSEN) ÜBERSÄTTIGT (GESTOSSEN) MIT HOLZ (ZISCHEN)
WASSER DURCH ETWAS ANDERES ALS ERDE BEREICHERT (NOCHMAL GESTOSSEN)

... UND DANN VERWIESEN AUF EIN ANDERES GESCHLECHT
... UND DANN VERWENDET IN HINSICHT AUF EIN ANDERES GESCHLECHT

UND DANN VERNACHLÄSSIGT WIE ...

HAVING BEEN IN A STRONG PROGRESSION 0333-0341
HAVING A STRONG PROGRESSION
HAVING BEEN IN AN ASCENDING PROGRESSION
HAVING AN ASCENDING PROGRESSION
HAVING BEEN IN A DESCENDING PROGRESSION
HAVING A DESCENDING PROGRESSION
HAVING BEEN IN A SUPERSTRONG PROGRESSION
HAVING A SUPERSTRONG PROGRESSION
HAVING BEEN IN A DECEPTIVE PROGRESSION
HAVING A DECEPTIVE PROGRESSION
HAVING BEEN IN A SUBSTITUTE PROGRESSION
HAVING A SUBSTITUTE PROGRESSION
HAVING BEEN IN AN ENRICHED PROGRESSION
HAVING AN ENRICHED PROGRESSION
HAVING BEEN IN A RETROGRADE PROGRESSION
HAVING A RETROGRADE PROGRESSION
HAVING BEEN IN A ROVING PROGRESSION
HAVING A ROVING PROGRESSION

MADE TO APPEAR AS 0363
(   ) MADE TO APPEAR AS (   )

MADE UNSUITABLE TO/FOR 0366-0369
PUT OUT OF PLACE TO/FOR
CATERED TO/FOR
NOT QUITE DONE TO/FOR

REVOKED FROM TIME TO TIME 0372

WITH AN ADVANCE DECLINED AT/TO (WITH OR WITHOUT LEVERAGE) 0374-0375
WITH AN ADVANCE REVERSED AT/FROM (WITH OR WITHOUT LEVERAGE)

WITH RELATION TO THE VARIOUS MANNERS OF USE FOR/OF VARIOUS THINGS: 0376-0378
HAVING HAD LEVERAGE FOR/OF (WITH OR WITHOUT DIRECTION)
HAVING HAD ADVANCEMENT FOR/OF (WITH OR WITHOUT DIRECTION)
HAVING HAD DIRECTION (WITH OR WITHOUT ...)

IN STARKEM FORTSCHREITEN GEWESEN SEIN
STARKES FORTSCHREITEN HABEN
IN ANSTEIGENDEM FORTSCHREITEN GEWESEN SEIN
ANSTEIGENDES FORTSCHREITEN HABEN
IN ABSTEIGENDEM FORTSCHREITEN GEWESEN SEIN
ABSTEIGENDES FORTSCHREITEN HABEN
IN EXTRASTARKEM FORTSCHREITEN GEWESEN SEIN
EXTRASTARKES FORTSCHREITEN HABEN
IN TRÜGERISCHEM FORTSCHREITEN GEWESEN SEIN
TRÜGERISCHES FORTSCHREITEN HABEN
IN ERSATZWEISEM FORTSCHREITEN GEWESEN SEIN
ERSATZWEISES FORTSCHREITEN HABEN
IN ANGEREICHERTEM FORTSCHREITEN GEWESEN SEIN
ANGREICHERTES FORTSCHREITEN HABEN
IN RÜCKLÄUFIGEM FORTSCHREITEN GEWESEN SEIN
RÜCKLÄUFIGES FORTSCHRHEITEN HABEN
IN UMHERSTREIFENDEM FORTSCHREITEN GEWESEN SEIN
UMHERSTREIFENDES FORTSCHREITEN HABEN

SOLL ERSCHEINEN ALS
( ) SOLL ERSCHEINEN ALS ( )

UNBRAUCHBAR GEMACHT FÜR/UM
WEGGESTELLT FÜR/UM
VORBEREITET FÜR/UM
NICHT GANZ FERTIG FÜR/UM

WIDERRUFEN VON ZEIT ZU ZEIT

MIT EINEM VORANGEHEN GEBEUGT BEI/NACH (MIT ODER OHNE HEBELDREHUNG)
MIT EINEM VORANGEHEN UMGEKEHRT BEI/VON (MIT ODER OHNE HEBELDREHUNG)

MIT BEZIEHUNG ZU DEN VERSCHIEDENEN ARTEN DES GEBRAUCHS FÜR/VON VERSCHIEDENARTIGE(N) DINGEN:
HEBELWIRKUNG GEHABT HABEND FÜR/VON (MIT ODER OHNE RICHTUNG)
FORTSCHRITT GEHABT HABEND FÜR/VON (MIT ODER OHNE RICHTUNG)
RICHTUNG GEHABT HABEND (MIT ODER OHNE ...)

WITH A RELATION TO THE VARIOUS MANNERS OF RESONANCE: 0380-0383
HAVING BEEN MOVED TO A POINT OF DISCORDANCE
(WITH OR WITHOUT PURPOSE)
HAVING BEEN VIBRATED TO A POINT OF DESTRUCTION
(WITHIN OR WITHOUT PURPOSE)
HAVING BEEN PLACED AS A MEANS TOWARDS RESONANCE
(DESPITE EFFECTIVENESS)
HAVING BEEN PLACED AS A MEANS AGAINST RESONANCE
(WITHIN THE CONTEXT OF EFFECTIVENESS)

HAVING BEEN REVOLVED 0384
(WITH OR WITHOUT A RESOLUTION)
(WITHIN OR WITHOUT)
(   ) REVOLVED
[BEING THEN WITHIN A CONTEXT OF REVOLUTION]

PLACED UPON A STONE 0389
[   ] UPON A STONE
(HAVING THUS BEEN ALTERED)

UP ON (IN) THE AIR 0393-0394
DOWN ON [IN] THE GROUND
BEING WITHIN THE CONTEXT OF [A] REACTION

BEING WITH THE CONTEXT OF REACTION:
UP ON (IN) THE AIR
DOWN ON [IN] THE GROUND

(SOMETIMES FOUND) 0397
WITHIN THE CONTEXT OF CHANGE:
ARRANGED AS (TO)
ARRANGED AS TO

OFTEN REPLAYED (PLAYED AGAIN) 0401

MIT EINEM BEZUG ZU DEN VERSCHIEDENEN ARTEN UND WEISEN VON RESONANZ:
BEWEGT BIS ZU EINEM PUNKT VON DISSONANZ
(MIT ODER OHNE VORSATZ)
IN SCHWINGUNG VERSETZT BIS ZU EINEM PUNKT VON ZERSTÖRUNG
(INNERHALB ODER AUSSERHALB EINES VORSATZES)
EINGESETZT ALS MITTEL GEGEN RESONANZ HIN
(TROTZ WIRKSAMKEIT)
EINGESETZT ALS MITTEL GEGEN RESONANZ
(IM KONTEXT VON WIRKSAMKEIT)

UMGEDREHT WORDEN
(MIT ODER OHNE ENTSCHLUSS)
(INNERHALB ODER AUSSERHALB)
(   ) UMGEDREHT
[DANN IN <u>EINEM</u> KONTEXT VON UMDREHUNG]

GELEGT AUF EINEN STEIN
[   ] AUF EINEN STEIN
(UND SO VERÄNDERT WORDEN)

HINAUF AUF (IN) DIE LUFT
HINUNTER AUF [IN] DIE ERDE
INNERHALB DES KONTEXTS VON [EINER] REAKTION

MIT DEM KONTEXT VON REAKTION:
HINAUF AUF (IN) DIE LUFT
HINUNTER AUF [IN] DIE ERDE

(MANCHMAL GEFUNDEN)
IM ZUSAMMENHANG VON VERÄNDERUNG:
ANGELEGT (UM ZU)
ANGELEGT UM ZU

OFT WIEDERHOLT (NOCHMALS GESPIELT)

UNCOVERED 0402
COVERED OVER
COVERED UP
WITH RELATION TO [A] VIEW

ON A ROUGH ______________ 0403-0405
BEING WITHIN THE CONTEXT OF [A] PLACE
ON A SMOOTH ____________
BEING WITHIN THE CONTEXT OF [A] PLACE
IN THE ROUGH
BEING WITHIN THE CONTEXT OF [A] PLACE

HAVING BRIDGED A (THE) GAP 0406
HAVING AVOIDED A (THE) PITFALL
HAVING MADE THE (A) POINT
ALL WITH AN END IN VIEW

hell ALSO dunkel	**hell ALSO dunkel**	0413
6 of one	**“6 ______________”**	
1/2 dozen	**“1/2 ____________”**	
of another	**of another**	

[BOTH WITHIN A RHYTHM OF SORTS (i.e.: THE TANGO)]

100 ROCKS ON A WALL 0414-0418
CUT
(TO A DOUBLED STANDARD)
99 ROCKS ON A WALL
FADED
(TO A DOUBLED STANDARD)
98 ROCKS ON A WALL
UPSTAGED
(TO A DOUBLED STANDARD)
97 ROCKS ON A WALL
WASHED OUT
(TO A DOUBLED STANDARD)
96 ROCKS ON A WALL
BLACKED OUT
(TO A DOUBLED STANDARD)

UNBEDECKT
ÜBERDECKT
AUFGEDECKT
IN BEZUG AUF [EINE] SICHT

INNERHALB DES ZUSAMMENHANGES VON [EINEM] ORT SICH BEFINDEND
AUF EINEM/EINER GROBEN ______________
INNERHALB DES ZUSAMMENHANGES VON [EINEM] ORT SICH BEFINDEND
AUF EINEM/EINER GLATTEN ______________
INNERHALB DES ZUSAMMENHANGES VON [EINEM] ORT SICH BEFINDEND
IM GROBEN

EINE (DIE) SCHLUCHT [KLUFT] ÜBERBRÜCKT
EINER (DER) FALLGRUBE [FALLE] ENTGANGEN
DEN (EINEN) PUNKT GEMACHT
ALLES MIT EINEM ENDE IN SICHT

hell ALSO dunkel	hell ALSO dunkel
6 of one	"6 ________________"
1/2 dozen	"1/2 ______________"
of another	of another

[BOTH WITHIN A RHYTHM OF SORTS (i.e.: THE TANGO)]

100 FELSBROCKEN AUS EINER WAND
GESCHNITTEN
(NACH EINEM DOPPELTEN STANDARD)
99 FELSBROCKEN AUF EINER WAND
AUSGEBLICHEN
(NACH EINEM DOPPELTEN STANDARD)
98 FELSBROCKEN AUF EINE WAND
AUFGESETZT
(NACH EINEM DOPPELTEN STANDARD)
97 FELSBROCKEN AUF EINER WAND
AUSGEWASCHEN
(NACH EINEM DOPPELTEN STANDARD)
96 FELSBROCKEN AUF EINER WAND
ABGEDUNKELT
(NACH EINEM DOPPELTEN STANDARD)

CARRIED TO GREAT LENGTHS. 0419
CARRIED TO (RELATIVELY) GREAT LENGTHS.
BROUGHT UP (RELATIVELY) SHORT.
BROUGHT UP SHORT.
ALL OVER A MATTER OF TIME

BENT TO A STRAIGHT AND NARROW AT A POINT OF PASSAGE 0422

HAVING A RELATION TO PROGRESS (OF A SORT): 0426
LEFT HERE
PUT THERE
FOR A LIMITED TIME

A BIT OF MATTER AND A LITTLE BIT MORE 0430

WITH A TOUCH OF PINK 0431
WITH A BIT OF VIOLET
WITH A HINT OF GREEN

ONE BEHIND THE OTHER 0436
ONE ON TOP OF THE OTHER
ONE IN FRONT OF THE OTHER
UNDER ANY CIRCUMSTANCE

BLOWN AWAY UNDER CERTAIN CIRCUMSTANCES 0437

RESTED UPON QUITE HEAVILY 0440
WITHIN A PROBABILITY OF COLLAPSE
(i.e. a corner stone)

HAVING BEEN MARKED WITH (i.e. decorated) 0443
HAVING BEEN DECORATED WITH (i.e. marked)
WITH A PROBABILITY OF BEEING SEEN

SEHR WEIT GETRAGEN.
(RELATIV) SEHR WEIT GETRAGEN.
(RELATIV) NICHT WEIT GEBRACHT.
NICHT WEIT GEBRACHT.
ALLES EINE FRAGE DER ZEIT

GEKRÜMMT ZU EINER GERADEN UND ENGEN AN EINEM DURCHGANGSPUNKT

IN DER MÖGLICHKEIT EINER BEZIEHUNG (IRGENDEINER ART) ZU ENTWICKELN:
HIER GELASSEN
DORT HINGELEGT
FÜR BEGRENZTE ZEIT

EIN BISSCHEN MATERIE UND EIN KLEINES BISSCHEN MEHR

MIT EINEM HAUCH VON ROSA
MIT EINEM BISSCHEN VIOLETT
MIT EINER SPUR VON GRÜN

EINER HINTER DEM ANDEREN
EINER ÜBER DEM ANDEREN
EINER VOR DEM ANDEREN
UNTER JEDER BEDINGUNG

WEGGEBLASEN UNTER GEWISSEN UMSTÄNDEN

ZIEMLICH SCHWER DARAUF GESTÜTZT
INNERHALB EINER WAHRSCHEINLICHKEIT DES ZUSAMMENBRUCHS
(d. h. ein Eckstein)

GEZEICHNET SEIN MIT (z. B. dekoriert)
DEKORIERT SEIN MIT (z. B. gezeichnet)
MIT DER MÖGLICHKEIT GESEHEN ZU WERDEN

ABOVE BELOW THE LEVEL OF WATER 0446
WITH A PROBABILITY OF FLOODING
(i.e. a dike)

COVERED WITH RED AND GREEN 0447
PAINTED WITH BLUE AND PUCE
PLACED UPON YELLOW AND RED
(ALL WITH A PROBABILITY OF BEING SEEN)

BLACK, ORANGE, YELLOW WITHIN A HORIZONTAL RELATIONSHIP 0450
(i.e. placed edge to edge)

REGARDING INSCRIPTIONS 0453
(OF A SORT):
INSCRIBED UPON
TO A DEGREE
CUT INTO

HAVING BEEN BUILT ON SAND WITH ANOTHER BASE (BASIS) IN FACT 0454

WITH RELATION TO THE VARIOUS MANNERS OF USE: 0457

1. PREPARATION FOR
   AND
2. PRESENTATION OF
3. POSITIONED OVER
4. HIDDEN FROM VIEW
5. RENOVATED
   etc.

ALTERED TO SUIT
(i.e. preparation for presentation)

DONE FAR AND AWAY 0458

MANY COLORED OBJECTS PLACED SIDE BY SIDE TO FORM A ROW OF MANY COLORED OBJECTS 0462

OBERHALB UNTERHALB DES WASSERSTANDES
MIT DER WAHRSCHEINLICHKEIT DES ÜBERFLUTENS
(i. e. EIN DEICH)

ÜBERZOGEN MIT ROT UND GRÜN
ANGEMALT MIT BLAU UND BRAUNROT
PLAZIERT AUF GELB UND ROT
(ALLES MIT DER WAHRSCHEINLICHKEIT GESEHEN ZU WERDEN)

SCHWARZ, GOLDGELB, GELB IN EINER HORIZONTALEN BEZIEHUNG
(d. h. Rand an Rand)

HINSICHTLICH INSCHRIFTEN
(EINER ART):
DARAUFGESCHRIEBEN
ZIEMLICH TIEF
EINGEKERBT

AUF SAND GEBAUT TATSÄCHLICH (AUS) AUF ANDEREM GRUND

MIT BEZIEHUNG ZU DEN VERSCHIEDENEN ARTEN DES GEBRAUCHS:
1. VORBEREITUNG FÜR
   UND
2. DARBIETUNG VON
3. PLAZIERT ÜBER
4. DEM BLICK ENTZOGEN
5. ERNEUERT
   usw.

GEEIGNET VERÄNDERN
(d. h. Vorbereitung für die Darbietung)

GEMACHT WEIT UND WEG

VIELE FARBIGE DINGE NEBENEINANDER ANGEORDNET BILDEN EINE REIHE VIELER FARBIGER DINGE

VARIOUS LIQUIDS CARRIED BY VIRTUE OF THEIR OWN WEIGHT FROM VARIOUS POINTS TO FORM A POOL OF VARIOUS LIQUIDS AT A POINT OF ACCUMULATION 0463

THAT WHICH WHEN IN PLACE IMPAIRS PROGRESS 0468-0469
THAT WHICH BY PRESENTATION IMPLIES AN IMPASSE

AN ACCUMULATION OF SUFFICIENT ABRASION TO REMOVE ENOUGH OF AN OPAQUE SURFACE TO LET LIGHT THROUGH WITH MORE INTENSITY 0476

AN OBJECT MADE TO RESEMBLE ANOTHER 0477
BY THE ADDITION OF A SUFFICIENT QUANTITY
OF EXTERNAL QUALITIES

A FORCE OF SUFFICIENT FORCE TO WEAR THROUGH A SURFACE (i.e. FRAYED) 0478

A GROUPING OF THAT WHICH IS CONNECTED 0480
WITH USE IN A TEMPERATE CLIMATE
A GROUPING OF THAT WHICH IS CONNECTED
WITH USE IN A HOT CLIMATE
A GROUPING OF THAT WHICH IS CONNECTED
WITH USE IN A COLD CLIMATE

TAKEN FROM HERE TO WHERE IT CAME FROM AND TAKEN TO A PLACE AND USED 0481
IN SUCH A MANNER THAT IT CAN ONLY REMAIN AS A REPRESENTATION OF WHAT IT WAS
WHERE IT CAME FROM

SHAPED UP SUFFICIENTLY 0487
TO ASSUME SOME SHAPE
(EJUSDEM GENERIS)

THE SALT OF THE EARTH MINGLED WITH THE SALT OF THE SEA 0488

VERSCHIEDENARTIGE FLÜSSIGKEITEN DURCH DIE WIRKUNG IHRES EIGENEN GEWICHTS VON VERSCHIEDENEN PUNKTEN AUS AUF EINEN SAMMELPUNKT HIN BEWEGT UM DORT EINE LACHE AUS VERSCHIEDENEN FLÜSSIGKEITEN ZU BILDEN

DAS WAS SOBALD ANGEBRACHT FORTSCHRITT BEEINTRÄCHTIGT
DAS WAS DURCH DARSTELLUNG EINEN STILLSTAND ANDEUTET

EINE AUSREICHENDE ANSAMMLUNG VON ABRIEB UM VON EINER UNDURCHSICHTIGEN OBERFLÄCHE GENUG ZU ENTFERNEN UM LICHT MIT HÖHERER INTENSITÄT HINDURCH ZU LASSEN

EINEN GEGENSTAND GEMACHT EINEM ANDEREN ZU GLEICHEN
DURCH DIE BEIFÜGUNG EINER HINREICHENDEN MENGE
ÄUSSERLICHER EIGENSCHAFTEN

EINE KRAFT VON GENÜGENDER STÄRKE UM SICH DURCH EINE OBERFLÄCHE HINDURCHZUARBEITEN
(d. h. ABGENUTZT)

EINE GRUPPIERUNG DESSEN WAS MIT DER BENUTZUNG
IN ENEM GEMÄSSIGTEN KLIMA ZU TUN HAT
EINE GRUPPIERUNG DESSEN WAS MIT DER BENUTZUNG
IN EINEM HEISSEN KLIMA ZU TUN HAT
EINE GRUPPIERUNG DESSEN WAS MIT DER BENUTZUNG
IN EINEM KALTEN KLIMA ZU TUN HAT

VON HIER GENOMMEN ZUM PUNKT WOHER ES KAM UND ZU EINER STELLE GEBRACHT
UND GEBRAUCHT IN DER ART UND WEISE DASS ES NUR EINE REPRÄSENTATION DESSEN BLEIBEN
KANN WAS ES WAR WO ES HER KAM

HINREICHEND GEFORMT
UM IRGENDEINE GESTALT ANZUNEHMEN
(EJUSDEM GENERIS)

DAS SALZ DER ERDE MIT DEM SALZ DES MEERES VERMENGT

A MASS OF SUFFICIENT QUANTITY MOVED A SUFFICIENT DISTANCE TO LEAVE HUMPS AND BOSSES IN THE WAKE OF PROGRESS (ROCHES MOUTONNÉES) 0489

PRESSURE SUFFICIENT TO FORM AN ICE OF MASS ENOUGH TO CARRY UPON WITHIN AND BENEATH ITSELF SOME OF THAT WITHIN THE VECTOR OF MOTION 0490

AN ARCH AFFORDED IN A WALL OF STONE WITH A KEYSTONE OF CHALK AND IMPOSTS OF SLATE 0494

STILL WATER PLACED UPON THE STREAM 0497

STONE UPON STONE UPON FALLEN STONE 0498

PEBBLES AND STRAW STREWN ON A LEVEL WITH THE SURFACE OF THE WATER 0500

WATER SPILLED FROM SOURCE TO USE 0510

ENOUGH PUSH AND PULL TO MAKE A STRUCTURE GO TO PIECES 0517

MASSES OF SOFT MATTER PUT UNDER A STONE 0518

TWO SEPARATE METALS ATTACHED WITHOUT A SEAM 0519

GOLD ENOUGH TO TIP THE BALANCE 0520

HUNG OVER THE SIDE & LOWERED INTO THE DEPTHS 0521

TENSION ENOUGH TO HOLD A STONE ABOVE THE RHINE 0526

ENCASED BY + REDUCED TO RUST 0533

EINE AUSREICHEND GROSSE MASSE BEWEGT ÜBER EINE AUSREICHEND LANGE STRECKE
UM IM GEFOLGE DES FORTSCHRITTS HÖCKER UND BUCKEL ZU HINTERLASSEN (FELS-HÖCKER)

HINREICHENDER DRUCK ZU FORMEN GENÜGEND MASSE EIS ZU TRAGEN AUF IHR IN IHR UNTER IHR
INNERHALB DES VEKTORS DER BEWEGUNG

EIN BOGEN ERMÖGLICHT IN EINER WAND AUS STEINEN MIT EINEM SCHLUSSSTEIN AUS KREIDE
UND AUFLAGEN AUS SCHIEFER

RUHENDES WASSER AUF DEM STROM PLAZIERT

STEIN AUF STEIN AUF GEFALLENEN STEIN

KIESEL UND STROH GESTREUT ÜBER DIE EBENE DER WASSER-OBERFLÄCHE

WASSER VERGOSSEN ZWISCHEN QUELLE UND VERBRAUCH

GENUG STOSS UND ZUG EINE STRUKTUR IN TEILE FALLEN ZU LASSEN

MASSEN WEICHER MATERIE UNTER EINEN STEIN GESTECKT

ZWEI VERSCHIEDENE METALLE OHNE EINE NAHT VERBUNDEN

GOLD GENUG DAS GLEICHGEWICHT ZU KIPPEN

ÜBER DIE SEITE GEHÄNGT & IN DIE TIEFE GESENKT

SPANNUNG GENUG EINEN STEIN ZU HALTEN ÜBER DEM RHEIN

UMHÜLLT VON + ZU ROST REDUZIERT

PAINTED STONES RINGING THE RUBBLE OF A STRUCTURE MADE OF STONES NOT PAINTED 0534

WATER UNDER A BRIDGE 0544

DROPS OF BLUE WATER FORCED OVER THE RIM OF A POT MADE OF CLAY 0548

AS FAR AS THE EYE CAN SEE 0585

ON TOP OF THE TREES 0587-0589
THE SOUNDS MADE OF TREES MADE TO FALL
COVERED OVER WITH LEAVES & LEFT TO ROT

STACKS OF BRICK HOLDING A ROOF ABOVE THE GROUND 0591
SOME BAMBOO LASHED TO SOME BAMBOO TO KEEP ITSELF ABOVE THE GROUND
A PIECE OF STEEL HOLDING A LOT OF GLASS ABOVE THE GROUND
CONCRETE POURED UNTIL IT SETS ITSELF ABOVE THE GROUND
LENGTHS OF SILK HUNG ON POLES ABOVE THE GROUND

A BIT + A BIT UNTIL A POT IS FULL 0592

BEMALTE STEINE DIE TRÜMMER EINES GEBILDES GEBAUT AUS NICHT BEMALTEN STEINEN UMRINGEND

WASSER UNTER EINER BRÜCKE

TROPFEN VON BLAUEM WASSER ÜBER DEN RAND EINES TONTOPFES GETRIEBEN

SO WEIT WIE DAS AUGE KANN

ÜBER DEN WIPFELN DER BÄUME
DAS KRACHEN VON ZU FALL GEBRACHTEN BÄUMEN
MIT BLÄTTERN ÜBERDECKT & DEM VERMODERN ÜBERLASSEN

BACKSTEINPFEILER HALTEN EIN DACH ÜBER DEM BODEN
ETWAS BAMBUS AN ETWAS BAMBUS GEBUNDEN UM SICH SELBST ÜBER DEM BODEN ZU HALTEN
EIN STÜCK STAHL HÄLT EINE MENGE GLAS UBER DEM BODEN
BETON GEGOSSEN BIS ER EINE FORM ÜBER DEM BODEN ANNIMMT
SEIDENBAHNEN AUF STANGEN ÜBER DEN BODEN GEHANGEN

EIN WENIG + EIN WENIG BIS EIN TOPF VOLL IST

SOME STONE TO STAND ON 0593
SOME STONE TO HOLD
SOME STONE TO THROW
SOME WOOD TO STAND ON
SOME WOOD TO HOLD
SOME WOOD TO THROW
SOME GLASS TO STAND ON
SOME GLASS TO HOLD
SOME GLASS TO THROW
SOME STEEL TO STAND ON
SOME STEEL TO HOLD
SOME STEEL TO THROW
SOME GOLD TO STAND ON
SOME GOLD TO HOLD
SOME GOLD TO THROW
SOME EARTH TO STAND ON
SOME EARTH TO HOLD
SOME EARTH TO THROW
SOME COAL TO STAND ON
SOME COAL TO HOLD
SOME COAL TO THROW
SOME SALT TO STAND ON
SOME SALT TO HOLD
SOME SALT TO THROW
SOME LEAD TO STAND ON
SOME LEAD TO HOLD
SOME LEAD TO THROW
SOME ASHES TO STAND ON
SOME ASHES TO HOLD
SOME ASHES TO THROW
SOME RUBBER TO STAND ON
SOME RUBBER TO HOLD
SOME RUBBER TO THROW
SOME HEMP TO STAND ON
SOME HEMP TO HOLD
SOME HEMP TO THROW

IRON STEEL & GLASS STREWN UNDERFOOT 0598
UPON A PATH FROM PLACE TO PLACE

BAMBOO VINES & SHELLS STREWN UNDERFOOT
UPON A STREET FROM PLACE TO PLACE

ETWAS STEIN ZUM DARAUF STEHEN
ETWAS STEIN ZUM FESTHALTEN
ETWAS STEIN ZUM WERFEN
ETWAS HOLZ ZUM DARAUF STEHEN
ETWAS HOLZ ZUM FESTHALTEN
ETWAS HOLZ ZUM WERFEN
ETWAS GLAS ZUM DARAUF STEHEN
ETWAS GLAS ZUM FESTHALTEN
ETWAS GLAS ZUM WERFEN
ETWAS STAHL ZUM DARAUF STEHEN
ETWAS STAHL ZUM FESTHALTEN
ETWAS STAHL ZUM WERFEN
ETWAS GOLD ZUM DARAUF STEHEN
ETWAS GOLD ZUM FESTHALTEN
ETWAS GOLD ZUM WERFEN
ETWAS ERDE ZUM DARAUF STEHEN
ETWAS ERDE ZUM FESTHALTEN
ETWAS ERDE ZUM WERFEN
ETWAS KOHLE ZUM DARAUF STEHEN
ETWAS KOHLE ZUM FESTHALTEN
ETWAS KOHLE ZUM WERFEN
ETWAS SALZ ZUM DARAUF STEHEN
ETWAS SALZ ZUM FESTHALTEN
ETWAS SALZ ZUM WERFEN
ETWAS BLEI ZUM DARAUF STEHEN
ETWAS BLEI ZUM FESTHALTEN
ETWAS BLEI ZUM WERFEN
ETWAS ASCHE ZUM DARAUF STEHEN
ETWAS ASCHE ZUM FESTHALTEN
ETWAS ASCHE ZUM WERFEN
ETWAS GUMMI ZUM DARAUF STEHEN
ETWAS GUMMI ZUM FESTHALTEN
ETWAS GUMMI ZUM WERFEN
ETWAS HANF ZUM DARAUF STEHEN
ETWAS HANF ZUM FESTHALTEN
ETWAS HANF ZUM WERFEN

EISEN STAHL & GLAS UNTER DIE FUESSE GESTREUT
AUF EINEM PFAD VON ORT ZU ORT

BAMBUS REBEN & MUSCHELN UNTER DIE FUESSE GESTREUT
AUF EINER STRASSE VON ORT ZU ORT

TILES PILED UPON MORTAR 0610
PILED UPON TILES

HYDROGEN WITH WATER GYPSUM WITH WATER WINE WITH WATER 0616

(AND SO ON)

FLAGS FOLDED OUT OF SIGHT OF THE BARRICADE 0617

SMALL PILES OF THOSE THINGS THAT FALL THROUGH THE CRACKS IN THE FLOOR 0619

PUSHED OUT IN FRONT OF EACH OTHER 0622
(AUF DIE BARRIKADEN)

OVER THE WALL & IN FRONT OF THE NEXT 0623

MISCELLANEOUS OBJECTS (MADE BY HAND) 0625-0626
GIVEN TO THE TIDE FOR A TIME

MISCELLANEOUS MATERIALS BROUGHT BY THE TIDE TO THE SHORE
(AFTER A TIME IN THE SEA)

JUST ANOTHER MOVEMENT OF THE TIDE (IMPAIRED) 0627-0628
JUST ANOTHER ELAPSURE OF TIME (DESIGNATED)

KACHELN GESTAPELT ÜBER MÖRTEL
GESTAPELT ÜBER KACHELN

WASSERSTOFF MIT WASSER GIPS MIT WASSER WEIN MIT WASSER

(UND SO WEITER)

FAHNEN AUSSER SICHT DER BARRIKADEN GEFALTET

KLEINE HAUFEN JENER DINGE DIE DURCH DIE RITZEN IM BODEN FALLEN

PUSHED OUT IN FRONT OF EACH OTHER
(AUF DIE BARRIKADEN)

ÜBER DIE WAND & VOR DER NÄCHSTEN

VERSCHIEDENE OBJEKTE (HANDGEMACHT)
DER FLUT FÜR EINIGE ZEIT ÜBERLASSEN

VERSCHEDENE OBJEKTE (MIT DE HAND MOKT)
DE FLOT FÖR ENIGE TIED ÖBERLATEN

VERSCHIEDENE MATERIALIEN VON DER FLUT GEBRACHT AN DAS UFER
(NACH EINIGER ZEIT IM MEER)

VERSCHEDENET MATERIOL VON DE FLOT HERBROCHT AN DAT UFER
(NOH ENIGE TIED INT MEER)

NUR EINE ANDERE BEWEGUNG DER GEZEITEN (VERHINDERT)
NUR EIN ANDERES VERGEHEN VON ZEIT (BEZEICHNET)

(AWAY FROM IT ALL) 0631

HERE THERE & EVERYWHERE

(BENEATH IT ALL)

HERE THERE & EVERYWHERE

(ALL OVER IT ALL)

HERE THERE & EVERYWHERE

(ABOVE IT ALL)

HERE THERE & EVERYWHERE

HARD AS A ROCK 0634
OR (ASSUMING THE POSITION)
SOFT AS SILK

PUT TOGETHER
OR (ASSUMING THE POSITION)
SPREAD APART

PLACED ON TOP
OR (ASSUMING THE POSITION)
PLACED BELOW

TOSSED ASIDE
OR (ASSUMING THE POSITION)
CARRIED ALONG

(THIS & THAT) PUT (HERE & THERE) 0637
OUT OF SIGHT OF POLARIS

EIN BISSCHEN ZEIT + GANZ VIEL EBBE 0638
(TIME + TIDE)

(GONE WITH THE WIND 0640

UND SO WEITER...)

(WEG VON ALLEM)

HIER DORT & ÜBERALL

(UNTER ALLEM)

HIER DORT & ÜBERALL

(ALLES ÜBER ALLEM)

HIER DORT & ÜBERALL

(ÜBER ALLEM)

HIER DORT & ÜBERALL

HART WIE GESTEIN
ODER (IN ANNAHME DER POSITION)
WEICH WIE SEIDE

ZUSAMMENGETRAGEN
ODER (IN ANNAHME DER POSITION)
VERTEILT

ÜBEREINANDER GESTELLT
ODER (IN ANNAHME DER POSITION)
UNTEREINANDER GESTELLT

BEISEITE GESTOSSEN
ODER (IN ANNAHME DER POSITION)
MITGERISSEN

(DIES & DAS) HINGESTELLT (HIER & DORT)
AUSSERHALB DER SICHT VON POLARIS

EIN BISSCHEN ZEIT + GANZ VIEL EBBE
(TIME + TIDE)

(GONE WITH THE WIND

UND SO WEITER...)

(2 OBJECTS + A ROPE) 0641

GREEN GLASS 0643
BROKEN IN THE LIGHT OF DAY
[WHITE]

MILK GLASS
BROKEN IN THE LIGHT OF SUNSET
[RED]

BROWN GLASS
BROKEN IN THE MORNING LIGHT
[BLUE]

OUT ON THE ICE 0647
(THICK & THIN)

2 METAL BALLS + 2 METAL RINGS 0656
(SET DOWN IN THE GROOVE)

TAKEN TO A POINT IN TIME 0664
(SOMEPLACE)

TAKEN TO A POINT IN SPACE (PLACE)
(SOMETIME)

TAKEN TO ANOTHER POINT
(SOMEHOW)

SOME OF THIS + SOME OF THAT 0669
GENTLY PLACED
UNDER THE LIGHT OF POLARIS

SMASHED TO PIECES 0670
(IN THE STILL OF THE NIGHT)

(2 OBJEKTE + EINE SCHNUR)

GRÜNES GLAS
GEBROCHEN IM TAGESLICHT
[WEISS]

MILCHGLAS
GEBROCHEN IM LICHT DES SONNENUNTERGANGS
[ROT]

BRAUNES GLAS
GEBROCHEN IM MORGENLICHT
[BLAU]

DRAUSSEN AUF DEM EIS
(DICK & DÜNN)

2 METALLENE KUGELN + 2 METALLENE RINGE
(NIEDERGELGT IN DER FURCHE)

ZU EINER BESTIMMTEN ZEIT
(IRGENDWO)

IN EINEM BESTIMMTEN RAUM (ORT)
(IRGENDWANN)

AN EINER ANDEREN STELLE
(IRGENDWIE)

ETWAS HIERVON + ETWAS DAVON
VORSICHTIG
UNTER DAS LICHT VON POLARIS GESTELLT

ZERSCHMETTERT IN STÜCKE
(IM FRIEDEN DER NACHT)

( ) + ( ) 0672

(PLACED)

IN THE HEAT OF THE DAY

( ) + ( )

(PLACED)

IN THE HEAT OF THE NIGHT

SANDPAPER (COARSE) 0685

+

STONE (COLD)

&

MOVED ONE AGAINST THE OTHER

(   ) + (   )

PLATZIERT

IN DER HITZE DES TAGES

(   ) + (   )

PLATZIERT

IN DER HITZE DER NACHT

SANDPAPIER (RAUH)
+
STEIN (KALT)
&
GEGEN EINANDER BEWEGT

SOME MATERIAL
(LIGHTER THAN AIR)
AND
SOME MATERIAL
(HEAVIER THAN WATER)
THROWN SOMEPLACE (WET) 0694–0697

SOME MATERIAL
(HARDER THAN LEAD)
AND
SOME MATERIAL
(SOFTER THAN STEEL)
THROWN SOMEPLACE (DRY)

SOME MATERIAL
(THICKER THAN BLOOD)
AND
SOME MATERIAL
(CLEAR AS MUD)
THROWN SOMEPLACE (LOW)

SOME MATERIAL
(WHITER THAN SNOW)
AND
SOME MATERIAL
(DARKER THAN COAL)
THROWN SOMEPLACE (HIGH)

THE WEIGHT OF IT ALL 0701–0705

THE LENGTH OF IT ALL

THE BREADTH OF IT ALL

THE SOUND OF IT ALL

THE SMELL OF IT ALL

WOOD (AS HARD AS A ROCK) & WOOD (AS LIGHT AS CAN BE)
CRUSHED TOGETHER INTO DUST 0706

ETWAS MATERIAL
(LEICHTER ALS LUFT)
UND
ETWAS MATERIAL
(SCHWERER ALS WASSER)
IRGENDWOHIN GEWORFEN (NASS)

ETWAS MATERIAL
(HÄRTER ALS BLEI)
UND
ETWAS MATERIAL
(WEICHER ALS STAHL)
IRGENDWOHIN GEWORFEN (TROCKEN)

ETWAS MATERIAL
(DICKER ALS BLUT)
UND
ETWAS MATERIAL
(KLAR WIE SCHLAMM)
IRGENDWOHIN GEWORFEN (TIEF)

ETWAS MATERIAL
(WEISSER ALS SCHNEE)
UND
ETWAS MATERIAL
(SCHWÄRZER ALS KOHLE)
IRGENDWOHIN GEWORFEN (HOCH)

DAS GEWICHT VON ALLEM

DIE LÄNGE VON ALLEM

DIE BREITE VON ALLEM

DER KLANG VON ALLEM

DER GERUCH VON ALLEM

HOLZ (SO HART WIE EIN FELSEN) & HOLZ (SO LEICHT WIE ES SEIN KANN)
ZUSAMMENGESCHLAGEN ZU STAUB

ENERGY & BITS OF MATTER MADE TO FALL TO EARTH 0707

X ± X ± X	0713
ACROSS THE WATER	

1 LARGE 1 SMALL	0714
AT THE EDGE OF THE DRIED UP LAKE	

OUT ON THE OCEAN SHORE	0715
OUT ON THE BOTTOM OF THE MOUNTAIN	

AS LONG AS IT LASTS 0716

ONE POTATO TWO POTATO THREE POTATO & (MORE) 0724

TWO BLOCKS OF TEMPERED STEEL BOTH EQUALLY HEAVY 0725
ONE WET & THE OTHER DRY

PISS	&	GINGER	0726
	&		
APPLES	&	PEARS	

TO THE POINT & 0728

( ) (±) ( ) 0730
HELD TOGETHER WITH WATER

STEINE & STEINE & STEINE 0733
STONES & STONES & STONES

STEINE + STEINE + STEINE + STEINE
STONES + STONES + STONES + STONES

ENERGIE & STÜCKE AUS MATERIE GESCHAFFEN ZUR ERDE ZU FALLEN

X ± X ± X
DURCH DAS WASSER

1 GROSS 1 KLEIN
AM RAND DES AUSGETROCKNETEN SEES

DRAUSSEN AM UFER DES OZEANS
DRAUSSEN AM FUSS DES BERGES

SO LANGE ES WÄHRT

EIN KARTOFFEL ZWEI KARTOFFEL DREI KARTOFFEL & (MEHR)

ZWEI BLÖCKE AUS VERGÜTETEM STAHL BEIDE GLEICH SCHWER
EINER NASS & DER ANDERE TROCKEN

PISSE	&	INGWER
	&	
ÄPFELN	&	BIRNEN

ZUR SACHE &

( ) (±) ( )
ZUSAMMENGEHALTEN DURCH WASSER

STEINE & STEINE & STEINE
STONES & STONES & STONES

STEINE + STEINE + STEINE + STEINE
STONES + STONES + STONES + STONES

ENOUGH OF THIS 0734

e

ENOUGH OF THAT

GENOEG VAN DIT

OF

GENOEG VAN DAT

A HILL REMOVED OF GRASS & 0738-0741

A MOUND ENLARGED IN SURFACE &

A VALLEY MADE MORE DEEP &

A MOUNTAIN OPENED END TO END &

STRETCHED AS TIGHTLY AS IS POSSIBLE 0742

(SATIN) & (PETROLEUM JELLY)

MILK AND HONEY TAKEN FAR FAR AWAY 0744

STONES FOUND AND BROKEN SOMETIME IN THE FUTURE 0745

ROWS OF CABBAGES MARKED WITH RED INK AND BURIED TOMORROW 0746

DRY EARTH 0749

&

SCATTERED ASHES

OR

DRY EARTH

&

BURIED GOLD

OR

GENUG HIERVON

ODER

GENUG DAVON

EIN HÜGEL VON GRAS BEFREIT &

EINE ERHEBUNG IN DER OBERFLÄCHE VERGRÖSSERT &

EIN TAL TIEFER GEMACHT &

EIN BERG DURCH UND DURCH GEÖFFNET &

SO FESTGESPANNT WIE MÖGLICH

(SATIN) & (PETROLEUM PASTE)

MILCH UND HONIG WEIT WEIT WEGGEBRACHT

STEINE IRGENDWANN IN DER ZUKUNFT GEFUNDEN UND GEBROCHEN

REIHEN VON KOHL MIT ROTER TINTE MARKIERT UND MORGEN VERGRABEN

VERTROCKNETE ERDE

&

GESTREUTE ASCHE

ODER

VERTROCKNETE ERDE

&

VERGRABENES GOLD

ODER

\+ PEARLS ROLLED ACROSS THE FLOOR 0750
\+ CANNON BALLS STACKED AS HIGH AS THEY WILL GO
\+ BURNT CORK RUBBED UPON THE GARDEN WALL
\+ CONCRETE PUMMELED TO SAND UNDERFOOT
\+ GLASS SCRATCHED BY DIAMONDS (VW, WWW)

WATER / SALZ & SALT / WASSER WITH / OHNE + WITHOUT / MIT SAND 0751

FIRE / WATER & WASSER / FEUER WITH / OHNE + WITHOUT / MIT SAND

LIGNITE (OR) ANTHRACITE 0752
BURNT BURNT
WITH OTHER BROWN THINGS WITH OTHER BLACK THINGS
WITHOUT REGARD TO THE NATURE OF THINGS

LINEN (OR) WOOL 0753
DRAPED ON THE BANKS OF A RIVER
WITHOUT REGARD TO THE CONSEQUENCES

CAST IRON (OR) FORGED STEEL 0754
PLUNGED INTO WATER SET INTO SAND
BOTH ENDS TWISTED TO THE MIDDLE
WITHOUT REGARD TO THE CAPABILITIES OF THE MATERIAL

BALL BEARINGS (OR) ROUND STONES 0755
MADE TO ROLL
OUTSIDE OF WHAT THERE IS

+ PERLEN ÜBER DEN BODEN GEROLLT
+ KANONENKUGELN AUFGESTAPELT SO HOCH WIE MÖGLICH
+ GEBRANNTER KORK AN DIE GARTENMAUER GERIEBEN
+ BETON ZU SAND ZERTRAMPELT
+ GLAS VON DIAMANTEN ZERKRATZT

WATER / SALZ & SALT / WASSER WITH / OHNE + WITHOUT / MIT SAND

FIRE / WATER & WASSER / FEUER WITH / OHNE + WITHOUT / MIT SAND

BRAUNKOHLE (ODER) ANTHRAZIT
VERBRANNT VERBRANNT
MIT ANDEREN BRAUNEN DINGEN MIT ANDEREN SCHWARZEN DINGEN
OHNE RÜCKSICHT AUF DIE NATUR DER DINGE

LEINEN (ODER) WOLLE

AUSGEBREITET AN DEN UFERN EINES FLUSSES
OHNE RÜCKSICHT AUF DIE FOLGEN

GUSSEISEN (ODER) SCHMIEDESTAHL
IN WASSER GEGOSSEN IN SAND GEGOSSEN
BEIDE ENDEN BIS ZUR MITTE VERDREHT
OHNE RÜCKSICHT AUF DIE EIGENSCHAFTEN DES MATERIALS

KUGELLAGERKUGELN (ODER) RUNDE STEINE
ZUM ROLLEN GEBRACHT
AUSSERHALB ALLEN SEINS

LOST | AT SEA 0756

WITH IRON BALLS | & SOMETHING LIKE IT | MOVED ALONG 0757

& SOMETHING NOTHING LIKE IT | SWITCHED ON & OFF

WITH STEEL BALLS | BOLTED DOWN | BROUGHT BACK

TURNED AROUND

TAR 0759
+
HIGH WATER
(+)
(–)
TEER
+
LOW WATER

ZURÜCKGELASSEN AFTER THE WIND 0760

1 X 1 X 2 MORE 0761
1 X 1 X 2 MEHR

1 X ANOTHER & ANOTHER & ANOTHER
1 X EIN ANDERES & EIN ANDERES & EIN ANDERES

1 X SOMETHING ELSE & 2 OTHER THINGS
1 X ETWAS ANDERES & 2 ANDERE DINGE

1 X A FEW THINGS LIKE IT
1 X SO EIN PAAR DINGE

FROM POINT TO POINT 0762
WITHOUT THE QUALITIES
ATTRIBUTED TO STEEL
IRON & STONE

VERLOREN AUF SEE

MIT EISENKUGELN & ETWAS IN DER ART WEITERBEWEGT

& ETWAS GANZ ANDERES EIN & AUS (UM)GESTELLT

MIT STAHLKUGELN DURCHGEJAGT ZURÜCKGEBRACHT

HERUMGEDREHT

TEER
+
HOCHWASSER
(+)
(−)
TEER
+
NIEDRIGWASSER

ZURÜCKGELASSEN AFTER THE WIND

1 X 1 X 2 MORE
1 X 1 X 2 MEHR

1 X ANOTHER & ANOTHER & ANOTHER
1 X EIN ANDERES & EIN ANDERES & EIN ANDERES

1 X SOMETHING ELSE & 2 OTHER THINGS
1 X ETWAS ANDERES & 2 ANDERE DINGE

1 X A FEW THINGS LIKE IT
1 X SO EIN PAAR DINGE

VON PUNKT ZU PUNKT
OHNE DIE EIGENSCHAFTEN
VERBUNDEN MIT STAHL
EISEN & STEIN

A LINE DRAWN FROM THE FIRST STAR AT DUSK TO THE LAST STAR AT DAWN 0765

MEHR LA	MORE LA	PLUS LA	0770
MEHR DI	MORE DI	PLUS DI	
MEHR DA	MORE DA	PLUS DA	
UND SO WEITER	AND SO ON	ET AINSI DE SUITE	

PAST THE END OF THE DOCK 0771

BUILT TO SEE OVER THE EDGE 0773

THINGS MADE TO BE SEEN FORCEFULLY OBSCURED 0774

THINGS CAPABLE OF COMBUSTION COLLECTED AND BURNT TO A CRISP 0775

THINGS PUSHED DOWN TO THE BOTTOM AND BROUGHT UP AGAIN 0776

WOOD (WET & CARINTHIAN) 0777
STONE (SHINY & CARINTHIAN)
WOOD (DRY & CARINTHIAN)

A STONE WITH WOOD
ON THE TOP & WOOD
ON THE BOTTOM

GRAPHITE + WOOD	&	IN A PILE	0778
GRAPHITE + STEAL	&	IN MOTION	
GRAPHITE + STONE	&	IN A BOX	
GRAPHITE + PAPER	&	IN A LINE	
GRAPHITE + WATER	&	IN A PUDDLE	

EINE LINIE GEZOGEN VOM ERSTEN STERN DER ABENDDÄMMERUNG BIS ZUM LETZTEN STERN DER MORGENDÄMMERUNG

MEHR LA	MORE LA	PLUS LA
MEHR DI	MORE DI	PLUS DI
MEHR DA	MORE DA	PLUS DA
UND SO WEITER	AND SO ON	ET AINSI DE SUITE

NACH DEM ENDE VON DEM KAI

GEBAUT UM ÜBER DEN RAND ZU SEHEN

DINGE GEMACHT UM GESEHEN ZU WERDEN GEWALTSAM VERBORGEN

DINGE DIE BRENNBAR SIND GESAMMELT UND VÖLLIG VERKOHLT

DINGE AUF DEN BODEN GESTOSSEN UND WIEDER AUFGEHOBEN

HOLZ (NASS & IN KÄRNTEN)
STEIN (GLÄNZEND & IN KÄRNTEN)
HOLZ (TROCKEN & IN KÄRNTEN)

EIN STEIN MIT HOLZ
DARÜBER & HOLZ
DARUNTER

GRAPHIT + HOLZ	&	AUF EINEM HAUFEN
GRAPHIT + STAHL	&	IN BEWEGUNG
GRAPHIT + STEIN	&	IN EINER SCHACHTEL
GRAPHIT + PAPIER	&	AUF EINER LINIE
GRAPHIT + WASSER	&	IN EINER PFÜTZE

IN ONE END & OUT THE OTHER (& THEN AGAIN) 0780

ROWS OF BROKEN BOTTLES SET INTO BADLY MIXED CONCRETE 0785

STONES TIED WITH STRING & PLACED EVERY WHICH WAY 0788

ROLLING STONES ADORNED WITH STARLIGHT 0791
(MORE OR LESS)

BUILT UP WITH STONES FALLEN DOWN FROM THE SKY 0795
DOWN ON

JUST ABOUT 0798
FULL CIRCLE

ALMOST AS FAR 0799
AS IT WILL

NOT QUITE 0800
BUT CLOSE

THE LONG & THE SHORT OF IT 0802

TAKEN APART 0805
& PUT BACK TOGETHER AGAIN

DILUTED & TEMPERED NEUTRALIZED 0808
& MODIFIED ALMOST STOPPED

DURCH EIN ENDE REIN & DURCH DAS ANDERE DURCH (& DANN NOCH EINMAL)

REIHEN VON ZERBROCHENEN FLASCHEN IN SCHLECHT GEMISCHTEN BETON GESETZT

STEINE MIT SEILEN GEBUNDEN & IN JEDER RICHTUNG VERORTET

ROLLENDE STEINE VON STERNENLICHT ANGESTRAHLT
(MEHR ODER WENIGER)

AUFGEBAUT MIT VOM HIMMEL GEFALLENEN STEINEN
HERUNTER HINAUF

GERADE EBEN
VOLLE RUNDUNG

FAST SO WEIT
ES GEHT

NICHT GANZ
ABER NAHEZU

DER LANGEN REDE KURZER SINN

AUSEINANDER GENOMMEN
& WIEDER ZUSAMMEN GESETZT

AUFGELÖST | & TEMPERIERT | NEUTRALISIERT

& VERÄNDERT | NAHEZU GESTOPPT

AGITATED BY & BLENDED WITH ALLOWED TO FLOW 0809
GENTLY MANIPULATED & LEFT TO COOL

WRITTEN ON THE WIND 0814

0817
ONE WAY
AUF EINE ART & WEISE
THEN ANOTHER WAY
DANN AUF EINE ANDERE ART & WEISE
THEN ANOTHER WAY
DANN AUF EINE ANDERE ART & WEISE

ILLUMINATED BY THE LIGHTS OF TWO SHIPS PASSING IN THE NIGHT 0818

HELD ABOVE THE HORIZON 0821

BUILT AT THE EDGE OF THE GRASS 0822

ARRANGED AT THE POINT WHERE ONE MOUNTAIN BECOMES ANOTHER 0823

PLACED DIRECTLY UNDER THE LIGHT 0826

PLACED AT AN ANGLE WITH THE LIGHT 0827

PLACED ON EITHER SIDE OF THE LIGHT 0828

BEWEGT VON | & VERMISCHT MIT | ERLAUBT ZU STRÖMEN

SANFT MANIPULIERT | & ZUR ABKÜHLUNG STEHENGELASSEN

AUF DEN WIND GESCHRIEBEN

ONE WAY

AUF EINE ART & WEISE

THEN ANOTHER WAY

DANN AUF EINE ANDERE ART & WEISE

THEN ANOTHER WAY

DANN AUF EINE ANDERE ART & WEISE

ANGESTRAHLT VON DEN LICHTERN ZWEIER SCHIFFE DIE IN DER NACHT VORBEI ZIEHEN

ÜBER DEN HORIZONT GEHALTEN

AM RANDE DES GRASES GEBAUT

DORT WO EIN BERG IN DEN ANDEREN ÜBERGEHT

DIREKT UNTER DAS LICHT GESTELLT

SCHRÄG ZUM LICHT GESTELLT

AUF BEIDE SEITEN DES LICHTS GESTELLT

THINGS THEMSELVES ON TOP OF OTHER THINGS ON TOP OF SOMETHING ELSE NOW & THEN 0829

BEFORE & AFTER 0833
A HOLE IN TIME

BEFORE THE SUN RISES 0838
HIDDEN FROM THE MOONLIGHT
LEFT IN THE WIND

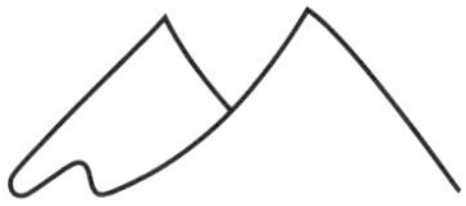

AT A DISTANCE 0839
TO THE FOREGROUND

CHANGED FIRST TO CONTAIN A GESTURE 0843
THEN TO FOLLOW A CURVE
& THEN TO SUPPORT A FOLD
EACH TRANSITION ACQUIRING A NEED
OF ITS OWN FULL CIRCLE

DINGE SELBER AUF ANDEREN DINGEN AUF ETWAS ANDEREM JETZT & DANN

VOR & NACH EINEM LOCH IN DER ZEIT

BEVOR DIE SONNE AUFGEHT
VOM MONDLICHT VERSTECKT
IM WIND GELASSEN

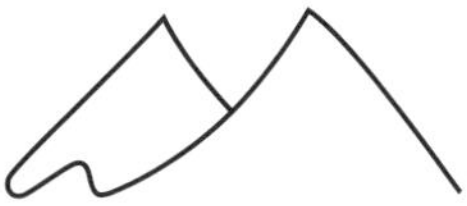

AUS EINEM ABSTAND ZU DEM VORDERGRUND

GEÄNDERT ZUERST UM EINE GESTE ZU ERLANGEN
DANN EINE KURVE ZU VERFOLGEN
& DANN EINE FALTE ZU STÜTZEN
JEDER DIESER ÜBERGÄNGE ERWIRBT DIE NOTWENDIGKEIT
SEINES VOLLEN KREISES

A BIG THING
A LITTLE THING
AFTER ALL
ANOTHER THING
SOMETHING

IN FRONT OF A POINT IN TIME

A CLEAR THING
A DENSE THING
AFTER ALL
ANOTHER THING
SOMETHING

REFLECTING THE SAME LIGHT

A THING OF SOME WEIGHT
A THING OF LESS WEIGHT
AFTER ALL
ANOTHER THING
SOMETHING

STANDING AT THE SAME PLACE

A BLACK THING
A WHITE THING
AFTER ALL
SOMETHING
ANYTHING

SEEN AT ANY GIVEN MOMENT

SOMETHING IN MOTION
SOMETHING IN STASIS
AFTER ALL
ANOTHER THING
SOMETHING

WITHIN THE SAME RESONANCE

SOMETHING OF FORMAL SUBSTANCE
SOMETHING OF INFORMAL SUBSTANCE
AFTER ALL
ANOTHER THING
SOMETHING

LEFT IN THE RAIN

ETWAS GROSSES
ETWAS KLEINES
NACH ALLES
ETWAS ANDERES
ETWAS

VOR EINEM PUNKT IN DER ZEIT

ETWAS KLARES
ETWAS DICHTES
NACH ALLES
ETWAS ANDERES
ETWAS

REFLEKTIEREN DASSELBE LICHT

ETWAS VON GEWICHT
ETWAS VON WENIGER GEWICHT
NACH ALLES
ETWAS ANDERES
ETWAS

STEHEN AM SELBEN ORT

ETWAS SCHWARZES
ETWAS WEISSES
NACH ALLES
ETWAS
IRGENDETWAS

SIND IN JEDEM BESTIMMTEN MOMENT ZU SEHEN

ETWAS IN BEWEGUNG
ETWAS IM STILLSTAND
NACH ALLES
ETWAS ANDERES
ETWAS

INNERHALB DERSELBEN RESONANZ

ETWAS VON FORMALER SUBSTANZ
ETWAS VON FORMLOSER SUBSTANZ
NACH ALLES
ETWAS ANDERES
ETWAS

STEHEN IM REGEN

FOUND ALONE AFTER ANY GIVEN TIME 0851
FOUND MIXED + MATCHED AFTER ANY GIVEN TIME
FOUND DUE TO PROXIMITY AFTER ANY GIVEN TIME
FOUND DUE TO ITS NATURE AFTER ANY GIVEN TIME
FOUND BY CHANCE AFTER ANY GIVEN TIME
FOUND TO MAKE DO WITH AFTER ANY GIVEN TIME
FOUND WHERESOEVER IT IS AFTER ANY GIVEN TIME

UNDER THE SUN 0852

BENT & BROKEN SHAFTS OF LIGHT 0853
AT A SUFFICIENT DISTANCE
NOT TO NEED TO KNOW
THE CAUSE OR THE CONSEQUENCE
SEEN AS RED & USED AS SUCH
SEEN AS BLUE & USED AS SUCH
SEEN AS GREEN & USED AS SUCH
SEEN AS VIOLET & USED AS SUCH
SEEN AS YELLOW & USED AS SUCH
BENT TO BE SEEN AS & USED AS A LUMINOUS ARC
FROM ONE ZONE OF TIME TO ANOTHER ZONE OF TIME
AT THE SAME TIME
KEPT STANDING STILL AS THE WORLD TURNS
BREAKING A LINE OF SIGHT EACH TIME

SILVER BARS BATHED IN BRIMSTONE FOR ANY GIVEN TIME 0861

BENT UNTIL STRAIGHT (→) 0863

EMPTIED UNTIL FULL (→) 0864

BATTERED UNTIL FORMED (→) 0865

TO THE EXTENT OF HOW DEEP THE VALLEY IS AT SOME GIVEN TIME 0866

ZU GEGEBENER ZEIT ALLEIN GEFUNDEN
ZU GEGEBENER ZEIT GEMISCHT + PASSEND GEFUNDEN
ZU GEGEBENER ZEIT DURCH NÄHE GEFUNDEN
ZU GEGEBENER ZEIT AUFGRUND SEINER ART GEFUNDEN
ZU GEGEBENER ZEIT DURCH ZUFALL GEFUNDEN
ZU GEGEBENER ZEIT UM AUSZUKOMMEN GEFUNDEN
ZU GEGEBENER ZEIT WO AUCH IMMER ES IST GEFUNDEN

UNTER DER SONNE

GEBEUGTE & GEBROCHENE LICHTSTRAHLEN
ALS ROT GESEHEN & ALS SOLCHES GEBRAUCHT
ALS BLAU GESEHEN & ALS SOLCHES GEBRAUCHT
ALS GRÜN GESEHEN & ALS SOLCHES GEBRAUCHT
ALS VIOLETT GESEHEN & ALS SOLCHES GEBRAUCHT
ALS GELB GESEHEN & ALS SOLCHES GEBRAUCHT
AUS GENÜGENDER FERNE
NICHT ZU WISSEN BRAUCHEN
DIE URSACHE ODER DIE FOLGE
GEBEUGT UM ALS STRAHLENDER BOGEN GESEHEN &
GEBRAUCHT ZU WERDEN
VON EINER ZONE DER ZEIT IN EINE ANDERE ZONE DER ZEIT
ZUR GLEICHEN ZEIT
STILL STEHEND WÄHREND DIE WELT SICH DREHT
BRICHT DIE SICHT ZU JEDER ZEIT

SILBERSTÄBE GETAUCHT IN SCHWEFEL FÜR UNBESTIMMTE ZEIT

GEBOGEN BIS GERADE (→)

GELEERT BIS VOLL (→)

ZERSCHLAGEN BIS GEFORMT (→)

GEMESSEN DARAN WIE TIEF DAS TAL IST ZU EINER BESTIMMTEN ZEIT

WAVE AFTER WAVE TOWARDS THE EARTH 0871
WAVE AFTER WAVE TOWARDS THE WATER
WAVE AFTER WAVE TOWARDS THE SKY
WAVE AFTER WAVE TOWARDS THE EDGE
WAVE AFTER WAVE TOWARDS THE BEGINNING
WAVE AFTER WAVE TOWARDS THE WAVE

PUT INTO A CONTEXT 0876
NOT PREVIOUSLY KNOWN
WHERESOEVER

PUT ASIDE OR PUT AWAY 0879
REACHING FOR THE MOON

PUT ASIDE OR PUT AWAY 0880
REACHING FOR THE STARS

PUT ASIDE OR PUT AWAY 0881
REACHING FOR THE CORE

THROUGH THE EYE OF A NEEDLE 0884
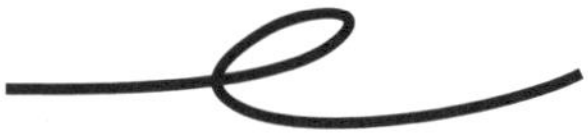 JUST ONE TIME

THROUGH A HOLE IN THE WALL
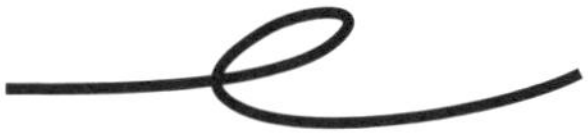 JUST ONE TIME

THROUGH A CRACK IN THE DOOR
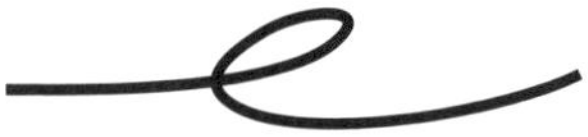 JUST ONE TIME
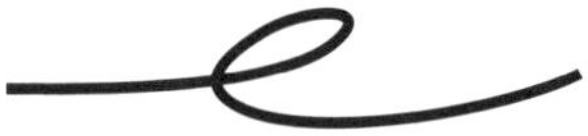 JUST ONE TIME

WELLE NACH WELLE NACH DIE ERDE
WELLE NACH WELLE NACH DAS WASSER
WELLE NACH WELLE NACH DER HIMMEL
WELLE NACH WELLE NACH DIE GRENZE
WELLE NACH WELLE NACH DER ANFANG
WELLE NACH WELLE NACH DIE WELLE

IN EINEN KONTEXT GESTELLT
VORHER NICHT BEKANNT
WOHIN AUCH IMMER

AUFGESCHOBEN ODER AUFGEHOBEN
NACH DEM MOND GREIFEN

AUFGESCHOBEN ODER AUFGEHOBEN
NACH DEN STERNEN GREIFEN

AUFGESCHOBEN ODER AUFGEHOBEN
NACH DEM KERN GREIFEN

DURCH EIN NADELÖHR

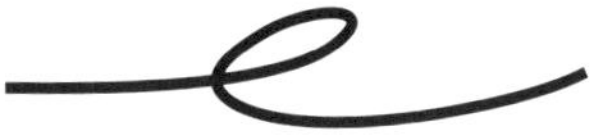
NUR EINMAL

DURCH EIN LOCH IN DER WAND

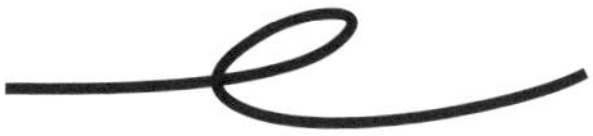
NUR EINMAL

DURCH EINEN RISS IN DER TÜR

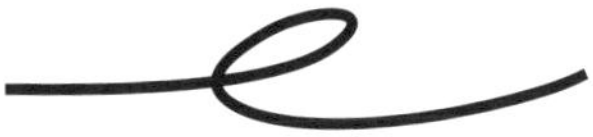
NUR EINMAL

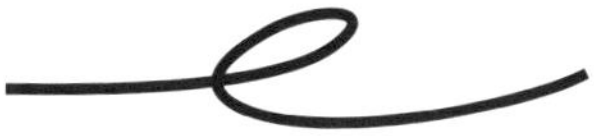
NUR EINMAL

MATTER SO SHAKEN TO ITS CORE TO LEAD TO A CHANGE IN INHERENT FORM TO THE EXTENT OF BRINGING ABOUT A CHANGE IN THE DESTINY OF THE MATERIAL 0885

PRIMARY SECONDARY TERTIARY

A PURSUIT OF HAPPINESS 0898

ASAP

EN ROUTE 0900

AT ANOTHER TIME

EN ROUTE

TO ANOTHER STAGE

EN ROUTE

IN ANOTHER COURT

EN ROUTE

ON ANOTHER PLANE

EN ROUTE

VIA ANOTHER ROUTE

MATERIE DERART BIS IN DEN KERN ERSCHÜTTERT DASS ES ZU EINER VERÄNDERUNG DER INHÄRENTEN FORM FÜHRT IN DEM AUSMASS DASS ES EINE ÄNDERUNG IM SCHICKSAL DES MATERIALS BEWIRKT

PRIMÄR SEKUNDÄR TERTIÄR

EIN STREBEN NACH GLÜCK

SO BALD WIE MÖGLICH

UNTERWEGS
ZU EINER ANDEREN ZEIT

UNTERWEGS
AUF EINER ANDEREN STRECKE

UNTERWEGS
IN EINEM ANDEREN HOF

UNTERWEGS
IN EINEM ANDEREN FLUGZEUG

UNTERWEGS
AUF EINEM ANDEREN WEG

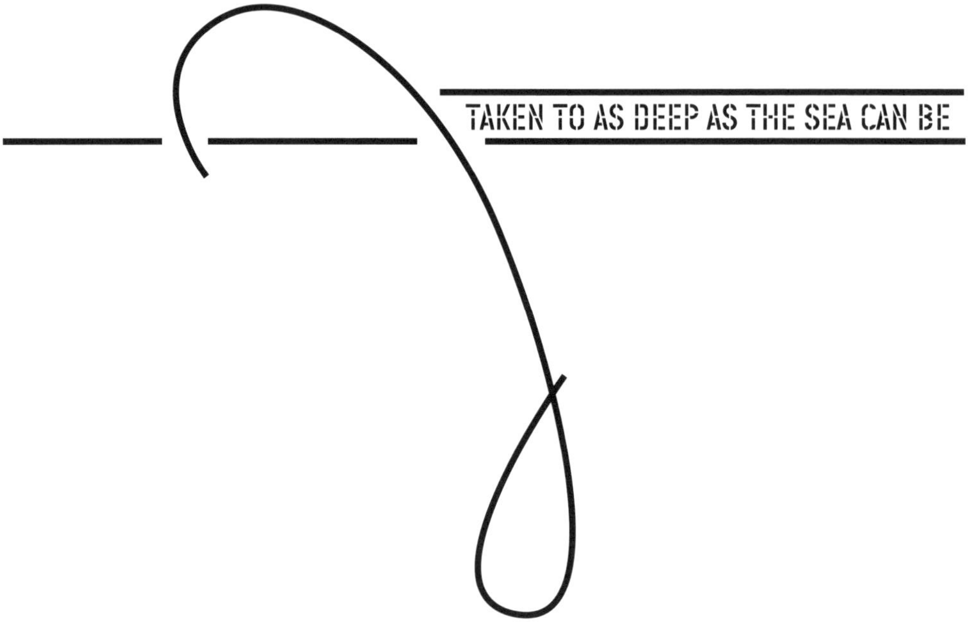
 0908

& FROM THE ABOVE 0915
& FROM THE BETWEEN
& FROM THE BENEATH

SOMETHING ABOVE WHAT BELOW IS 0916
+
SOMETHING BELOW WHAT ABOVE IS

ALL THE ABOVE 0917

A CHIP TAKEN OFF OF AN OLD BLOCK 0919

MITGENOMMEN BIS ZUR TIEFSTEN STELLE DES MEERES

& VON XXX OBEN
& VON XXX ZWISCHEN
& VON XXX UNTEN

ETWAS OBEN WAS UNTEN IST
+
ETWAS UNTEN WAS OBEN IST

ALL DAS OBEN STEHENDE

EIN SPAN GENOMMEN VON EINEM ALTEN KLOTZ

BENEATH 0925

RESOLVED MASS

BETWEEN

CRYSTALLIZED WITH THE DRIPPINGS 0946

FROM THE TREES THAT CAME FROM THE LAND

(FOREVER AMBER)

0949

SOME FLOWERS
CUT AND STREWN

UPON SOME APPLES
FALLEN FROM THE TREE

& LAID TO REST

UNTEN

AUFGELÖSTE MASSE

ZWISCHEN

KRISTALLISIERT AUS DEN TROPFEN
VON DEN BÄUMEN DIE VOM LAND KAMEN

(FÜR IMMER BERNSTEIN)

EINIGE BLUMEN
GESCHNITTEN UND GESTREUT

ÜBER EINIGE ÄPFEL
DIE VOM BAUM GEFALLEN SIND

& SICH ZUR RUHE GELEGT HABEN

2 MASSES OF MAGMA WHICH FAR FROM THE EDGE OF THE VENT FELL 0973

+

2 MASSES OF MAGMA WHICH CLOSE TO THE EDGE OF THE VENT FELL

PLACED SIDE BY SIDE WITH A MASS OF MAGMA THAT FELL INTO THE SEA

2 BROCKEN MAGMA DIE WEIT VOM RANDE DES SCHLUNDES NIEDERFIELEN

+

2 BROCKEN MAGMA DIE NAH AM RANDE DES SCHLUNDES NIEDERFIELEN

PLAZIERT SEITE AN SEITE MIT EINEM BROCKEN MAGMA DER INS MEER NIEDERFIEL

2 MASSES DE MAGMA LOIN DU BORD DE LA CHEMINÉE SONT TOMBÉES

+

2 MASSES DE MAGMA PRÈS DU BORD DE LA CHEMINÉE SONT TOMBÉES

PLACEES COTE A COTE D'UNE MASSE DE MAGMA QUI DANS LA MER EST TOMBEE

0981-0985

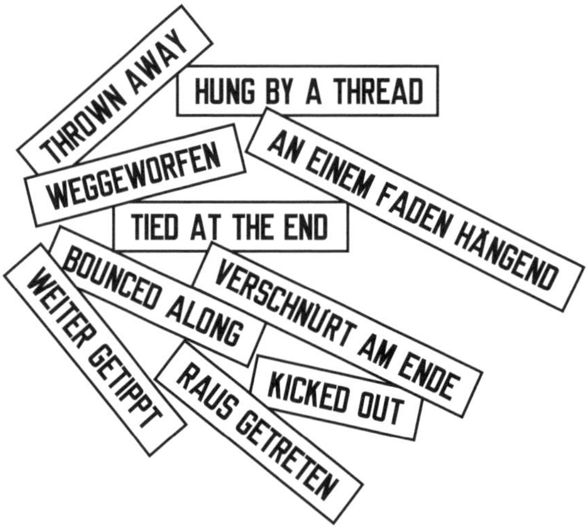

2 MASSES OF MAGMA WHICH FAR FROM THE EDGE OF THE VENT FELL
+
2 MASSES OF MAGMA WHICH CLOSE TO THE EDGE OF THE VENT FELL

PLACED SIDE BY SIDE WITH A MASS OF MAGMA THAT FELL INTO THE SEA

2 BROCKEN MAGMA DIE WEIT VOM RANDE DES SCHLUNDES NIEDERFIELEN
+
2 BROCKEN MAGMA DIE NAH AM RANDE DES SCHLUNDES NIEDERFIELEN

PLAZIERT SEITE AN SEITE MIT EINEM BROCKEN MAGMA DER INS MEER NIEDERFIEL

2 MASSES DE MAGMA LOIN DU BORD DE LA CHEMINÉE SONT TOMBÉES
+
2 MASSES DE MAGMA PRÈS DU BORD DE LA CHEMINÉE SONT TOMBÉES

PLACEES COTE A COTE D'UNE MASSE DE MAGMA QUI DANS LA MER EST TOMBEE

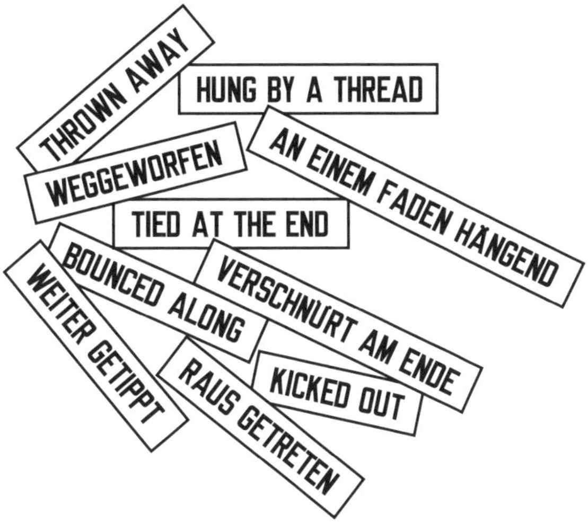

1006

BROUGHT TO TOUCH
DICHT BEI

WITH WHATEVER MEANS
ARE AT HAND
DICHT BEI

ONE & THE SAME
DICHT BEI

EILE MIT WEILE

ON THE TOP OF IT 1007
& THEN
NOT ON
THE TOP
OF IT

ON THE BANKS
OF THE DANUBE

PULLED ALONG 1008
& THEN
ALLOWED TO
DRIFT

ON THE BANKS
OF THE DANUBE

BROUGHT TO TOUCH
DICHT BEI

WITH WHATEVER MEANS
ARE AT HAND
DICHT BEI

ONE & THE SAME
DICHT BEI

EILE MIT WEILE

OBEN DRAUF
& DANN
NICHT
OBEN
DRAUF

AN DEN UFERN
DER DONAU

ENTLANG GEZOGEN
& DANN
TREIBEN
LASSEN

AN DEN UFERN
DER DONAU

SPLIT IN TWO 1009
& THEN
LEFT WHOLE

ON THE BANKS
OF THE DANUBE

THROW INTO 1010
& THEN
DREDGED OUT

ON THE BANKS
OF THE DANUBE

ATTACHED TO THE TREES 1011
& THEN
NOT ATTACHED
ON THE OTHER
SIDE

ON THE BANKS
OF THE DANUBE

HANDLED WITH CARE & SO WEITER 1024

SORGFÄLTIG GEHANDELT & SO WEITER

IN ZWEI GETEILT

& DANN

GANZ GELASSEN

AN DEN UFERN

DER DONAU

HINEINGEWORFEN

& DANN

HERAUSGEZOGEN

AN DEN UFERN

DER DONAU

AN DEN BÄUMEN FEST

& DANN

DRÜBEN

NICHT FEST

AN DEN UFERN

DER DONAU

HANDLED WITH CARE & SO WEITER

SORGFÄLTIG GEHANDELT & SO WEITER

THE SUM OF THE PARTS DICHT BEI 1025

BROUGHT FORTH BY THE RESONANCE OF A DISSONANCE 1026

DICHT BEI

PUSHED FORWARD CLOSE BY 1027

PUSHED ASIDE CLOSE BY

WITH GRACEFUL HASTE

IN & OUT 1047
OF PLACE
CARRIED BY ITS OWN WEIGHT

THE SUM OF THE PARTS DICHT BEI

HERVORGEBRACHT DURCH DIE RESONANZ EINER DISSONANZ

DICHT BEI

PUSHED FORWARD DICHT BEI

PUSHED ASIDE DICHT BEI

EILE MIT WEILE

EIN & AUS
VOM ORT
GETRAGEN VOM EIGENEN GEWICHT

The body of this text is based on the following publications: *Works* (Hamburg, 1977), *Specific & General Works* (Villeurbanne, 1993), and the more complete and up-to-date catalogue of Lawrence Weiner's works in language compiled by Moved Pictures Archive, overseen by Alice Zimmerman in New York. The initial cataloguing technique is explained in *Specific & General Works*: "The works have never been dated but catalogued, and they have been catalogued not from initial conception but from their first public presentation." Since 1993 and the advent of the computer, this cataloguing method has changed and dating the work is now a component in the archive's records. In order to catalogue all translations of works presented in the German-speaking world—*Specific & General Works* is almost twenty years old—on the basis of the two last sources mentioned (*Works*, 1977, is in English only), exhibitions in the German-speaking world were looked at to the extent they are documented in catalogues, posters, invitations, Internet sites, or in museum archives, exhibition halls, galleries, projects, or competitions. This way of proceeding reflects the subtitle of the book formulated by Lawrence Weiner on the title page, designed by the artist: WORKS PRESENTED IN THE GERMAN LANGUAGE / ARBEITEN VORGESTELLT IM DEUTSCHSPRACHIGEN RAUM.

A work *en route* per se represents a challenge in editorial terms, to the extent that the work is subject to ever changing contexts, especially to changes in perception and, on occasion, meaning. Individual works are not always presented the same way, rather it is by the particular application of the work to its context, whether it is an installation, a book, a poster, etc. Weiner also does not have many rules regarding line breaks. For example, the line breaks in Weiner's contribution to Documenta 5 in 1972, *A Primer / Ein Elementarbuch*, a volume in DIN A6, vary drastically from the catalogue *Specific & General Works* from 1993. Accordingly, if not prescribed by the work itself, the line breaks of this study do not follow the format of a particular exhibition. The typography of any specific presentation was ignored as Weiner's works are subject to constant change in this respect. The typographical execution and book cover design were placed in the hands of the artist and at his suggestion all works in German are set in Franklin Gothic Extra Condensed, while the works in English were set in FF Offline or Margaret Seaworthy Gothic. Weiner's standard usage of capital letters was followed, and also his aversion to the use of commas, found in normal text, was followed when replicating his work.

Translations are not subject to a set of rules in Weiner's work. They are produced with the conviction that the work can never not be translated, meaning that the integral link between the language used and its corresponding material will always be found. While a great deal of his translations have been done by Weiner himself, quite often they come from an engagement with bartenders and collectors and even from poets like Ferdinand Schmatz. In so doing, the German language works reflect a spectrum of translation practice and theory. There are strictly interlinear versions as well as translations oriented toward the target language. Any attempt here to make the translations consistent would conceal this and have been precluded, if only out of respect for the interpretational approach of the translator qua author in question, even if, as Stefan Weidner suggests, a translation "tends invariably . . . to claim to be a translation, and thus claims to be accessing something else." Weiner's well-known 1969 work A 36" X 36" REMOVAL TO THE LATHING OR SUPPORT WALL OF PLASTER OR WALLBOARD FROM A WALL, for example, exists in five different Germanic translations: EIN QUADRATMETER WAND-VERKLEIDUNG VON EINER WAND ENTFERNT (*Lawrence Weiner: Jahresgabe 1972*, Westfälischer Kunstverein, Münster, 1973), EIN AUSSCHNITT VON 36 X 36 INCHES AUS EINER GIPSWAND ODER WANDPLATTE BIS AUF DAS LATTENWERK ODER DAS MAUERWERK (*Einige Werke von Lawrence Weiner*, supplement to *Lawrence Weiner*, exh. cat. Kunsthalle Basel, 1976), EIN 36 X 36 INCHES GROSSER AUSSCHNITT BIS AUF DEN GRUND DES LATTEN- ODER MAUERWERKS AUS EINER GIPSWAND ODER WANDPLATTE (*Werke & Re-Konstruktionen / Works & Re-Constructions*, exh. cat. Kunsthalle Bern, 1983), EINE ENTFERNUNG VON 91,5 X 91,5 CM DES PUTZES ODER DER WANDVERKLEIDUNG AUS EINER WAND BIS ZUM LATTENWERK ODER MAUERWERK (*Minimal Maximal: Die Minimal Art und ihr Einfluß auf die internationale Kunst der 90er Jahre*, exh. cat. Neues Museum Weserburg, Bremen, Heidelberg, 1998), EINE 36 X 36 INCHES GROSSE ABTRAGUNG AUF DEN GRUND DES LATTEN ODER MAUERWERKS AUS EINER GIPSWAND ODER WANDPLATTE (*Lawrence Weiner: As Far as the Eye Can See*, exh. cat. K21 Kunstsammlung Nordrhein-Westfalen, Düsseldorf, 2008).

How should DISPLACED be translated? With VERSCHOBEN (*As Far as the Eye Can See*), VERLEGT (*Einige Werke von Lawrence Weiner*) or VERSETZT (*Werke & Re-Konstruktionen*)? Does PAINTED mean GEMALT (*Jahresgabe 1972*) or ANGESTRICHEN (*Einige Werke von Lawrence Weiner*)? EN ROUTE AT ANOTHER TIME EN ROUTE TO ANOTHER STAGE EN ROUTE IN ANOTHER COURT EN ROUTE ON ANOTHER PLANE EN ROUTE VIA ANOTHER ROUTE was translated at the exhibition *Lawrence Weiner: As Far as the Eye Can See*, with UNTERWEGS ZU EINER ANDEREN ZEIT UNTERWEGS AUF EINER ANDEREN STRECKE UNTERWEGS IN EINEM ANDEREN HOF UNTERWEGS IN EINEM ANDEREN FLUGZEUG UNTERWEGS AUF EINEM ANDEREN WEG, but could also be translated as UNTERWEGS ZU EINER ANDEREN ZEIT UNTERWEGS ZU EINER ANDEREN BÜHNE UNTERWEGS AUF EINEM ANDEREN PLATZ UNTERWEGS AUF EINER ANDEREN EBENE UNTERWEGS ÜBER EINEN ANDEREN WEG. The first translation would be a biographic reading, the second a reading based on a nomadic art. Each translation represents a different approach.

The representation of all variants, here only listed by way of example, both in terms of presentation and translation is, given the limited scope of this publication, neither possible nor desired. At issue is an overview of Weiner's English/German-language works, not a historical-critical edition primarily intended for academic purposes. Each English/German work only appears in one version. This is understood in the context of this catalogue of works presented in the German language that it is expressly not meant as a definitive version, but rather presented as a possible version of the pieces, statements, works, sculptures that have gone through many hands and many stages—even the terms and conditions used for Weiner's language works are variable. The selection was not made according to a range of criteria about what is a good translation, however defined, but according to the criterion of taking into account the various sources as broadly as possible, which in its variation is best suited to the task of documenting a work *en route* in a catalogue of limited scope. An author's source list of references is provided for further information about translations in question.

Specific & General Works, published in 1993, provides an overview of the dating of works with the indication: "Persons wishing to ascertain the date of a work may use the following rough method." This method has been adopted for this volume and brought up to date from the Moved Pictures Archive.

0001-0042	**1968**	0497-0504	**1983**	0806-0823	**1998**
0043-0142	**1969**	0505-0516	**1984**	0824-0843	**1999**
0143-0232	**1970**	0517-0526	**1985**	0844-0858	**2000**
0233-0261	**1971**	0527-0551	**1986**	0859-0876	**2001**
0262-0332	**1972**	0552-0576	**1987**	0877-0885	**2002**
0333-0364	**1973**	0577-0610	**1988**	0886-0894	**2003**
0365-0396	**1974**	0611-0634	**1989**	0895-0899	**2004**
0397-0419	**1975**	0635-0669	**1990**	0900-0913	**2005**
0420-0430	**1976**	0670-0711	**1991**	0914-0938	**2006**
0431-0448	**1977**	0712-0725	**1992**	0939-0965	**2007**
0449-0458	**1978**	0726-0733	**1993**	0966-0994	**2008**
0459-0469	**1979**	0734-0761	**1994**	0995-1032	**2009**
0470-0478	**1980**	0762-0769	**1995**	1033-1046	**2010**
0479-0482	**1981**	0770-0788	**1996**	1047-	**2011**
0483-0496	**1982**	0789-0805	**1997**		

Grundlage des Textkorpus sind die Publikationen *Works* (Hamburg, 1977), *Specific & General Works* (Villeurbanne 1993) und das aktuelle Gesamtverzeichnis der katalogisierten Spracharbeiten des von Alice Zimmerman geführten Moved Pictures Archive, New York. Das ursprüngliche Verfahren der Katalogisierung ist in *Specific & General Works* erläutert: »Die Arbeiten sind nicht datiert, sondern katalogisiert. Maßgeblich für die Katalogisierung ist nicht die ursprüngliche Konzeption, sondern die erste öffentliche Präsentation.« Seit 1993 und mit dem Aufkommen des Computers wurde das Verfahren der Katalogisierung geändert, und die Datierung der Arbeiten ist nunmehr Bestandteil der Aufzeichnungen des Archivs. Um die Übersetzungen der im deutschsprachigen Raum gezeigten Arbeiten zu erfassen – das letzte Werkverzeichnis liegt fast zwanzig Jahre zurück –, wurden auf der Basis der beiden letztgenannten Quellen (*Works* ist ein rein englischsprachiges Werkverzeichnis) die Ausstellungen im deutschsprachigen Raum gesichtet, sofern sie in Katalogen, auf Plakaten, Einladungskarten, Internetseiten oder in Archiven von Museen, Ausstellungshallen, Galerien, Projekten oder Wettbewerben dokumentiert sind. Dieses Auswahlverfahren spiegelt der von Lawrence Weiner formulierte Untertitel des Buches auf der von dem Künstler gestalteten Titelseite: WORKS PRESENTED IN THE GERMAN LANGUAGE / ARBEITEN VORGESTELLT IM DEUTSCHSPRACHIGEN RAUM.

Ein Werk en route stellt editorisch an sich schon eine Herausforderung dar, da es Gegenstand sich ständig verändernder Kontexte ist und damit eine andere Rezeption und gelegentlich auch andere Bedeutung erfährt. Einzelne Arbeiten werden nicht immer in der gleichen Form präsentiert. Vielmehr hängt die spezifische Umsetzung der Arbeit von dem jeweiligen Kontext ab, sei es eine Installation, ein Buch oder ein Plakat. Entsprechend gibt es bei Weiner hinsichtlich des Zeilenumbruchs keine feste Regel, und so weicht in diesem Punkt sein Beitrag zur *documenta* 5 von 1972 *A Primer / Ein Elementarbuch,* ein Heft in DIN-A6-Größe, stark von dem Verzeichnis *Specific & General Works* von 1993 ab, um nur ein Beispiel zu nennen. Sofern also von der Arbeit selbst nicht vorgegeben, folgt der Zeilenbruch in der Zusammenstellung der englisch-deutschen Arbeiten nicht zwingend dem Format einer bestimmten Ausstellung. Als nicht bindend wird auch die Typografie einer bestimmten Präsentation betrachtet, da Weiners Arbeiten hier ebenfalls einem ständigen Wandel unterliegen. Die typografische Umsetzung und Covergestaltung des vorliegenden Buches lagen im Sinn einer Werkausführung in den Händen des Künstlers, und auf seinen Vorschlag hin sind alle Arbeiten in Franklin Gothic Extra Condensed gesetzt – mit Ausnahme der in FF Offline und Margaret Seaworthy Gothic gesetzten grafisch gestalteten englischen Arbeiten. Weiners standardmäßiger Verwendung von Versalien sowie auch seiner Abneigung gegen den Gebrauch von Kommata wurde bei der Darstellung der Werke Rechnung getragen.

Übersetzungen unterliegen bei Weiner ebenfalls keinem starren Schema. Sie sind getragen von der Überzeugung, dass jede Arbeit aufgrund des unmittelbaren Bezugs der Sprache zum Material übersetzbar ist. Obwohl die Übersetzungen zu einem großen Teil vom Künstler selbst stammen, sind auch Barkeeper oder Sammler beteiligt und sogar Dichter wie Ferdinand Schmatz. Damit spiegeln die deutschsprachigen Arbeiten eine Bandbreite an Übersetzungspraxis und -theorie. Es gibt die strengen Interlinearversionen ebenso wie die an der Idiomatik der Zielsprache orientierten Übersetzungen. Jeglicher Versuch eines vereinheitlichenden Eingriffs würde genau dies verschleiern und verbietet sich schon allein aus dem Respekt vor dem Interpretationsansatz des jeweiligen Übersetzers qua Autor von selbst, wenn mit Stefan Weidner eine Übersetzung »tendenziell immer [...] Behauptung von Übersetzung, und damit Behauptung des Zugangs zu etwas Anderem« ist.

Weiners bekannte 1969 in Bern ausgeführte Arbeit A 36" X 36" REMOVAL TO THE LATHING OR SUPPORT WALL OF PLASTER OR WALLBOARD FROM A WALL beispielsweise liegt in fünf unterschiedlichen Übersetzungen ins Deutsche vor: EIN QUADRATMETER WAND-VERKLEIDUNG VON EINER WAND ENTFERNT (*Lawrence Weiner. Jahresgabe 1972,* Westfälischer Kunstverein, Münster 1973), EIN AUSSCHNITT VON 36 X 36 INCHES AUS EINER GIPSWAND ODER WANDPLATTE BIS AUF DAS LATTENWERK ODER DAS MAUERWERK (*Einige Werke von Lawrence Weiner,* Beilage zu *Lawrence Weiner,* Ausst.-Kat. Kunsthalle Basel, Basel 1976), EIN 36 X 36 INCHES GROSSER AUSSCHNITT BIS AUF DEN GRUND DES LATTEN- ODER MAUERWERKS AUS EINER GIPSWAND ODER WANDPLATTE (*Werke & Re-Konstruktionen / Works & Re-constructions,* Ausst.-Kat. Kunsthalle Bern, Bern 1983), EINE ENTFERNUNG VON 91,5 X 91,5 CM DES PUTZES ODER DER WANDVERKLEIDUNG AUS EINER WAND BIS ZUM LATTENWERK ODER MAUERWERK (*Minimal Maximal. Die Minimal Art und ihr Einfluß auf die internationale Kunst der 90er Jahre,* Ausst.-Kat. Neues Museum Weserburg, Bremen, u. a., Heidelberg 1998), EINE 36 X 36 INCHES GROSSE ABTRAGUNG AUF DEN GRUND DES LATTEN ODER MAUERWERKS AUS EINER GIPSWAND ODER WANDPLATTE (*Lawrence Weiner. As Far as the Eye Can See,* K21 Kunstsammlung Nordrhein-Westfalen, Düsseldorf, 2008). Wie übersetzt man DISPLACED? Mit VERSCHOBEN (*Lawrence Weiner. As Far as the Eye Can See*), VERLEGT (*Einige Werke von Lawrence Weiner*) oder VERSETZT (*Werke & Re-Konstruktionen*)? Meint PAINTED GEMALT (*Lawrence Weiner. Jahresgabe 1972*) oder ANGESTRICHEN (*Einige Werke von Lawrence Weiner*)?

EN ROUTE AT ANOTHER TIME EN ROUTE TO ANOTHER STAGE EN ROUTE IN ANOTHER COURT EN ROUTE ON ANOTHER PLANE EN ROUTE VIA ANOTHER ROUTE wurde in der Ausstellung *As Far as the Eye Can See* übersetzt mit UNTERWEGS ZU EINER ANDEREN ZEIT UNTERWEGS AUF EINER ANDEREN STRECKE UNTERWEGS IN EINEM ANDEREN HOF UNTERWEGS IN EINEM ANDEREN FLUGZEUG UNTERWEGS AUF EINEM ANDEREN WEG, ließe sich aber auch übertragen in: UNTERWEGS ZU EINER ANDEREN ZEIT UNTERWEGS ZU EINER ANDEREN BÜHNE UNTERWEGS AUF EINEM ANDEREN PLATZ UNTERWEGS AUF EINER ANDEREN EBENE UNTERWEGS ÜBER EINEN ANDEREN WEG. Die erste Übersetzung wäre eine biografische, die zweite eine auf die nomadisierende Kunst selbst zurückgewandte Lesart. Jede Übersetzung stellt einen anderen, eigenen Zugang dar.

Die Darstellung aller, hier nur exemplarisch aufgezeigten Varianten, sowohl von der Präsentation als auch von der Übersetzung her, ist in dem begrenzten Umfang dieser Publikation nicht möglich und auch nicht das Ziel. Es geht um einen Überblick über die englisch-deutschen Spracharbeiten Weiners, nicht um eine primär für wissenschaftliche Zwecke erstellte historisch-kritische Ausgabe. Jede englisch-deutsche Arbeit erscheint in nur einer Version. Diese Version versteht sich im Kontext dieses Werkverzeichnisses ausdrücklich nicht als die maßgebliche, sondern wird als eine mögliche der durch viele Hände und viele Etappen gegangenen Pieces / Statements / Works / Sculptures präsentiert – auch die Bezeichnungen für Weiners Spracharbeiten sind variabel. Die Auswahl erfolgte nicht nach einem Kriterienkatalog einer wie auch immer zu definierenden guten Übersetzung, sondern nach Maßgabe einer möglichst breiten Berücksichtigung der unterschiedlichen Quellen, die in ihrer Varianz am ehesten der Aufgabe der Dokumentation eines Werks en route in einem Werkverzeichnis begrenzten Umfangs gerecht werden kann. Über die Herkunft der jeweiligen Übersetzung gibt das Quellenverzeichnis Auskunft.

Hinsichtlich der Frage nach der Datierung der Arbeiten findet sich in dem 1993 veröffentlichten Buch *Specific & General Works* eine kurze Übersicht mit dem Hinweis: »Das Datum einzelner Arbeiten lässt sich näherungsweise anhand nachstehender Tabelle ermitteln.« Dieses Verfahren wurde hier übernommen und von dem Moved Pictures Archive aktualisiert.

0001-0042	1968	0497-0504	1983	0806-0823	1998
0043-0142	1969	0505-0516	1984	0824-0843	1999
0143-0232	1970	0517-0526	1985	0844-0858	2000
0233-0261	1971	0527-0551	1986	0859-0876	2001
0262-0332	1972	0552-0576	1987	0877-0885	2002
0333-0364	1973	0577-0610	1988	0886-0894	2003
0365-0396	1974	0611-0634	1989	0895-0899	2004
0397-0419	1975	0635-0669	1990	0900-0913	2005
0420-0430	1976	0670-0711	1991	0914-0938	2006
0431-0448	1977	0712-0725	1992	0939-0965	2007
0449-0458	1978	0726-0733	1993	0966-0994	2008
0459-0469	1979	0734-0761	1994	0995-1032	2009
0470-0478	1980	0762-0769	1995	1033-1046	2010
0479-0482	1981	0770-0788	1996	1047-	2011
0483-0496	1982	0789-0805	1997		

TRANSLATION SOURCES
QUELLENVERZEICHNIS DER ÜBERSETZUNGEN

0001-0003 *Lawrence Weiner. Jahresgabe 1972*, Westfälischer Kunstverein, Münster, 1973
0004 *Lawrence Weiner. As Far as the Eye Can See*, K21 Kunstsammlung Nordrhein-Westfalen, Düsseldorf, 2008 (Label)*
0006 **see** wie 0001
0007 *Works & Re-Constructions / Werke & Re-Konstruktionen*, Kunsthalle Bern, 1983
0008 **see** wie 0001
0009 **see** wie 0007
0011 **see** wie 0001
0014 **see** wie 0007
0015-0017 **see** wie 0001
0018 *Lawrence Weiner*, Kunsthalle Basel, 1976
0021 **see** wie 0007
0024 **see** wie 0004 (Label)
0026 **see** wie 0007
0027-0028 **see** wie 0001
0029 *Lawrence Weiner*, Konrad Fischer Galerie, Düsseldorf, 1969
0035 **see** wie 0001
0044 **see** wie 0001
0046 **see** wie 0001
0049 **see** wie 0018
0051-0054 **see** wie 0029
0055 **see** wie 0007
0056 **see** wie 0004
0062 **see** wie 0018
0071 **see** wie 0007
0073 **see** wie 0001
0074 **see** wie 0018
0075 **see** wie 0004
0077 **see** wie 0001
0078 *Conception / Konzeption*, Städtisches Museum, Leverkusen, 1969
0082 **see** wie 0004 (**Label and accompanying publication** Label und Begleitpublikation)
0083 **see** wie 0007
0084 **see** wie 0078
0087 **see** wie 0078
0088 **see** wie 0001
0097 **see** wie 0078
0098 **see** wie 0001
0102 **see** wie 0001
0110 **see** wie 0001
0115 **see** wie 0001
0129 **see** wie 0001
0142-0143 **see** wie 0001
0151 **see** wie 0001
0153-0154 **see** wie 0007
0157-0166 *Lawrence Weiner: An Exhibition / Eine Ausstellung*, Gegenverkehr, Aachen, Zentrum für aktuelle Kunst, 1970
0167-0168 **see** wie 0001
0169 **see** wie 0018
0185 **see** wie 0001
0188 **see** wie 0004 (Label)
0206 **see** wie 0001
0210 **see** wie 0001
0215 **see** wie 0007
0216-0221 *6 Sculptures*, Konrad Fischer Galerie, Düsseldorf, 1970
0224-0226 **see** wie 0004 (Label)
0229 **see** wie 0001
0234 **see** wie 0018
0240 **see** wie 0001
0244 **see** wie 0001
0245 *Concept Art*, von Klaus Honnef, **Cologne** Köln, 1971
0251 **Postcard, GDR, 1969, expanded in a temporary installation, Salzhaus, Sindelfingen, 1989** Postkarte, DDR, 1969, erweitert in einer temporären Installation, Salzhaus Sindelfingen, 1989
0261 **see** wie 0001
0264 **see** wie 0001
0267 **see** wie 0001
0278 **see** wie 0001
0280 **see** wie 0018
0282-0285 **see** wie 0007
0287 **see** wie 0001
0289-0293 **Temporary installation** Temporäre Installation, Akademisches Gymnasium Graz, 2006
0295 **see** wie 0001
0300-0302 **Permanent installation** Permanente Installation, Städtisches Museum Mönchengladbach, 1995
0303-0310 *8 Works of Lawrence Weiner / 8 Arbeiten von Lawrence Weiner*, Städtisches Museum Mönchengladbach, 1973
0311-0312 **see** wie 0004 (Label)
0332 **see** wie 0004 (Label)
0333-0341 **Permanent installation** Permanente Installation, Hallen für Neue Kunst, Schaffhausen, 1996
0363 **see** wie 0018
0366-0369 **see** wie 0004 (Label)
0372 **see** wie 0018
0374-0375 *Projekt 74*, **Cologne** Köln 1974
0376-0378 **see** wie 0007
0380-0383 Galerie Rolf Preisig, Basel, 1974
0384 **see** wie 0018
0389 **see** wie 0018
0393-0394 **see** wie 0007
0397 **see** wie 0018
0401 **see** wie 0004 (Label)
0402 **see** wie 0018
0403-0405 *3 Works in Relation to Place / 3 Arbeiten in Beziehung zum Ort*, Konrad Fischer Galerie, Düsseldorf, 1975
0406 *Towards a Reasonable End /Auf ein vernünftiges Ende zu*, Kabinett für aktuelle Kunst, Bremerhaven, 1975
0413 **Private collection** Privatsammlung
0414-0418 **see** wie 0004 (Label)
0419 *Eine Arbeit von Lawrence Weiner bei Rolf Preisig*, Galerie Rolf Preisig, Basel, 1975
0422 **see** wie 0007
0426 *Words: Gebrauch der Sprache in der Kunst*, Museum Bochum, 1979
0430 **see** wie 0007
0431 *With a Touch of Pink / Mit einem Hauch von Rosa Ein neues Buch von Lawrence Weiner und dem Kabinett für aktuelle Kunst*, Kabinett für aktuelle Kunst, Bremerhaven, 1978
0436 *Eine Ausstellung von Lawrence Weiner bei Galerie Schöttle*, Galerie Rüdiger Schöttle, **Munich** München, 1976
0437 *Rosenfest. Worte, Bilder, Musik, Theater*, DAAD Galerie, Berlin, 1984
0440 **see** wie 0007
0443 *Lawrence Weiner*, Konrad Fischer Galerie, Düsseldorf, 1977
0446 *Leere X Vision*, MARTa Herford, 2003
0447 **see** wie 0004
0450 *"Salon" Presents / »Salon« stellt vor*, Museum Folkwang, Essen, 1979
0453 **see** wie 0007
0454 *Tatsächlich. Skulpturen und Bücher von Lawrence Weiner*, Kabinett für aktuelle Kunst, Bremerhaven, 1999
0457 **see** wie 0007
0458 **see** wie 0450
0462 *Documenta 7*, Kassel, 1982
0463 **see** wie 0007
0468-0469 *A Presentation Within the Context of an Installation*, Galerie Rüdiger Schöttle, **Munich** München, 1979
0476 **see** wie 0004
0477 **see** wie 0007
0478 **see** wie 0007
0480 *Lawrence Weiner*, Konrad Fischer Galerie, Düsseldorf, 1981
0481 **see** wie 0004 **Label and accompanying publication and presented in conjunction with the exhibition in** Label und Begleitpublikation und präsentiert zur Ausstellung in: *Neue Rhein Zeitung*, 26.11.2008
0487 **see** wie 0007
0488 *Bilder sind nicht verboten*, Kunsthalle Düsseldorf, 1982
0489 *Rites of Passage / Riten des Übergangs*, Städtische Galerie im Lenbachhaus, **Munich** München, 1992
0490 Sammlung Klaar, **Vienna** Wien, 1981
0494 **see** wie 0004
0497-0498 wie 0007
0500 *In Other Words*, Museum am Ostwall, Dortmund, 1989
0510 **Permanent installation** Permanente Installation, Biel, 1991
0517-0521 *5 Sculptures*, Konrad Fischer Galerie, Düsseldorf, 1985
0526 **Permanent installation** Permanente Installation, Museum Haus Esters, Krefeld, 1985
0533 **see** wie 0004 (Label)
0534 **Permanent installation** Permanente Installation, Kunstmuseum Winterthur, 1995
0544 **see** wie 0004
0548 **see** wie 0004 (Label)
0585 **see** wie 0004, **Translation by Lawrence Weiner in the accompanying publication** Übersetzung von Lawrence Weiner in der Begleitpublikation
0587-0589 *On Top of the Trees*, Galerie Mai 36, **Lucerne** Luzern, 1988
0591 *Altered to Suit / Passend gemacht*, Museum Haus Esters, Krefeld, 1988
0592 *Concept Art*, Galerie Brigitte March, Stuttgart, 1989
0593 **see** wie 0004 (Label)
0598 **Permanent installation** Permanente Installation, Hallen für Neue Kunst, Schaffhausen, 1994
0610 *Zwei Blöcke / Two Blocks*, Städtische Galerie Nordhorn, 1993
0616 *Lawrence Weiner bei Konrad Fischer*, Konrad Fischer Galerie, Düsseldorf, 1989
0617 *Flags Folded out of Sight of the Barricade*, Galerie Brigitte March, Stuttgart, 1989
0619 *From Point to Point / Von Punkt zu Punkt*, Kunstmuseum St. Gallen, 1995
0622 *Schwerpunkt Skulptur*, Kaiser Wilhelm Museum, Krefeld, 1992

0623 wie 0004
0625-0626 *Lawrence Weiner,* Galerie Ascan Crone, Hamburg, 1989
0627-0628 *Lawrence Weiner. Locus Solus XII,* Galerie Hubert Winter, **Vienna** Wien, 1989
0631 **see** wie 0004 (Label)
0634 **see** wie 0004 (Label)
0637 **see** wie 0004 (Label)
0638 *Einleuchten,* Deichtorhallen Hamburg, 1990
0640 **Temporary installation, Venloer Strasse, Cologne** Temporäre Installation, Venloer Straße, Köln
0641 **see** wie 0610
0643 *Broken Glass,* Jablonka Galerie, **Cologne** Köln, 1990
0647 *Außenraum Innenstadt,* Sprengelmuseum Hannover, 1991
0656 **see** wie 0610
0664 *Sometime Someplace Somehow,* Galerie Anselm Dreher, Berlin, 1990
0669 **see** wie 0004 (Label)
0670 **Permanent installation, Flak tower** Permanente Installation, Flakturm, **Vienna** Wien, 1991
0672 **see** wie 0004 **and presented in conjunction with the exhibition in** und präsentiert zur Ausstellung in: *Neue Rhein Zeitung,* 26.11.2008
0685 *8. Triennale Kleinplastik,* Fellbach, 2001
0694-0697 **see** wie 0004
0701-0705 **see** wie 0004 (**Label and accompanying publication** Label und Begleitpublikation)
0706 **see** wie 0610
0707 *Made to Fall to Earth / Geschaffen zur Erde zu fallen,* Galerie Hubert Winter, **Vienna** Wien, 1993
0713-0715 *Denkräume.* Museion – Museum für moderne und zeitgenössische Kunst, **Bolzano** Bozen, 1992
0716 **see** wie 0004 (Label)
0724 *Platzverführung,* KulturRegion Stuttgart, 1992
0725 **see** wie 0610
0726 *Piss & Ginger & Apples & Pears,* Galerie Klemens Gasser, **Bolzano** Bozen, 1993
0728 *Zeitgleich,* Kunsthalle Tirol, Hall, 1994
0730 **Permanent installation** Permanente Installation, Foyer Verbund-Hauptgebäude, **Vienna** Wien, 2005
0733 **Permanent installation** Permanente Installation, Schloss Hohenkammer, **Munich** München, 2007
0734 *KünstlerInnen,* Kunsthaus Bregenz, 1997
0738-0741 **see** wie 0619
0742 **see** wie 0004 (Label)
0744-0746 *Tomorrow & Tomorrow & Tomorrow,* Konrad Fischer Galerie, Düsseldorf, 1994
0749 *Skulptur. Projekte in Münster 1997,* Westfälisches Landesmuseum für Kunst und Kulturgeschichte, Münster, 1997
0750 *Rosebud,* Städtische Galerie im Lenbachhaus, **Munich** München, 1994
0751 *Vorstellungsrealitäten,* Galerie Dorothea von der Koelen, Mainz, 1994
0752-0755 *Or without Regard / Oder ohne Rücksicht,* Städtische Kunstsammlungen Chemnitz, 1994
0756 *Pocket Knife,* Edition, Düsseldorf, 1994
0757 *Terminal / Kopfbahnhof,* Hauptbahnhof Leipzig, 1995
0759 **Temporary installation** Temporäre Installation, Kunsthalle Kiel, 1994
0760 Edition Galerie Brigitte March, Stuttgart, 1994
0761 **Permanent installation, Cathedral Square and Venloer Strasse, Cologne** Permanente Installation, Domplatte und Venloer Straße, Köln, 1995
0762 **see** wie 0619
0765 **Temporary installation, City tram** Temporäre Installation, Städtische Straßenbahn, Düsseldorf, 2008, **and see** und wie 0004 (Label)
0770 *Feedbackstage,* Galerie Thomas Schulte, Berlin, 2009
0771 *Nach dem Ende von dem Kai,* Kunsthalle Krems, 1997
0773 **see** wie 0004 (Label)
0774-0776 *Just One Time / Nur einmal,* Galerie Klosterfelde, Berlin, 2002
0777 *Slipping & Sliding / Rutschen & Schlittern,* Kärntner Landesgalerie, Klagenfurt, 1996, **and permanent installation** und permanente Installation, Alpen-Adria-Universität Klagenfurt, 2002
0778 *Bernd Lohaus – Lawrence Weiner,* Haus Bill, Zumikon **near Zurich** bei Zürich, 1996
0780 *Interventionen 13,* Museum in Progress, **Vienna** Wien, **presented in** präsentiert in: *Der Standard,* 1.8.1996
0785 *Badly Mixed Concrete,* Galerie Hubert Winter, **Vienna** Wien, 1996
0788 *Crossings,* Kunsthalle Wien, **Vienna,** 1998
0791 *HeimWeh – FernLust,* Galerie Hubert Winter, **Vienna** Wien, 2000
0795 **Permanent installation, building façade** Permanente Installation, Wohnhaus-Fassade, Düsseldorf, 1997
0798-0800 *Henceforth Thus / Von nun an also,* Konrad Fischer Galerie, Düsseldorf, 1997
0802 *Sarajevo 2000,* MUMOK Museum moderner Kunst Stiftung Ludwig Wien, 1998
0805 *Gäste / Guests,* Galerie Friedrich, Bern, 1997
0808-0809 *5 Elements 2 Times,* Galerie Dorothea van der Koelen, Mainz, 1998
0814 *Written on the Wind / Auf den Wind geschrieben,* Kunsthalle Nürnberg, 1998
0817 *Zeit / Los: Zur Kunstgeschichte der Zeit,* Kunsthalle Krems, 1999
0818 **see** wie 0004 (Label)
0821-0823 *Lost & Found,* Galerie Ascan Crone, Hamburg, 1999
0826-0828 *Under the Sun,* Buchmann Galerie, **Cologne** Köln, 1999
0829 *Walls / Wände,* Konrad Fischer Galerie, Düsseldorf, 1999
0833 *Chronos und Kairos,* Museum Fridericianum, Kassel, 1999
0838 **Permanent installation** Permanente Installation, Schloss Zuoz, 2007
0839 Galerie Dorothea van der Koelen, Mainz, 1999
0843 *Full Circle,* Galerie Hubert Winter, **Vienna** Wien, 2000
0850 *Nach alles / After All,* Deutsche Guggenheim, Berlin, 2000
0851 *Ideal City,* Frankfurt am Main, 2000
0852 Buchmann Galerie, **Cologne** Köln, 2000
0853 *Bent & Broken Shafts of Light / Gebeugte und gebrochene Lichtstrahlen,* Kunstmuseum Wolfsburg, 2000
0861 **Private collection** Privatsammlung, Innsbruck
0863-0865 *The Concept Sublime: 35 Years Brigitte March International Contemporary Art,* Galerie Brigitte March, Stuttgart, 2011
0866 **see** wie 0004
0871 Wettbewerb Deutsche Welle, Bonn, 2001
0876 Tiroler Landesmuseum Innsbruck, 2001
0879-0881 *Put Aside or Put Away,* Buchmann Galerie, **Cologne** Köln, 2002
0884 *Just One Time / Nur einmal,* Galerie Klosterfelde, Berlin, 2002
0885 *Primary Secondary Tertiary / Primär Sekundär Tertiär,* Kunstverein Rhein Ruhr, Essen, 2002
0898 **see** wie 0004 (**Label and accompanying publication** Label und Begleitpublikation)
0900 **see** wie 0004 (Label)
0908 **see** wie 0004 (**Label and accompanying publication** Label und Begleitpublikation)
0915-0916 *X Y & Z,* Bawag Foundation, **Vienna** Wien, 2006
0917 **see** wie 0004 (Label)
0919 *Lawrence Weiner,* Konrad Fischer Galerie, Düsseldorf, 2006
0925 *Into a Journey,* Galerie Meyer Riegger, Karlsruhe, 2006
0946 **see** wie 0004 (Label)
0949 **see** wie 0004 (Label)
0973 *Lawrence Weiner – Eine Installation,* Institut français, **Cologne** Köln, 2007
0981-0985 *Lawrence Weiner,* Konrad Fischer Galerie, Berlin, 2008
1006 *Graceful Haste / Eile mit Weile,* Galerie Mai 36, **Zurich** Zürich, 2010
1007-1011 *Die Ebbe und der Strom,* Galerie Hubert Winter, **Vienna** Wien, 2009
1024 *Personal Structures. Time – Space – Existence,* Galerie Georg Kargl, **Vienna** Wien, 2010
1025 **Radio station** Radiostation, Bad Deutsch-Altenburg, 2011
1026 **Permanent installation, Johanneskirche Stadtkirche** Permanente Installation, Johanneskirche Stadtkirche, Düsseldorf, 2010
1027 *When Ideas Become Form,* Galerie van der Koelen, **Venice and Mainz** Venedig und Mainz, 2009
1047 *Belvedere,* Arp Museum Bahnhof Rolandseck, Remagen, 2011

* **The typography of the labels of the works by Weiner were part of the bilingual exhibition and accompanied in English those in German and in German those in English.** Die in der Typografie der jeweiligen Arbeit Weiners ausgeführten Labels waren Bestandteil der zweisprachig konzipierten Ausstellung und begleiteten auf Englisch die in deutscher Sprache und auf Deutsch die in englischer Sprache präsentierten Arbeiten.

SOLO EXHIBITIONS IN THE GERMAN-SPEAKING WORLD (SELECTION)
EINZELAUSSTELLUNGEN IM DEUTSCHSPRACHIGEN RAUM (AUSWAHL)

1969 Konrad Fischer Galerie, Düsseldorf

1970 Gegenverkehr. Zentrum für aktuelle Kunst, Aachen
Konrad Fischer / Fernsehgalerie Gerry Schum, Art Cologne, Köln
Galerie Folker Skulima, Berlin
Konrad Fischer Galerie, Düsseldorf

1971 *Broken off / Abgebrochen*, Ost-Berlin

1972 Konrad Fischer Galerie, Düsseldorf
Westfälischer Kunstverein, Münster

1973 Kabinett für aktuelle Kunst, Bremerhaven
Städtisches Museum, Mönchengladbach

1975 Konrad Fischer Galerie, Düsseldorf
Kabinett für aktuelle Kunst, Bremerhaven
Galerie Rolf Preisig, Basel

1976 Galerie Rüdiger Schöttle, München
Kunsthalle Basel

1977 Konrad Fischer Galerie, Düsseldorf

1978 Galerie Rolf Preisig, Basel
Galerie Rüdiger Schöttle, München
Kabinett für aktuelle Kunst, Bremerhaven

1979 Galerie Rüdiger Schöttle, München

1980 Forum Kunst, Rottweil

1981 Kabinett für aktuelle Kunst, Bremerhaven
Konrad Fischer Galerie, Düsseldorf

1983 Kunsthalle Bern

1985 Konrad Fischer Galerie, Düsseldorf

1988 Galerie Mai 36, Luzern
Museum Haus Esters, Krefeld

1989 Konrad Fischer Galerie, Düsseldorf
Galerie Brigitte March, Stuttgart
Galerie Ascan Crone, Hamburg
Galerie Hubert Winter, Wien
Portikus, Frankfurt a. M.
Salzhaus, Sindelfingen

1990 Jablonka Galerie, Köln
Galerie Anselm Dreher, Berlin

1991 Galerie Mai 36, Luzern

1992 Städtische Galerie im Lenbachhaus und Kunstforum, München

1993 Galerie Klemens Gasser, Bozen
Galerie Hubert Winter, Wien
Städtische Galerie Nordhorn
Hochschule für Angewandte Kunst in Wien

1994 Galerie Brigitte March, Stuttgart
Galerie Mai 36, Zürich
Schule und Museum für Gestaltung, Zürich
Konrad Fischer Galerie, Düsseldorf
Jablonka Galerie, Köln
Städtische Kunstsammlungen Chemnitz
Zeitgleich, Kunsthalle Tirol, Hall

1995 Kunstmuseum Winterthur
Kunstmuseum St. Gallen
Kunsthof WBK, Zürich
Museum Ludwig, Köln

1996 Projektraum, Berlin
Haus Bill, Zumikon bei Zürich (mit Bernd Lohaus)
Kärntner Landesgalerie in der Kunsthalle Ritter, Klagenfurt
museum in progress, Wien
Galerie Hubert Winter, Wien
Secession, Wien

1997 Konrad Fischer Galerie, Düsseldorf

1998 Galerie Dorothea van der Koelen, Mainz
Kunsthalle Wien
Kunsthalle Nürnberg
Kunstbunker. Forum für zeitgenössische Kunst, Nürnberg

1999 Galerie Ascan Crone, Hamburg
Galerie Buchmann, Köln
Kunstverein Bergisch Gladbach
Neues Museum Weserburg, Bremen
Galerie Mai 36, Zürich

2000 Galerie Hubert Winter, Wien
Künstlerhaus, Wien
museum in progress, Wien
Deutsche Guggenheim, Berlin
Kölnischer Kunstverein und Kunstverein Heilbronn
Galerie Anselm Dreher, Berlin
Nationalgalerie im Hamburger Bahnhof – Museum für Gegenwart – Berlin und Kunst- und Ausstellungshalle der Bundesrepublik Deutschland, Bonn (mit Peter Gordon)
Kunstmuseum Wolfsburg

2001 Galerie Brigitte March, Stuttgart

2002 Galerie Buchmann, Köln
Konrad Fischer Galerie, Düsseldorf
Tiroler Landesmuseum, Innsbruck
Die Tiroler Sparkasse, Innsbruck
Alpen-Adria-Universität Klagenfurt
Galerie Klosterfelde, Berlin
Synagoge Stommeln, Pulheim

2003 Kunstverein Ruhr, Forum Kunst & Architektur, Essen

2004 Neuer Jungfernstieg, Hamburg
Galerie Mai 36, Zürich
Hochschule für Gestaltung und Kunst, Zürich
Permanente Installation, Kraftfutterwerk der A. Rieper AG, Vintl

2005 Galerie Johann Widauer, Innsbruck
Museum der Moderne und Galerie Thaddaeus Ropac, Salzburg

2006 Konrad Fischer Galerie, Düsseldorf
Bawag Foundation, Wien

2007 Haus der Kunst, München
Kunstparterre, München
Permanente Installation, Schloss Hohenkammer, München
Permanente Installation, Bellevue, Helvetia- und Limmatplatz, Zürich
Institut français, Köln

2008 Konrad Fischer Galerie, Berlin
El Sourdog Hex, Berlin
Galerie Hubert Winter, Wien
K21 Kunstsammlung Nordrhein-Westfalen, Düsseldorf

2010 Permanente Installation, Johanneskirche Stadtkirche, Düsseldorf
Galerie Mai 36, Zürich

GROUP EXHIBITIONS IN THE GERMAN-SPEAKING WORLD (SELECTION)
GRUPPENAUSSTELLUNGEN IM DEUTSCHSPRACHIGEN RAUM (AUSWAHL)

1969 *When Attitudes Become Form*, Kunsthalle Bern u. a. (Katalog)
Vorstellungen nehmen Form an, Museum Haus Lange, Krefeld (Katalog)
Op Losse Schroeven / Verborgene Strukturen, Stedelijk Museum Amsterdam und Museum Folkwang, Essen (Katalog)
Prospect 69, Städtische Kunsthalle Düsseldorf (Katalog)
Konzeption / Conception, Städtisches Museum Leverkusen (Katalog)
Pläne und Projekte als Kunst, Kunsthalle Bern (Katalog)

1970 *Umwelt-Akzente. Die Expansion der Kunst*, Kunstkreis Monschau (Katalog)
Identifications, Fernsehgalerie von Gerry Schum, Erstes Deutsches Fernsehen, Südwestfunk, Baden-Baden

1971 *Situation Concepts*, Galerie im Taxispalais, Innsbruck, und Galerie Nächst St. Stephan, Wien (Katalog)
Concept Konzept, 2. Biennale von Nürnberg, Kunsthalle Nürnberg (Katalog)
Experimenta 4, Frankfurter Kunstverein (Katalog)
Prospect 71, Städtische Kunsthalle Düsseldorf (Katalog)

1972 *»Konzept«-Kunst*, Kunstmuseum Basel (Katalog)
Das Konzept ist die Form, Westfälischer Kunstverein, Münster
documenta 5, Kassel (Katalog)

1973 *Bilder – Objekte – Filme – Konzepte*, Städtische Galerie im Lenbachhaus, München (Katalog)
Prospect 73, Städtische Kunsthalle Düsseldorf (Katalog)

1974 *Concept Art*, Kunstverein Braunschweig (Katalog)
To Seperate = Trennen, Teilen, Amerika-Haus, Berlin
Kunst – Über Kunst, Kölnischer Kunstverein (Katalog)
Aspekte internationaler Kunst am Anfang der 70er Jahre. Projekt '74, Wallraf-Richartz-Museum u. a., Köln (Katalog)
Prospect 74, Städtische Kunsthalle Düsseldorf (Katalog)

1975 *Today Together*, Kölner Kunstmarkt, Sonderausstellung, Köln

1976 *Prospect – Retrospect. Europa 1946–1976*, Städtische Kunsthalle Düsseldorf (Katalog)
New York in Europa: Amerikanische Kunst aus europäischen Sammlungen, Neue Nationalgalerie, Berlin (Katalog)

1977 *documenta 6*, Kassel (Katalog)
10 Jahre Kabinett für aktuelle Kunst Bremerhaven, Kunsthalle Bremerhaven

1978 *Works from the Crex Collection*, InK, Zürich u. a. (Katalog)
Museum des Geldes, Städtische Kunsthalle Düsseldorf und Kunstverein für die Rheinlande und Westfalen, Düsseldorf (Katalog)

1979 *Words: Gebrauch der Sprache in der Kunst während des letzten Jahrzehntes / Words: L'uso del linguaggio nell'arte del'ultimo decennio*, Museum Bochum (Katalog)
»Salon« stellt vor / "Salon" presents, Museum Folkwang, Essen (Reprints der Salon-Ausgaben, Köln 2007)
Künstlerbücher, Produzentengalerie, München, u. a. (Katalog)

1980 *Das Bild einer Geschichte. 1956–1976. Die Sammlung Panza di Biumo*, Kunstsammlung Nordrhein-Westfalen, Düsseldorf u. a. (Katalog)
Minimal und Conceptual Art aus der Sammlung Giuseppe Panza di Biumo, Museum für Gegenwartskunst, Basel (Katalog)
Avantgarden – Retrospektiv, Westfälischer Kunstverein, Münster (Katalog)
Westkunst, Museen der Stadt Köln (Katalog)
Künstlerbücher, Frankfurter Kunstverein

1982 *documenta 7*, Kassel (Katalog)
Bilder sind nicht verboten, Städtische Kunsthalle Düsseldorf und Kunstverein für die Rheinlande und Westfalen, Düsseldorf (Katalog)

1983 Hallen für Neue Kunst, Schaffhausen
Bücher, Bilder, Objekte aus der Sammlung Speck, Museen Haus Lange und Haus Esters, Krefeld (Katalog)
Master Works of Conceptual Art, Galerie Paul Maenz, Köln (Katalog)

1984 *Idea*, Galerie Tanja Grunert, Stuttgart (Katalog)
1984 im Toten Winkel, Kunstverein in Hamburg (Katalog)
Rosenfest. Worte, Bilder, Musik, Theater, DAAD Galerie, Berlin (Katalog)

1985 *Dreißig Jahre durch die Kunst*, Museum Haus Lange, Krefeld (Katalog)
Zugehend auf eine Biennale des Friedens, Kunsthaus und Kunstverein, Hamburg (Katalog)

1986 *Wien Fluss 1986*, Wiener Festwochen, Wien (Katalog)
Ohne die Rose tun wir's nicht ... Grüße an Beuys von 199 Künstlern, Haus Koekkoek, Kleve, u. a. (Katalog)

1987 *Musée St. Pierre, Lyon*, Frankfurter Kunstverein (Katalog)

1988 *Der Hund in mir / The Dog Within*, Galerie Hubert Winter
Skulpturenrepublik, Kunstraum Wien (Katalog)
Broken Music. Artist's Recordworks, DAAD Galerie, Berlin (Katalog)
Balkon mit Fächer. 25 Jahre Berliner Kulturprogramm des DAAD, DAAD Galerie, Berlin (Katalog)

1989 *Concept Art*, Galerie Brigitte March, Stuttgart, u. a. (Katalog)
Bilderstreit. Widerspruch, Einheit, Fragment, Museums Ludwig in den Rheinhallen der Kölner Messe, Köln (Katalog)
Furkart 1989, Hotel Furkartblick, Furkart
Skulpturen für Krefeld I, Museum Haus Esters, Krefeld (Katalog)
In Other Words, Museum am Ostwall, Dortmund (Katalog)
Hier wird getanzt, XPO Galerie, Hamburg (Katalog)
Hamburg Projekt 1989. Künstler realisieren Arbeiten im öffentlichen Raum, Hamburg
Die letzten 22 Jahre, Kunstverein in Hamburg
Acchrochage für Tatlin, Städtische Kunsthalle Düsseldorf
Musée d'Art Contemporain Lyon. Werke aus der Sammlung, Musée d'Art Contemporain Lyon und Städtische Galerie Göppingen, Göppingen (Katalog)
Einleuchten. Will, Vorstel & Simul in HH, Deichtorhallen Hamburg (Katalog)

1990 *Concept Art – Minimal Art – Arte Povera – Land Art*, Kunsthalle Bielefeld
Arte Conceptual, Paris und Madrid (1989/90), Deichtorhallen Hamburg u. a. (Katalog)
High Season I: A Multiple / Print Show, Galerie Hubert Winter, Wien
The Ready Made Boomerang. The 8th Biennale of Sydney, DAAD Galerie, Berlin (Katalog)

1991 *Tabula Rasa. 25 Künstler im Stadtraum von Biel*, Biel (Katalog)
Meta Memphis. Möbel und Gebrauchsobjekte aus den Kollektionen 1989 und 1991, Institut Mathildenhöhe, Darmstadt (Katalog)
Topographie I, Wiener Festwochen, Wien
Außenraum Innenstadt, Sprengel Museum Hannover (Katalog)

1992 *Die Künstlerpostkarte*, Altonaer Museum, Hamburg, u. a. (Katalog)
Platzverführung, KulturRegion Stuttgart (Katalog)
Force Sight. Brigitte March. Internationale Kunst der Gegenwart, Schloss Presteneck, Neustadt / Stein (Katalog)
Vorhut aus dem Hinterland. Künstler aus 25 Jahren, Kabinett für aktuelle Kunst, Bremerhaven (Katalog)
Territorium Artis, Kunst- und Ausstellungshalle der Bundesrepublik Deutschland, Bonn (Katalog)

Stars Don't Stand Still in the Sky. Hommage à Stéphane Mallarmé, Kunstmuseum Winterthur (Katalog)

1993 *Künstler: Bücher*, Kunstmuseen Krefeld Kunstmuseen, Krefeld (Katalog)
Amerikanische Kunst im 20. Jahrhundert. Malerei und Plastik 1913–1993, Martin-Gropius-Bau, Berlin (Katalog)
Bright Light. Brigitte March. Internationale Kunst der Gegenwart, Schloss Presteneck, Neustadt / Stein (Katalog)
Die Sprache der Kunst. Die Beziehung von Bild und Text in der Kunst des 20. Jahrhunderts, Kunsthalle Wien und Frankfurter Kunstverein (Katalog)
I am you: Künstler gegen Gewalt, Goethe-Institut und Beck-Forum, München
Trigon 93, Neue Galerie Graz (Katalog)

1994 *Drawing-Room. Zeichnungen und Skulpturen aus der Sammlung Speck*, Neue Galerie Graz (Katalog)
Children in Crisis, Kunstverein Hamburg
Minimal Art?, Hallen für Neue Kunst, Schaffhausen
Das Jahrhundert des Multiples. Von Duchamp bis zur Gegenwart, Deichtorhallen Hamburg (Katalog)
Rosebud. Jenny Holzer, Matt Mullican, Lawrence Weiner, Städtische Galerie im Lenbachhaus, München (Katalog)
Setzen – Stellen – Legen, Galerie Anselm Dreher, Berlin
Vorstellungsrealitäten, Galerie Dorothea van der Koelen, Mainz (Katalog)
Wide White Space. Hinter dem Museum / Behind the Museum. 1966–1976, Palais voor Schone Kunsten / Palais des Beaux-Arts, Brüssel, u. a. (Katalog)

1995 *Kopfbahnhof / Terminal. Maria Eichhorn, Douglas Gordon*, Hauptbahnhof Leipzig (Katalog)
Signierstunde der Damen, Rathaus Wien
Die Sammlung Marzona. Arte Povera, Minimal Art, Concept Art, Land Art, MUMOK – Museum moderner Kunst Stiftung Ludwig Wien im Palais Liechtenstein, Wien (Katalog)
DO IT – TV-Version, 10, museum in progress, Wien

1996 *Rita McBride and Piggybackback* (Kollaboration mit Catherine Opie und Lawrence Weiner), Galerie Béla Jarzyk, Köln
Chaos, Wahnsinn. Permutationen der zeitgenössischen Kunst, Kunsthalle Krems (Katalog)
Abenteuer Kunst, Städtische Galerie Göppingen (Katalog)
Sammlung Speck, Museum Ludwig, Köln (Katalog)
How the Chicken Crossed the Road, Galerie Mai 36, Zürich
Schwere-los. Skulpturen, Landesgalerie Linz (Katalog)
Interventionen, 13, museum in progress, Wien

1997 *Schauplatz Museumsquartier. Zur Transformation eines Ortes*, Kunsthalle Wien
Views From Abroad / Die Entdeckung des Anderen, MMK – Museum für Moderne Kunst, Whitney Museum of American Art, New York (1996) und Frankfurt a. M. (Katalog)
Notfalls leben wir auch ohne Herz. Exemplarisches aus der Sammlung Speck, Kunsthalle Wien (Katalog)
Diskland, Snowscape, Shed im Eisenwerk, Frauenfeld bei Winterthur
Multiple Identity. Amerikanische Kunst 1975–1995 aus dem Whitney Museum of American Art, Kunstmuseum Bonn (Katalog)
504: ein Ausstellungsprojekt der Klasse John Armleder, Hochschule für Bildende Künste, Braunschweig
3 Wege zum See, Künstlerhaus Klagenfurt (Katalog)
Skulptur. Projekte in Münster 1997, Westfälisches Landesmuseum, Münster (Katalog)
KünstlerInnen. 50 Positionen zeitgenössischer internationaler Kunst. Videoporträts und Werke, Kunsthaus Bregenz u. a. (Katalog)
Raum Zeichen Licht, Kärntner Landesgalerie, Klagenfurt
Gäste / Guests, Galerie Friedrich, Bern
And Then There Were None, Galerie Meyer Riegger, Karlsruhe
Konkrete Poesie – Konzeptkunst, Kunstverein Rosenheim (Katalog)

1998 *Berlin / Berlin. 1. Berlin Biennale*, Akademie der Künste Berlin u. a.
Crossings. Kunst zum Hören und Sehen, Kunsthalle Wien (Katalog)
Kunst mit durch über Schrift, Atterseehalle, Attersee
Zeichnen ist eine andere Art von Sprache. Neuere amerikanische Zeichnungen aus einer New Yorker Privatsammlung, Kunstmuseum Winterthur u. a. (Katalog)
Minimal Maximal – die Minimal Art und ihr Einfluss auf die Kunst der 90er Jahre, Neues Museum Weserburg, Bremen (Katalog)
Sarajevo 2000. Schenkungen von Künstlern für ein neues Museum in Sarajevo, MUMOK – Museum moderner Kunst Stiftung Ludwig Wien (Katalog)

1999 *Collection 99*, Galerie für zeitgenössische Kunst Leipzig
Positionen / Posizion. Werke aus der Sammlung / Opere dalla collezione i, Museion – Museum für moderne und zeitgenössische Kunst Bozen (Katalog)
Wände / Walls, Konrad Fischer Galerie, Düsseldorf
My House is Your House …, Galerie Hubert Winter, Wien
Zeit / Los: Zur Kunstgeschichte der Zeit, Kunsthalle Krems (Katalog)
Stop the Violence!!, Akademie der Bildenden Künste, Wien
Chronos & Kairos. Die Zeit in der zeitgenössischen Kunst, Museum Fridericianum, Kassel (Katalog)
Get Together. Kunst als Teamwork, Kunsthalle Wien (Katalog)
Die Kunst der Linie. Möglichkeiten des Graphischen, Landesgalerie Linz (Katalog)

2000 *HeimWeh – FernLust*, Galerie Hubert Winter, Wien
Die Natur der Dinge, NRW-Forum Kultur und Wirtschaft, Düsseldorf (Katalog)
Von Edgar Degas bis Gerhard Richter. Arbeiten auf Papier aus der Graphischen Sammlung, Kunstmuseum Winterthur u. a. (Katalog)
Stanze. Werke aus der Sammlung des Museums für Moderne Kunst Bozen, Museion – Museum für moderne und zeitgenössische Kunst Bozen (Katalog)
TransAct. Interventionen zur Lage in Österreich, museum in progress, Wien (Katalog)

2001 *Out of Print. An Archive as Artistic Concept*, Neues Museum Weserburg, Bremen, u. a. (Katalog)
Für Hanne, Galerie Crone, Berlin
DIN ART 4. 560 Künstler und ein Format, Museum für Kommunikation, Frankfurt a. M., u. a. (Katalog)
Wertwechsel. Zum Wert des Kunstwerks, Museum für Angewandte Kunst, Köln (Katalog)
Art Works. Sammlung Marzona, Kunsthalle Bielefeld (Katalog)
8. Triennale Kleinplastik. Vor-Sicht, Rück-Sicht, Fellbach (Katalog)

2002 *Privat Space*, Galerie Hubert Winter, Wien
Wasser Sand Weite / Water Sand Space, Galerie Dorothea van der Koelen, Mainz, u. a. (Katalog)
Take One, Two, Three … aus der Sammlung Speck, K21 Kunstsammlung Nordrhein-Westfalen, Düsseldorf (Katalog)
The Artists' Memory, Kunstsammlung Jena
Der Schock des 11. September und das Geheimnis des Anderen / The Shock of September 11 and the Mystery of the Other, Haus am Lützowplatz, Berlin (Katalog)
Waschsalon. Der Stoff aus dem die Bilder sind, Aargauer Kunsthaus / Halle Schönenwerder (Katalog)
The Music in Me, Chapter 1, Gesellschaft für aktuelle Kunst, Bremerhaven
What about Hegel (and you), Galerie Brigitte March, Stuttgart
Presence and Place, Galerie Anselm Dreher, Berlin
Startkapital, K21 Kunstsammlung Nordrhein-Westfalen Düsseldorf (Katalog)

2003 *Talking Pieces. Text und Bild in der Neuen Kunst*, Museum Morsbroich, Leverkusen (Katalog)
Projection, Konrad Fischer Galerie, Düsseldorf
Blickachsen 4. Skulpturen im Kurpark, Bad Homburg v. d. Höhe (Katalog)
Support 1 – Die Neue Galerie als Sammlung, Neue Galerie Graz
Adorno: die Möglichkeit des Unmöglichen / Adorno: the Possibility of the Impossible, Frankfurter Kunstverein (Katalog)
Partners, Haus der Kunst, München (Katalog)
Ready to Shoot – Fernsehgalerie Gerry Schum, Kunsthalle Düsseldorf (Katalog)

Leere X Vision. Körper und Gegenstände, MARTa Herford (Katalog)

2004 *Treasure Island. 10 Jahre Kunstmuseum Wolfsburg*, Kunstmuseum Wolfsburg
Utopia Station, Haus der Kunst, München
Support 2 – die Neue Galerie als Sammlung, Neue Galerie Graz
Where Are You Standing?, Kupferstichkabinett, Berlin
The Artist's Beautiful Language, Galerie Anselm Dreher, Berlin
15 Jahre Deichtorhallen, Deichtorhallen Hamburg
Parkett – 20 Years of Artist's Collaboration, Kunsthaus Zürich (Katalog)
Behind the Facts. Interfunktionen 1968–1975, Kunsthalle Fridericianum, Kassel (Katalog)
Minimale Konzepte / Minimal Concepts, Kunstmuseum Wolfsburg

2005 *Attitüden Bilder Konzepte*, Galerie Brigitte March, Stuttgart
Zur Vorstellung des Terrors: Die RAF-Ausstellung, KW Institute for Contemporary Art, Berlin
e-flux Video Rentals, KW Institute for Contemporary Art, Berlin, und Portikus, Frankfurt a. M.
Douglas Gordon's The Vanity of Allegory, Deutsche Guggenheim, Berlin (Katalog)
Sammel-Leidenschaften. Cusp / Scheitelpunkt (&) so weiter, Neues Museum Weserburg, Bremen (Katalog)
Vinyl. Records and Covers by Artists. A Survey, Neues Museum Weserburg, Bremen (Katalog)
Die Wahrnehmung der Horizontale, Museion – Museum für moderne und zeitgenössische Kunst Bozen (Katalog)
Fast Nichts – Minimalistische Werke aus der Friedrich Christian Flick Collection, Hamburger Bahnhof – Museum für Gegenwart – Berlin (Katalog)
(un)limited – Künstlerbücher aus der Sammlung Missmahl, Museum Bochum und Museum für Druckkunst, Leipzig (Katalog)
strips – Bilder in Folge, Kunstverein Hannover u. a.

2006 *Mental Image / Wortwerke und Textbilder*, Kunstmuseum und Kunstverein St. Gallen
sculpture@CityNord. Das temporäre Skulpturenprojekt in der City Nord, Hamburg
6 Monuments with a Horizon Line I, Buchmann Galerie, Berlin
On the Ball, Galerie Anselm Dreher, Berlin
John Armleder u. a., Galerie Mezzanin, Wien
Public Space / Two Audiences. Werke und Dokumente aus der Sammlung Herbert. Inventaire, MACBA, Barcelona, und Kunsthaus Graz 2006 (Katalog)
Moving on Motion, Galerie Thomas Schulte, Berlin
The Guggenheim Collection, Kunst- und Ausstellungshalle der Bundesrepublik Deutschland, Bonn (Katalog)
Plane / Figure. Amerikanische Kunst aus Schweizer Privatsammlungen und aus dem Kunstmuseum Winterthur, Kunstmuseum Winterthur (Katalog)
Ideal City – Invisible City. 41 International Artists in Public Spaces and Several Exhibition Spaces in Two Cities. An Exhibition by European Art Projects, Potsdam (Katalog)
I (Ich) / Performative Ontology, Secession, Wien (Katalog)
Am Anfang war das Wort, Haus der Kunst, München
Into a Journey, Meyer Riegger Galerie, Karlsruhe
Into Me / Out Of Me, KW Institute for Contemporary Art, Berlin (Katalog)
Konzept. Aktion. Sprache, MUMOK – Museum moderner Kunst Stiftung Ludwig Wien (Katalog)

2007 *The Fit*, Nüans, Düsseldorf
Modelle für morgen: Köln, European Kunsthalle, Köln (Katalog)
Held Together With Water. Kunst aus der Sammlung Verbund, MAK – Österreichisches Museum für Angewandte Kunst / Gegenwartskunst, Wien (Katalog)
Romantischer Konzeptionalismus / Romantic Conceptualism, Kunsthalle Nürnberg und BAWAG Foundation, Wien (Katalog)
MARTa schweigt. Garde le silence, le silence te gardera. Die Kunst der Stille von Duchamp bis heute. Das Mysterium der Etrusker, MARTa Herford (Katalog)
Im Fluss. Künstlerpublikationen mit Blick aufs Wasser, Neues Museum Weserburg, Bremen
Lange nicht gesehen. Begegnungen mit dem Museum auf Abruf, MUSA, Wien
25 Jahre Galerie Crone, Galerie Crone, Berlin
Out of Time, Neues Museum Weserburg, Bremen
Beziehungsweise, Galerie Hubert Winter, Wien

2008 *Genau + anders. Mathematik in der Kunst von Dürer bis Sol LeWitt*, MUMOK – Museum moderner Kunst Stiftung Ludwig Wien
Die Hände der Kunst – Artist's Handbook, MARTa Herford (Katalog)
Ridiculously Modest, 032c Workshop, Berlin
Clinch / Cross / Cut. Team 404 & John Armleder, New Jerseyy, Basel
No Leftovers, Kunsthalle Bern
Lawrence Weiner, Konrad Fischer Galerie, Berlin
German Angst, Neuer Berliner Kunstverein
»Ich kann mir nicht jeden Tag ein Ohr abschneiden«. Dekonstruktionen des Künstlermythos. Werke aus der Friedrich Christian Flick Collection im Hamburger Bahnhof, den Sammlungen der Staatlichen Museen zu Berlin und anderen Sammlungen, Hamburger Bahnhof – Museum für Gegenwart – Berlin (Katalog)
2 x [(2 x 20) + (2 x 2)] + 2 = X x (Desperately) Trying to Figure out the World, Galerie Mai 36, Zürich, und Brooke Alexander, New York
Made in Munich, Haus der Kunst, München

2009 *Desire Acquire*, Galerie Bob van Orsouw, Zürich
Moments of the Horizon Line II, Buchmann Galerie, Berlin
Après Crepuscule – Na Schemering – After Twilight – Nach Dämmerung, Kölnischer Kunstverein
The Porn Identity, Kunsthalle Wien
Feedbackstage, Galerie Thomas Schulte, Berlin
1968. Die große Unschuld, Kunsthalle Bielefeld (Katalog)
Discover US! Carnival Within – An Exhibition Made in America, Uferhallen, Berlin (Katalog)
Double. Gregor Schneider. 40 Jahre Kabinett für aktuelle Kunst, Bremerhaven. Lawrence Weiner, MMK – Museum für Moderne Kunst, Frankfurt a. M. (Katalog)
Curated by Vienna 09, Gianni Jetzer u. a., Wien
Twilight Zone – Art Hits Design, Kunstraum Noe, Wien
Gegen den Strich! 15 Jahre Sammlung des Kunstmuseum Wolfsburg, Kunstmuseum Wolfsburg
Konzeptuelle Kunst auf Papier, Städtisches Museum Abteiberg, Mönchengladbach
When Ideas Become Form, Galerie Dorothea van der Koelen, Venedig und Mainz
Time, Konrad Fischer Galerie, Düsseldorf
Rencontres Internationales. Paris / Berlin / Madrid, Haus der Kulturen, Berlin
Learn to Read Art: A History of Printed Matter (1976–2009), Badischer Kunstverein, Karlsruhe
Die Kunst ist super!, Hamburger Bahnhof – Museum für Gegenwart – Berlin

2010 *Personal Structures. Space Time Existenz*, Künstlerhaus Palais Thurn & Taxis, Bregenz, und Galerie Georg Kargl, Wien
Compilation, Galerie Bernhard Knaus, Frankfurt a. M.
Radical Conceptual, MMK – Museum für moderne Kunst, Frankfurt a. M.
Gipfeltreffen der Moderne – Das Kunstmuseum Winterthur, Museum der Moderne Salzburg (Katalog)
Funktionen der Zeichnung, MMK – Museum für moderne Kunst, Frankfurt a. M.
1. Biennale für Internationale Lichtkunst / 1st Biennale for International Light Art – Open Light in Private Spaces, Unna (Katalog)
Weniger ist mehr. Bilder, Objekte, Konzepte aus Sammlung und Archiv von Herman und Nicole Daled / Less is More. Pictures, Objects, Concepts from the Collection and the Archives of Herman and Nicole Daled, 1966–1978, Haus der Kunst, München (Katalog)
Filmschönheit, Galerie Mezzanin, Wien, u. a.
Emscherkunst.2010. Eine Insel für die Kunst / An Island for the Arts, Ruhr.2010, Essen (Katalog)

Happy End, Kunsthalle Göppingen
Die Natur der Kunst, Kunstmuseum Winterthur
Mit der Möglichkeit gesehen zu werden Dorothee und Konrad Fischer: Archiv einer Haltung / With a Probability of Being Seen. Dorothee and Konrad Fischer: Archives of an Attitude, MACBA, Barcelona, und Museum Kurhaus Kleve (Katalog)
20 Jahre Texte zur Kunst: Mit Deiner Kunst, Editionen 1990–2010, Sammlung Haubrok, Berlin

2011 *Kompass. Zeichnung aus dem Museum of Modern Art, New York. The Judith Rothschild Foundation. Contemporary Drawings Collection*, Martin-Gropius-Bau, Berlin (Katalog)
Bild / Objekt: Neuere Amerikanische Kunst aus der Sammlung, Kunstmuseum Winterthur
time / bank, Portikus, Frankfurt a. M.
MMK 1991–2011. 20 Jahre Gegenwart, MMK – Museum für Moderne Kunst, Frankfurt a. M.
Umwelt-Akzente 1970–2011, Monschau
Belevedere. Warum ist Landschaft schön? Arp Museum Bahnhof Rolandseck, Remagen
The Concept Sublime: 35 Years Brigitte March International Contemporary Art, Galerie Brigitte March, Stuttgart
Museum der Wünsche, MUMOK – Museum moderner Kunst Stiftung Ludwig Wien
Farbe im Fluss. 20 Jahre Weserburg, Neues Museum Weserburg, Bremen
Denken – eine Ausstellung über Wege, die Welt zu erfahren. Künstlerbücher Sammlung Missmahl, Kolumba, Köln (Katalog)

ARTIST'S BOOKS AND MONOGRAPHS (SELECTION)
KÜNSTLERBÜCHER UND MONOGRAFIEN (AUSWAHL)

Terminal Boundaries, Satzfahne mit dem Vermerk: »© Lawrence Weiner 1969. Gedruckt in West Deutschland«, damals nicht veröffentlicht (vgl. Lucy R. Lippard, *Six Years: The Dematerialization of the Art Object from 1966 to 1972*, London 1973: »Dummy lost and book never published.«), als wissenschaftliches Quellenmaterial zugänglich in: http://opus.kobv.de/udk/volltexte/2008/33/pdf/marschall_maria.pdf (19.8.2011)

Lawrence Weiner. An Exhibition / Eine Ausstellung, Ausst.-Kat. Gegenverkehr. Zentrum für aktuelle Kunst, Aachen 1970

A Primer / Ein Elementarbuch, Kassel 1972

8 Works of Lawrence Weiner / 8 Arbeiten von Lawrence Weiner, Kassettenkatalog Städtisches Museum, Mönchengladbach 1973

Lawrence Weiner. Jahresgabe 1972, Westfälischer Kunstverein, Münster 1973

Within Forward Motion / Mit vorwärts gerichteter Bewegung, Ausst.-Kat. Kabinett für aktuelle Kunst, Bremerhaven 1973

Towards a Reasonable End / Auf ein vernünftiges Ende zu, Kabinett für aktuelle Kunst, Bremerhaven 1975

Lawrence Weiner, Ausst.-Kat. Kunsthalle Basel, Basel 1976 (mit Beilage: Einige Werke von Lawrence Weiner)

Works. Catalogue raisonné, Hamburg 1977

Regarding Inscriptions (of a Sort) / Hinsichtlich Inschriften (einer Art), Ausst.-Kat. Galerie Rolf Preisig, Basel 1978

With a Touch of Pink / Mit einem Hauch von Rosa, Ausst.-Kat. Kabinett für aktuelle Kunst, Bremerhaven 1978

Works & Re-Constructions / Werke & Re-Konstruktionen, Ausst.-Kat. Kunsthalle Bern, Bern 1983

Nach Themyscira. Texte aus Penthesilea von Heinrich von Kleist. Libretto zur Wiener Erstaufführung »Nach Themyscira« von Carlo Quartucci u. Carla Tato in einem Kontext von Lawrence Weiner, Wiener Festwochen, Wien 1986

Altered to Suit / Passend gemacht, Ausst.-Kat. Museum Haus Esters, Krefeld 1988

On Top of the Trees, Ausst.-Kat. Galerie Mai 36 Luzern, Vitznau 1988

Books 1969–1989. Catalogue raisonné, Köln 1989

Flags Folded out of Sight of the Barricade 1789–1989. Fahnen außer Sicht der Barrikaden gefaltet, Ausst.-Kat. Galerie Brigitte March, Stuttgart 1989

In the Crack of the Dawn (mit Matt Mullican), Ausst.-Kat. Galerie Mai 36, Luzern 1991

In the Still of the Night / Im Frieden der Nacht. Lawrence Weiner, Wiener Festwochen, Wien 1991

All Fall Down, Ausst.-Kat. Museion – Museum für moderne und zeitgenössische Kunst Bozen, Bozen 1992

Rites of Passage / Riten des Übergangs, Ausst.-Kat. Städtische Galerie im Lenbachhaus, München 1992

Ingrid Burgbacher-Krupka, *öffentlich / public freehold. Lawrence Weiner. Ulrich Rückriem*, Ostfildern-Ruit 1992

Two Blocks / Zwei Blöcke, Ausst.-Kat. Städtische Galerie Nordhorn, Nordhorn 1993

& or & oder & o, München 1994

Lawrence Weiner / Rachel Whiteread (= Parkett, 42), Zürich 1994

Or without Regard / Oder ohne Rücksicht, Ausst.-Kat. Städtische Kunstsammlungen Chemnitz, Stuttgart 1994

Up & All about Eve / Über und alles wegen Eva (1993) und Fly by Night / Fliege bei Nacht. With the Wind – The Voyage of the Bremen (1989), Ausst.-Kat. Galerie Brigitte March, Stuttgart 1994

From Point To Point / Von Punkt zu Punkt, Ausst.-Kat. Kunstverein und Kunstmuseum St. Gallen, Stuttgart 1995

To Build a Square in the Rhineland / Ein Quadrat im Rheinland bauen, Köln 1995

To Build a Square in the Rhineland / 1) Ein Quadrat im Rheinland bauen 2) Ein Viereck anlegen im Rheinland, Köln 1995

2. Ausstellung Haus Bill. Bernd Lohaus / Lawrence Weiner, Katalogkassette Haus Bill, Zumikon bei Zürich 1996

Slipping & Sliding / Rutschen & Schlittern, Ausst.-Kat. Kärntner Landesgalerie, Klagenfurt 1996

I Met a Stranger (mit Birgit Jürgenssen), Wien 1996

A Tale of a Maiden or Two, Köln 1996

Written on the Wind / Auf den Wind geschrieben, Katalogplakat, Kunsthalle Nürnberg 1998

Tatsächlich. Skulpturen und Bücher von Lawrence Weiner, Neues Museum Weserburg, Bremen 1999

Lawrence Weiner. 5 Elements 2 Times, Ausst.-Kat. Galerie Dorothea van der Koelen, Mainz und München 1999

The Metaphor Problem Again (mit John Baldessari), Küsnacht und Zürich 1999

Bent and Broken. Shafts of Light / Gebeugte und gebrochene Lichtstrahlen, Ausst.-Kat. Kunstmuseum Wolfsburg 2000

After All / Nach alles, Ausst.-Kat. Deutsche Guggenheim, Berlin 2000

The Society Architect Ponders the Golden Gate Bridge oder: Wie sie kriegen was sie nicht verdienen (mit Peter Gordon), Köln 2000

Any Given Time / Irgendwann, Ausst.-Kat. Synagoge Stommeln, Pulheim 2002

Primary Secondary Tertiary / Primär Sekundär Tertiär, Ausst.-Kat. Kunstverein Ruhr, Essen 2003

Having Been Said. Writings & Interviews of Lawrence Weiner 1968–2003, hrsg. von Gerti Fietzek und Gregor Stemmrich, Ostfildern-Ruit 2004

Gefragt und gesagt. Schriften und Interviews von Lawrence Weiner 1968–2003, hrsg. von Gerti Fietzek and Gregor Stemmrich, Ostfildern-Ruit 2004

Bremerhaven, Köln 2005

X Y & Z, Ausst.-Kat. Bawag Foundation, Wien 2006

Something to Put Something on, Göttingen 2007

As Far as the Eye Can See, Begleitpublikation, K21 Kunstsammlung Nordrhein-Westfalen, Düsseldorf 2008

If In Fact There Is a Context (Documenta 13: 100 Notes—100 Thoughts / 100 Notizen – 100 Gedanken, 8), Ostfildern 2011

Editor Herausgeber: Gabriele Wix
Copyediting Lektorat: Jonathan Fox (**English** Englisch), Regina Dorneich, Hatje Cantz (**German** Deutsch)
Translations from German Übersetzungen aus dem Deutschen: Brian Currid
Graphic design and typesetting Grafische Gestaltung und Satz: Anja Lutz // Book Design **in consultation with** in Absprache mit Lawrence Weiner
Typeface Schrift: PMN Caecilia; **for the works of** für die Arbeiten von Lawrence Weiner: Franklin Gothic Extra Condensed, Margaret Seaworthy, FF Offline
Production Herstellung: Ines Sutter, Hatje Cantz
Reproductions Reproduktionen: LVD Gesellschaft für Datenverarbeitung mbH, Berlin
Printing Druck: sellier druck GmbH, Freising
Paper Papier: Maxioffset 150 g/m²
Binding Buchbinderei: Conzella Verlagsbuchbinderei, Urban Meister GmbH, Aschheim-Dornach **near Munich** bei München

Published by Erschienen im
Hatje Cantz Verlag
Zeppelinstrasse 32
73760 Ostfildern
Deutschland / Germany
Tel. +49 711 4405-200
Fax +49 711 4405-220
www.hatjecantz.com

A special Collector's Edition is available. Please contact Hatje Cantz for more information. Es erscheint eine Collector's Edition. Nähere Informationen erhalten Sie beim Verlag.

Hatje Cantz books are available internationally at selected bookstores. For more information about our distribution partners, please visit our website at www.hatjecantz.com.

ISBN 978-3-7757-2979-6

Printed in Germany

Cover illustration Umschlagabbildung:
Lawrence Weiner, NACH BILDENDE KUNST / AFTER FINE ART, 2011

Photo credits Fotonachweis
Unless otherwise stated, all photographs are property of the Moved Pictures Archive, New York.
Wenn nicht anders vermerkt, stammen alle Fotografien aus dem Moved Pictures Archive, New York.
Editor: pp. 24/25, 27 left, 52/53, 54 bottom left and right, 55 bottom left and right
Courtesy Galerie Gisela Capitain, Estate Martin Kippenberger, Cologne: p. 10
Courtesy Galerie Hubert Winter, Vienna: pp. 12 top, 13, 14 top, 58 right
Courtesy Galerie Mezzanin, Vienna: p. 12 bottom
Courtesy Institut für Gegenwartskunst der ZHdK, Zurich (Stefan Altenburger): p. 22
Stefanie Jansen: pp. 54 top
Peter Kogler, Vienna: p. 57 bottom
Courtesy Konrad Fischer Galerie, Düsseldorf: pp. 11, 17 top right and bottom, 33 bottom left, 34/35
Achim Kukulies, Düsseldorf: pp. 4/5, 23, 39, 44/45, 63
Courtesy Fotoarchiv des MBN, Bau und Aktiengesellschaft, Georgsmarienhütte: p. 68
Nora Schoeller, Vienna: pp. 27 right, 57 top
Guido Wix, Bonn: pp. 14 bottom, 15, 18, 19, 21 right, 30, 32 top left and right, 36 top right and bottom left, 55 top and right

Acknowledgments
I would like to thank first and foremost Lawrence Weiner and the team at his studio in New York: Bethany Izard and Lauren Wolchik, as well as Alice Zimmerman, Kirsten Vibeke Thueson Weiner, Tae Hwang, and Alyssa Gorelick at Moved Pictures Archive, New York. I owe them all the greatest gratitude for their support of this project from its very inception.
It would be impossible to list all the institutions, museums, exhibition halls, galleries, and individuals that contributed to this project, but I wish to mention in particular Cologne's Kunst- und Museumsbibliothek, which with its rich and meticulously administered holdings greatly contributed to the realization of this volume; and Hatje Cantz Verlag and all those who worked on the project.
Finally, I would like to mention the Landschaftsverband Rheinland, an institution whose dedication is a testament to the significance Lawrence Weiner and American art holds for the Rhineland.

Dank
Der erste Dank gilt dem Künstler und dem Lawrence Weiner Studio, New York, mit Bethany Izard und Lauren Wolchik sowie Alice Zimmerman, Kirsten Vibeke Thueson Weiner, Tae Hwang und Alyssa Gorelick vom Moved Pictures Archive, New York. Ich bin ihnen zu größtem Dank verpflichtet, da sie alle das Projekt von Anfang an auf jede erdenkliche Weise unterstützt haben.
Stellvertretend für alle an der Recherche beteiligten Institutionen, Museen, Ausstellungshallen und Galerien, die namentlich nicht aufgeführt werden können, sei die Kunst- und Museumsbibliothek, Köln, genannt, die mit ihrem reichen und sorgfältig verwalteten Bestand maßgeblich zur Verwirklichung des Buchs beigetragen hat, wie auch der Hatje Cantz Verlag mit allen am Projekt beteiligten Mitarbeiterinnen und Mitarbeitern.
Der Landschaftsverband Rheinland hat mit seinem Engagement die Bedeutung Lawrence Weiners und der amerikanischen Kunst für das Rheinland nachdrücklich gewürdigt.

LVR
Qualität für Menschen